Myth and Southern History

Volume 2: The New South

Myth and Southern History

Volume 2: The New South

Second Edition

Edited by **Patrick Gerster**
and **Nicholas Cords**

University of Illinois Press
Urbana and Chicago

Illini Books edition, 1989
©1974, 1989 by Patrick Gerster and Nicholas Cords
Manufactured in the United States of America
P 5 4 3 2 1

This book is printed on acid-free paper.

Library of Congress Cataloging-in-Publication Data

Myth and Southern history / edited by Patrick Gerster and Nicholas
    Cords. —2nd ed.
       p.   cm.
    Includes bibliographies and indexes.
    Contents: v. 1. The Old South—v. 2. The New South.
    ISBN 0-252-06024-5 (v. 1). ISBN 0-252-06025-3 (v. 2)
    1. Southern States—History. 2. Southern States—Historiography.
    I. Gerster, Patrick. II. Cords, Nicholas.
    F209.M95 1989   88-4871
    975'.0072—dc19   CIP

For
Mark, Jennifer, Jason, James,
John, Nicholas, and Daniel

"Those are the Confederate dead," said Sally Carrol simply.

They walked along and read the inscriptions, always only a name and a date, sometimes quite indecipherable.

"The last row is the saddest—see, 'way over there. Every cross has just a date on it, and the word 'Unknown.'"

She looked at him and her eyes brimmed with tears.

"I can't tell you how real it is to me, darling—if you don't know."

"How you feel about it is beautiful to me."

"No, no, it's not me, it's them—that old time that I've tried to have live in me. These were just men, unimportant evidently or they wouldn't have been 'unknown'; but they died for the most beautiful thing in the world—the dead South. You see," she continued, her voice still husky, her eyes glistening with tears, "people have these dreams they fasten onto things, and I've always grown up with that dream. It was so easy because it was all dead and there weren't any disillusions comin' to me. I've tried in a way to live up to those past standards of noblesse oblige—there's just the last remnants of it, you know, like the roses of an old garden dying all around us— streaks of strange courtliness and chivalry in some of these boys an' stories I used to hear from a Confederate soldier who lived next door and a few old darkies. Oh, Harry, there was something, there was something! I couldn't ever make you understand, but it was there."

F. SCOTT FITZGERALD, *The Ice Palace*

There was something in the very air of a small town in the Deep South, something spooked-up and romantic, which did funny things to the imagination of its bright and resourceful boys. It had something to do with long and heavy afternoons with nothing doing, with rich slow evenings when the crickets scratched their legs and the frogs made delta music, with plain boredom, perhaps with an inherited tradition of making plots or playing practical jokes. I believe this hidden influence has something to do also with the Southern sense of fantasy and the absurd. We had to work our imaginations out on *something,* and the less austere, the better.

WILLIE MORRIS, *Good Old Boy*

Contents

Introduction to the Second Edition   xi

Introduction to the First Edition   xiii

1. GEORGE B. TINDALL, Mythology: A New Frontier
   in Southern History   1

2. PAUL M. GASTON, The New South Creed: A Study
   in Southern Mythmaking   17

3. DAVID M. POTTER, The Enigma of the South   33

4. PATRICK GERSTER AND NICHOLAS CORDS, The Northern
   Origins of Southern Mythology   43

5. ARTHUR S. LINK, The Progressive Movement in the
   South, 1870–1914   59

6. ANNE FIROR SCOTT, After Suffrage: Southern Women
   in the Twenties   81

7. JOHN HOPE FRANKLIN, The Great Confrontation: The
   South and the Problem of Change   101

8. C. VANN WOODWARD, The Search for Southern Identity   119

9. FRED C. HOBSON, The Savage South: An Inquiry into the
   Origins, Endurance, and Presumed Demise of an Image   133

10. SARA M. EVANS, Myth Against History: The Case
    of Southern Womanhood   141

11. CHARLES P. ROLAND, The Ever-Vanishing South   155

Bibliography   173

Index   185

Acknowledgments

As is the case with any project based on secondary sources, we have incurred many debts. Because this work is thematic, we are especially indebted to all those historians whose works have contributed either directly or indirectly to our developing interest in the relationship between myth and history. The work being regional in focus, we are most indebted to southern historians' contributions, and most particularly to those whose works are included herein. We also extend our thanks to Lawrence Malley, editor in chief, University of Illinois Press, who early developed a sustaining interest in the project. It is gratifying to note that he was instrumental in bringing the first edition from dream to reality and again plays a crucial role in this second edition. Further, he gave consistent encouragement during the book's long odyssey between editions. We would like also to thank Theresa Sears, our manuscript editor. Finally, we express deep gratitude to our wives and children for their usual support and diversions, however directly or indirectly they contributed to this edition.

Introduction to the Second Edition

The enthusiastic response to *Myth and Southern History* makes this second edition possible. In receiving both words of praise and suggestions for improvement from users of the first edition, our conviction about the relevance of a mythic perspective on the American South has, if anything, become even more firm. We feel secure in saying that perception of a mythic dimension to southern history has proven itself viable, as scholars continue to explore its frontiers and probe its subtleties. The mythological approach to southern history continues to be both relevant and exciting. It most assuredly has come of age, or at least it has assumed its proper place alongside the more traditional perspectives on the southern past.

Since the publication of the first edition of *Myth and Southern History*, we have had occasion to comment further—in classroom lectures, when presenting professional papers, and with the publication of articles, books, and reviews—on the elusive relationship of myth and southern history. What the intervening experiences have effected, in fact, is an even broader awareness of the reality myth contains. We continue to see myth and reality as complementary elements of the historical record. Indeed, even though southern myths may well emanate from historical inaccuracies, they are deeply imbedded in the fundamental explanations the South continues to hold about the mandates of its traditions. Their most important role is their persistent ability to control continuing social and political realities. In short, we stand convinced of our earlier stated belief, that many historical myths are factually false and psychologically true at one and the same time; and that their psychological truth is by far the more important.

Given the opportunity to completely revise *Myth and Southern History,* as editors we would have insisted on gender-neutral language and substitution of "black" for "Negro." We have found, however, good reason to retain the basic style of the first edition in the interests of sustaining the integrity of selections as originally published. Moreover, it is inevitable and proper, given the dynamic nature of southern scholarship, that we would add a number of new selections and drop several others. We have been guided by a desire to choose essays that voice our mythological theme in a scholarly way yet are readable and interesting.

This second edition contains new selections that deal with slavery in a colonial context, the nature of the slave debate (in both a historical and a historiographical sense), antebellum southern women, patterns of abolitionism and unionism in the Civil War era, the matter of the South's (indeed the nation's) reconstruction, the postbellum development of a civil religion, the role of the North in southern mythology, as well as new perspectives on such traditionally debated issues as the so-called Savage South, twentieth-century southern women both black and white, and the South's persistent Edenic impulse in the context of a continually emerging New South.

Introduction to the First Edition

Students of the southern past have long sought to identify a central theme in southern history. It was out of such a concern, for example, that historian Ulrich B. Phillips spoke of the sustained southern commitment to white supremacy; journalist Wilbur J. Cash sought to tap the inner workings of "the mind" of the South; and others have concluded the inner logic of southern history to be climate, geography, or its seemingly distinctive economic, political, social, or religious patterns. Indeed the debate over the central theme of southern history is a continuing one, with the only consensus being that there does exist a common thread of experience somewhere in the deep recesses of the southern past.

In 1964, while in pursuit of this central theme, George B. Tindall isolated "mythology" as a "new frontier" in southern history.[1] Acknowledging the work of earlier historians such as Francis Pendelton Gaines (*The Southern Plantation: A Study in the Development and Accuracy of a Tradition,* 1925), and anticipating the verdict of southern historians to come, Tindall's essay enthusiastically endorsed mythology as a tool for analyzing the rather blatant ambiguities, ironies, and paradoxes inherent in the southern past. The lens of myth had indeed been applied to the South before Professor Tindall's seminal work, but it was left for him to suggest that such an approach might well result in a new synthesis and a perspective worthy of sustained application. In short, Tindall's article posed the question: Is myth indeed one of the more important psychological determinants of southernism?

To what extent George B. Tindall's suggested approach to southern history will withstand the long-term erosion of historical scholarship is a question only future generations of scholars can answer with any full degree of certitude. It is the opinion of the editors, however, that an affirmative yet tentative judgment is now possible given the body of historical literature which has arisen clearly vindicating the Tindall thesis. An impressive array of southern scholars prior to and since Tindall's seminal essay have sought to determine the parameters of myth within what C. Vann Woodward has labeled "that twilight zone between living memory and written history." This volume brings together a sampling of their findings. Such scholars

---

[1] George B. Tindall, "Mythology: A New Frontier in Southern History," in Frank E. Vandiver (ed.), *The Idea of the South: Pursuit of a Central Theme* (Chicago, 1964).

are representative of an expanding and distinguished group of American historians who have come to see important distinctions between what might be termed "history as actuality" and "history as perceived."[2]

But perhaps further clarification and explanation are needed before this work can indeed provide the measure of historical insight which the "new frontier of mythology" potentially holds. The term "myth," as presented in this set of readings, is viewed in two ways. In the first instance, some of the authors seem to have Thomas A. Bailey's definition in mind as they speak of the myths of southern history: "a historical myth is . . . an account or belief that is demonstrably untrue, in whole or substantial part."[3] Those reflecting this definition tend to emphasize the negative aspects of myth, to isolate, and when the occasion warrants to debunk the results of misguided scholarship. Second, others appear more consistent with Henry Nash Smith's view of myth as "an intellectual construction that fuses concept and emotion into an image."[4] Briefly stated, one school seeks to emphasize historical inaccuracies while the other approaches the problem from the vantage point of social psychology. One sees myth as the by-product of historical scholarship (or lack of it), while the other shows a marked concern for the ways in which myth serves the decidedly positive function of unifying experience providing, in the words of Mark Schorer, "a large controlling image that gives philosophical meaning to the facts of ordinary life. . . ."[5] Certainly, at times both definitions are present—on occasion they tend to blend to the point of becoming almost indistinguishable. Both notions of myth are germane to the South and its history.

It is also important to note that the existence of a southern mythology in no way sets the South apart as distinctive or unique. It has been demonstrated in other quarters that much behavior and belief based on myth survives, and in fact thrives, in the contemporary world. The preeminent mythic scholar, Mircea Eliade, has observed that "certain aspects and functions of mythical thought are constituents of the human being."[6] Fundamental to the "human condition," myths in their infinite variety and complexity serve a supportive role to the dreams, ideals, and values of every society. Accordingly, "southern mythology" must be seen as differing from

[2] For a view of myth in its larger American context see Nicholas Cords and Patrick Gerster (eds.), *Myth and the American Experience*, 2 vols. (New York and Beverly Hills, 1973).

[3] Thomas A. Bailey, "The Mythmakers of American History," *The Journal of American History*, 55 (June 1968), p. 5.

[4] Henry Nash Smith, *Virgin Land: The American West as Symbol and Myth* (New York, 1950), p. v.

[5] Mark Schorer, "The Necessity of Myth," in Henry A. Murray (ed.), *Myth and Mythmaking* (New York, 1960), p. 355.

[6] Mircea Eliade, "Survivals and Camouflages of Myth," *Diogenes*, 41 (Spring 1963), p. 1.

its American equivalent only in degree not in kind, just as "American mythology" stands in relation to that of the world at large. Paul M. Gaston concurred with this judgment in his recent work, *The New South Creed: A Study in Southern Mythmaking:*

> What does distinguish the South, at least from other parts of the United States, is the degree to which myths have been spawned and the extent to which they have asserted their hegemony over the Southern mind.[7]

In this sense, at least, the American South has successfully transcended the strictures of regionalism.

Finally, the identification of myth as an important element in the historical process demonstrates anew that history is the dual product of documentation and imagination—both the record of the past *and* the dialogue among historians. The basic documents and the personal and professional prejudices of the historian (for Wendell H. Stephenson, "the fallacies of assumptions and methods") all find their way into the historical "record." The historian cannot dismiss the controlling images or myths of the society within which he writes. Because the serious historian must factor for all of these as he engages his discipline, this volume is as much a commentary on the writing of southern history—that is to say historiography—as it is on the viability of myth in the historical process. In these pages there is much support of the observation that "myth[s] have been used for centuries in writing history as well as making it."[8] The reader will find that "mythology" has provided, as well as suggests, new realms of scholarly speculation. More specifically, it becomes evident that such an approach applied to the South has come of age. It is an approach to southern history both relevant and exciting, deserving to *take its stand* beside the more traditional and validated perspectives long provided by historians of the marketplace, the political and diplomatic arenas, and the social record.

Some years ago Wilbur Cash wrote of the importance of the South's frontier experience: ". . . the history of the roll of frontier upon frontier— and on to the frontier beyond."[9] Given George B. Tindall's scholarly directive and the focus provided by the following selections, perhaps the South's enigmatic frontiers of the past—even that elusive central theme—can now find clearer explanation and synthesis in terms of her "new frontier of mythology."

---

[7] Paul M. Gaston, *The New South Creed: A Study in Southern Mythmaking* (New York, 1970), p. 8.

[8] Alfred Stern, "Fiction and Myth in History," *Diogenes,* 42 (Summer 1963), p. 98.

[9] Wilbur Cash, *The Mind of the South* (New York, 1941), p. 4.

1

Mythology: A New Frontier in Southern History

George B. Tindall

The "reality" of history, irrespective of time or place, remains an elusive commodity, especially as regards the American South. Indeed, as George B. Tindall, Professor of History at the University of North Carolina, Chapel Hill, argues in the selection which follows, the basic problem of distinguishing *objective reality* from *perceived reality* is ever present for the historian. Historical reality involves not only that which is demonstrably true but also that which one believes to be true. As such, the historian has a dual role: he remains at once a "custodian of the past and keeper of the public memory." The role of the historian involves both countering misguided scholarship and identifying the public dreams which do so much to orchestrate human behavior. Both of these facets of the historical enterprise inevitably lead the historian into the province of myth. Thus, in determining the dimensions of the southern experience, the historian must reckon not only with peculiar regional characteristics but also the myths which have conditioned them. As a significant unit of the region's experience, myth supplies an internal structure and a sustaining symmetry to our understanding of the South. Professor Tindall's exploration of this new frontier of mythology does much to establish the context—the perspective and technique—for this entire work.

From George Tindall, "Mythology: A New Frontier in Southern History," in Frank E. Vandiver (ed.), *The Idea of the South: Pursuit of a Central Theme*, pp. 1–15. Reprinted by permission of the author and the University of Chicago Press. Copyright © 1964 by William Rice University. All rights reserved. Published 1964. Composed and printed by the University of Chicago Press, Chicago, Illinois, U.S.A.

The idea of the South—or more appropriately, the ideas of the South—belong in large part to the order of social myth. There are few areas of the modern world that have bred a regional mythology so potent, so profuse and diverse, even so paradoxical, as the American South. But the various mythical images of the South that have so significantly affected American history have yet to be subjected to the kind of broad and imaginative historical analysis that has been applied to the idea of the American West, particularly in Henry Nash Smith's *Virgin Land: The American West as Symbol and Myth*. The idea of the South has yet to be fully examined in the context of mythology, as essentially a problem of intellectual history.

To place the ideas of the South in the context of mythology, of course, is not necessarily to pass judgment upon them as illusions. The game of debunking myths, Harry Levin has warned us, starts "in the denunciation of myth as falsehood from the vantage-point of a rival myth."[1] Mythology has other meanings, not all of them pejorative, and myths have a life of their own which to some degree renders irrelevant the question of their correlation to empirical fact. Setting aside for the moment the multiple connotations of the term, we may say that social myths in general, including those of the South, are simply mental pictures that portray the pattern of what a people think they are (or ought to be) or what somebody else thinks they are. They tend to develop abstract ideas in more or less concrete and dramatic terms. In the words of Henry Nash Smith, they fuse "concept and emotion into an image."[2]

They may serve a variety of functions. "A myth," Mark Schorer has observed, "is a large, controlling image that gives philosophical meaning to the facts of ordinary life; that is, which has organizing value for experience."[3] It may offer useful generalizations by which data may be tested. But being also "charged with values, aspirations, ideals and meanings,"[4] myths may become the ground for belief, for either loyalty and defense on the one hand or hostility and opposition on the other. In such circumstances a myth itself becomes one of the realities of history, significantly influencing the course of human action, for good or ill. There is, of course, always a danger of illusion, a danger that in ordering one's vision of reality, the myth may predetermine the categories of perception, rendering one blind to things that do not fit into the mental image.

---

[1] Harry Levin, "Some Meanings of Myth," in Henry A. Murray (ed.), *Myth and Mythmakers* (New York, 1960), p. 106.

[2] Henry Nash Smith, *Virgin Land: The American West as Symbol and Myth* (Vintage ed., New York, 1957), p. v.

[3] Mark Schorer, "The Necessity for Myth," in Murray (ed.), *Myth and Mythmakers*, p. 355.

[4] C. Vann Woodward, "The Antislavery Myth," *American Scholar*, XXXI (Spring, 1962), 325.

Since the Southern mind is reputed to be peculiarly resistant to pure abstraction and more receptive to the concrete and dramatic image, it may be unusually susceptible to mythology. Perhaps for the same reason our subject can best be approached through reference to the contrasting experiences of two Southerners—one recent, the other about forty-five years ago.

The first is the experience of a contemporary Louisiana writer, John T. Westbrook.

> During the thirties and early forties [Westbrook has written] when I was an English instructor at the University of Missouri, I was often mildly irritated by the average northerner's Jeeter-Lester-and-potlikker idea of the South. Even today the northern visitor inertia-headedly maintains his misconception: he hankers to see eroded hills and rednecks, scrub cotton and sharecropper shacks.
>
> It little profits me to drive him through Baton Rouge, show him the oil-ethyl-rubber-aluminum-chemical miles of industry along the Mississippi River, and say, "This . . . is the fastest-growing city of over 100,-000 in America. We can amply substantiate our claim that we are atomic target number one, that in the next war the Russians will obliterate us first. . . ."
>
> Our northerner is suspicious of all this crass evidence presented to his senses. It bewilders and befuddles him. He is too deeply steeped in William Faulkner and Robert Penn Warren. The fumes of progress are in his nose and the bright steel of industry towers before his eyes, but his heart is away in Yoknapatawpha County with razorback hogs and night riders. On this trip to the South he wants, above all else, to sniff the effluvium of backwoods-and-sand-hill subhumanity and to see at least one barn burn at midnight. So he looks at me with crafty misgiving, as if to say, "Well, you *do* drive a Cadillac, talk rather glibly about Kierkegaard and Sartre . . . but, after all, you *are* only fooling, aren't you? You do, don't you, sometimes, go out secretly by owl-light to drink swamp water and feed on sowbelly and collard greens?"[5]

The other story was the experience of a Southern historian, Frank L. Owsley, who traveled during World War I from Chicago via Cincinnati to Montgomery with a group of young ladies on the way to visit their menfolk at an army camp. He wrote later that, "despite everything which had ever been said to the contrary," the young ladies had a romantic conception of the "Sunny South" and looked forward to the journey with considerable ex-

John T. Westbrook, "Twilight of Southern Regionalism," *Southwest Review,* XLII (Summer, 1957), 231.

citement. "They expected to enter a pleasant land of white columned mansions, green pastures, expansive cotton and tobacco fields where negroes sang spirituals all the day through." Except in the bluegrass basins of central Kentucky and Tennessee, what they actually found "were gutted hillsides; scrub oak and pine; bramble and blackberry thickets, bottom lands once fertile now senile and exhausted, with spindling tobacco, corn, or cotton stalks . . . ; unpainted houses which were hardly more than shacks or here and there the crumbling ruins of old mansions covered with briars, the homes of snakes and lizards."[6] The disappointment of Dr. Owsley's ladies was, no doubt, even greater than that of Mr. Westbrook's friend in Baton Rouge.

There is a striking contrast between these two episodes, both in the picture of Southern reality and in the differing popular images that they present. The fact that they are four decades apart helps to account for the discrepancies, but what is not apparent at first is the common ancestry of the two images. They are not very distant cousins, collateral descendants from the standard image of the Old South, the plantation myth. The version of Owsley's lady friends is closer to the original primogenitor, which despite its advancing age and debility, still lives amid a flourishing progeny of legendary Southern gentility. According to Francis Pendleton Gaines, author of *The Southern Plantation,* the pattern appeared full-blown at least as early as 1832 in John Pendleton Kennedy's romance, *Swallow Barn.*[7] It has had a long career in story and novel and song, in the drama and motion picture. The corrosions of age seem to have ended its Hollywood career, although the old films still turn up on the late late. It may still be found in the tourist bait of shapely beauties in hoop skirts posed against the backdrop of white columns at Natchez, Orton, or a hundred other places.

These pictures are enough to trigger in the mind the whole euphoric pattern of kindly old marster with his mint julep; happy darkies singing in fields perpetually white to the harvest or, as the case may be, sadly recalling the long lost days of old; coquettish belles wooed by slender gallants in gray underneath the moonlight and magnolias. It is a pattern that yields all too easily to caricature and ridicule, for in its more sophisticated versions the figure of the planter carries a heavy freight of the aristocratic virtues: courtliness, grace, hospitality, honor, *noblesse oblige,* as well as many no less charming aristocratic vices: a lordly indifference to the balance sheet, hot temper, profanity, overindulgence, a certain stubborn obstinacy. The old-time Negro, when not a figure of comedy, is the very embodiment of

[6] Frank L. Owsley, "The Old South and the New," *American Review,* VI (February, 1936), 475.

[7] Francis Pendleton Gaines, *The Southern Plantation: A Study in the Development and Accuracy of a Tradition* (New York, 1925), p. 23.

loyalty. And the Southern belle: "Beautiful, graceful, accomplished in social charm, bewitching in coquetry, yet strangely steadfast in soul," Gaines
has written, "she is perhaps the most winsome figure in the whole field of
our fancy."[8] "The plantation romance," Gaines says, "remains our chief
social idyl of the past; of an Arcadian scheme of existence, less material,
less hurried, less prosaically equalitarian, less futile, richer in picturesqueness, festivity, in realized pleasure that recked not of hope or fear or un-
rejoicing labor."[9]

But there is still more to the traditional pattern. Somewhere off in the
piney woods and erosion-gutted clay hills, away from the white columns
and gentility, there existed Po' White Trash: the crackers; hillbillies; sand-
hillers; rag, tag, and bobtail; squatters; "po' buckra" to the Negroes; the
Ransy Sniffle of A. B. Longstreet's *Georgia Scenes* and his literary descendants like Jeeter Lester and Ab Snopes, abandoned to poverty and degeneracy—the victims, it was later discovered, of hookworm, malaria, and
pellagra. Somewhere in the pattern the respectable small farmer was lost
from sight. He seemed to be neither romantic nor outrageous enough to
fit in. His neglect provides the classic example in Southern history of the
blind spots engendered by the power of mythology. It was not until the
1930's that Frank L. Owsley and his students at Vanderbilt rediscovered
the Southern yeoman farmer as the characteristic, or at least the most
numerous, ante bellum white Southerner.[10] More about the yeoman pres-
ently; neglected in the plantation myth, he was in the foreground of another.

In contrast to the legitimate heirs of the plantation myth, the image of
John T. Westbrook's Yankee visitor in Baton Rouge seems to be descended
from what might be called the illegitimate line of the plantation myth, out
of abolition. It is one of the ironies of our history that, as Gaines put it, the
"two opposing sides of the fiercest controversy that ever shook national
thought agreed concerning certain picturesque elements of plantation life
and joined hands to set the conception unforgettably in public consciousness."[11] The abolitionists found it difficult, or even undesirable, to escape
the standard image. It was pretty fully developed even in *Uncle Tom's
Cabin.* Harriet Beecher Stowe made her villain a Yankee overseer, and has
been accused by at least one latter-day abolitionist of implanting deeply in
the American mind the stereotype of the faithful darkey. For others the
plantation myth simply appeared in reverse, as a pattern of corrupt opulence resting upon human exploitation. Gentle old marster became the ar-

[8] *Ibid.,* p. 16.
[9] *Ibid.,* p. 4.
[10] Frank L. Owsley, *Plain Folk of the Old South* (Baton Rouge, 1949).
[11] Gaines, *The Southern Plantation,* p. 30.

rogant, haughty, imperious potentate, the very embodiment of sin, the central target of the antislavery attack. He maintained a seraglio in the slave quarters; he bred Negroes like cattle and sold them down the river to certain death in the sugar mills, separating families if that served his purpose, while Southern women suffered in silence the guilty knowledge of their men's infidelity. The happy darkies in this picture became white men in black skins, an oppressed people longing for freedom, the victims of countless atrocities so ghastly as to be unbelievable except for undeniable evidence, forever seeking an opportunity to follow the North Star to freedom. The masses of the white folks were simply poor whites, relegated to ignorance and degeneracy by the slavocracy.

Both lines of the plantation myth have been remarkably prolific, but the more adaptable one has been that of the abolitionists. It has repeatedly readjusted to new conditions while the more legitimate line has courted extinction, running out finally into the decadence perpetrated by Tennessee Williams. Meanwhile, the abolitionist image of brutality persisted through and beyond Reconstruction in the Republican outrage mills and bloody shirt political campaigns. For several decades it was more than overbalanced by the Southern image of Reconstruction horrors, disarmed by prophets of a New South created in the image of the North, and almost completely submerged under the popularity of plantation romances in the generation before Owsley's trainload of ladies ventured into their "Sunny South" of the teens. At about that time, however, the undercurrents began to emerge once again into the mainstream of American thought. In the clever decade of the twenties a kind of neoabolitionist myth of the Savage South was compounded. It seemed that the benighted South, after a period of relative neglect, suddenly became an object of concern to every publicist in the country. One Southern abomination after another was ground through their mills: child labor, peonage, lynching, hookworm, pellagra, the Scopes trial, the Fundamentalist crusade against Al Smith. The guiding genius was Henry L. Mencken, the hatchet man from Baltimore who developed the game of South-baiting into a national pastime, a fine art at which he had no peer. In 1917, when he started constructing his image of "Baptist and Methodist barbarism" below the Potomac, he began with the sterility of Southern literature and went on from there. With characteristic glee he anointed one J. Gordon Coogler of South Carolina "the last bard of Dixie" and quoted his immortal couplet:

> Alas, for the South! Her books have grown fewer—
> She never was much given to literature.

"Down there," Mencken wrote, "a poet is now almost as rare as an oboe-player, a dry-point etcher or a metaphysician." As for "critics, musical composers, painters, sculptors, architects . . . there is not even a bad one between the Potomac mud-flats and the Gulf. Nor an historian. Nor a sociologist. Nor a philosopher. Nor a theologian. Nor a scientist. In all these fields the south is an awe-inspiring blank. . . ."[12] It was as complete a vacuity as the interstellar spaces, the "Sahara of the Bozart," "The Bible Belt." He summed it all up in one basic catalogue of Southern grotesqueries: "Fundamentalism, Ku Kluxry, revivals, lynchings, hog wallow politics— these are the things that always occur to a northerner when he thinks of the south."[13] The South, in short, had fallen prey to its poor whites, who would soon achieve apotheosis in the Snopes family.

It did not end with the twenties. The image was reinforced by a variety of episodes: the Scottsboro trials, chain gang exposés, Bilbo and Rankin, Senate filibusters, labor wars; much later by Central High and Orval Faubus, Emmett Till and Autherine Lucy and James Meredith, bus boycotts and Freedom Riders; and not least of all by the lush growth of literature that covered Mencken's Sahara, with Caldwell's *Tobacco Road* and Faulkner's *Sanctuary* and various other products of what Ellen Glasgow labeled the Southern Gothic and a less elegant Mississippi editor called the "privy school" of literature. In the words of Faulkner's character, Gavin Stevens, the North suffered from a curious "gullibility: a volitionless, almost helpless capacity and eagerness to believe anything about the South not even provided it be derogatory but merely bizarre enough and strange enough."[14] And Faulkner, to be sure, did not altogether neglect that market. Not surprisingly, he was taken in some quarters for a realist, and the image of Southern savagery long obscured the critics' recognition of his manifold merits.

The family line of the plantation myth can be traced only so far in the legendary gentility and savagery of the South. Other family lines seem to be entirely independent—if sometimes on friendly terms. In an excellent study, "The New South Creed, 1865–1900," soon to be published, Paul M. Gaston has traced the evolution of the creed into a genuine myth. In the aftermath of the Civil War, apostles of a "New South," led by Henry W. Grady, preached with almost evangelical fervor the gospel of industry. Their dream, Gaston writes, "was essentially a promise of American life for the South. It proffered all the glitter and glory and freedom from guilt that inhered in the American ideal."[15] From advocacy, from this vision of

---

[12] Henry L. Mencken, "The Sahara of the Bozart," in *Prejudices: Second Series* (New York, 1920), pp. 136, 137, 139.

[13] Henry L. Mencken, "The South Rebels Again," in Robert McHugh (ed.), *The Bathtub Hoax and Other Blasts & Bravos from the Chicago Tribune* (New York, 1958), p. 249. From a column in the Chicago *Tribune,* December 7, 1924.

[14] William Faulkner, *Intruder in the Dust* (New York, 1948), p. 153.

[15] Paul Morton Gaston, "The New South Creed, 1865–1900" (Ph.D. dissertation, Department of History, University of North Carolina, 1961), p. 193.

the future, the prophets soon advanced to the belief that "their promised land [was] at hand, no longer merely a gleaming goal." "By the twentieth century . . . there was established for many in the South a pattern of belief within which they could see themselves and their section as rich, success-oriented, and just . . . opulence and power were at hand . . . the Negro lived in the best of all possible worlds."[16]

As the twentieth century advanced, and wealth did in fact increase, the creed of the New South took on an additional burden of crusades for good roads and education, blending them into what Francis B. Simkins has called the "trinity of Southern progress": industrial growth, good roads, and schools. When the American Historical Association went to Durham in 1929 for its annual meeting, Robert D. W. Connor of the University of North Carolina presented the picture of a rehabilitated South that had "shaken itself free from its heritage of war and Reconstruction. Its self-confidence restored, its political stability assured, its prosperity regained, its social problems on the way to solution. . . ."[17] Two months before Connor spoke, the New York Stock Exchange had broken badly, and in the aftermath the image he described was seriously blurred, but before the end of the thirties it was being brought back into focus by renewed industrial expansion that received increased momentum from World War II and postwar prosperity.

Two new and disparate images emerged in the depression years, both with the altogether novel feature of academic trappings and affiliations. One was the burgeoning school of sociological regionalism led by Howard W. Odum and Rupert B. Vance at the University of North Carolina. It was neither altogether the image of the Savage South nor that of industrial progress, although both entered into the compound. It was rather a concept of the "Problem South," which Franklin D. Roosevelt labeled "the Nation's Economic Problem No. 1," a region with indisputable shortcomings but with potentialities that needed constructive attention and the application of rational social planning. Through the disciples of Odum as well as the agencies of the New Deal, the vision issued in a flood of social science monographs and programs for reform and development. To one undergraduate in Chapel Hill at the time, it seemed in retrospect that "we had more of an attitude of service to the South as the South than was true later. . . ."[18]

The regionalists were challenged by the Vanderbilt Agrarians, who de-

---

[16] *Ibid.,* pp. 195, 216.

[17] Robert D. W. Connor, "The Rehabilitation of a Rural Commonwealth," *American Historical Review,* XXXVI (October, 1930), 62.

[18] Alexander Heard, quoted in Wilma Dykeman and James Stokely, *Seeds of Southern Change: The Life of Will Alexander* (Chicago, 1962), p. 303.

veloped a myth of the traditional South. Their manifesto, *I'll Take My Stand,* by Twelve Southerners, appeared by fortuitous circumstance in 1930 when industrial capitalism seemed on the verge of collapse. In reaction against both the progressive New South and Mencken's image of savagery they championed, in Donald Davidson's words, a "traditional society . . . that is stable, religious, more rural than urban, and politically conservative," in which human needs were supplied by "Family, bloodkinship, clanship, folkways, custom, community. . . ."[19] The ideal of the traditional virtues took on the texture of myth in their image of the agrarian South. Of course, in the end, their agrarianism proved less important as a social-economic force than as a context for creative literature. The central figures in the movement were the Fugitive poets John Crowe Ransom, Donald Davidson, Allen Tate, and Robert Penn Warren. But, as Professor Louis Rubin has emphasized, "Through their vision of an agrarian community, the authors of *I'll Take My Stand* presented a critique of the modern world. In contrast to the hurried, nervous life of cities, the image of the agrarian South was of a life in which human beings existed serenely and harmoniously." Their critique of the modern frenzy "has since been echoed by commentator after commentator."[20]

While it never became altogether clear whether the Agrarians were celebrating the aristocratic graces or following the old Jeffersonian dictum that "Those who labor in the earth are the chosen people of God . . . ," most of them seemed to come down eventually on the side of the farmer rather than the planter. Frank L. Owsley, who rediscovered the ante bellum yeoman farmer, was one of them. Insofar as they extolled the yeoman farmer, the Agrarians laid hold upon an image older than any of the others—the Jeffersonian South. David M. Potter, a Southerner in exile at Stanford University, has remarked how difficult it is for many people to realize that the benighted South "was, until recently, regarded by many liberals as the birthplace and the natural bulwark of the Jeffersonian ideal. . . ."[21] The theme has long had an appeal for historians as well as others, Frederick Jackson Turner developed it for the West and William E. Dodd for the South. According to Dodd the democratic, equalitarian South of the Jeffersonian image was the norm; the plantation slavocracy was the great aberration. Dodd's theme has been reflected in the writing of other his-

[19] Donald Davidson, "Why the Modern South Has a Great Literature," *Vanderbilt Studies in the Humanities,* I (1951), 12.

[20] Louis D. Rubin, Jr., "Introduction to the Torchbook Edition," in Twelve Southerners, *I'll Take My Stand* (Torchbook ed.; New York, 1962), pp. xiv, xvii. See also Herman Clarence Nixon, "A Thirty Years' Personal View," *Mississippi Quarterly,* XIII (Spring, 1960), 79, for parallels in recent social criticism.

[21] David M. Potter, "The Enigma of the South," *Yale Review,* LI (Autumn, 1961), 143.

torians, largely in terms of a region subjected to economic colonialism by an imperial Northeast: Charles A. Beard, for example, who saw the sectional conflict as a struggle between agrarianism and industrialism; Howard K. Beale, who interpreted Reconstruction in similar terms; C. Vann Woodward, defender of Populism; Arthur S. Link, who first rediscovered the Southern progressives; and Walter Prescott Webb, who found the nation divided between an exploited South and West on the one hand, and a predatory Northeast on the other. Jefferson, like the South, it sometimes seems, can mean all things to all men, and the Jefferson image of agrarian democracy has been a favorite recourse of Southern liberals, just as his state-rights doctrines have nourished conservatism.

In stark contrast to radical agrarianism there stands the concept of monolithic conservatism in Southern politics. It seems to be a proposition generally taken for granted now that the South is, by definition, conservative—and always has been. Yet the South in the late nineteenth century produced some of the most radical Populists and in the twentieth was a bulwark of Wilsonian progressivism and Roosevelt's New Deal, at least up to a point. A good case has been made out by Arthur S. Link that Southern agrarian radicals pushed Wilson further into progressivism than he intended to go.[22] During the twenties Southern minority leadership in Congress kept up such a running battle against the conservative tax policies of Andrew Mellon that, believe it or not, there was real fear among some Northern businessmen during the 1932 campaign that Franklin D. Roosevelt might be succeeded by that radical Southern income-taxer, John Nance Garner![23] The conservative image of course has considerable validity, but it obscures understanding of such phenomena as Albert Gore, Russell Long, Lister Hill, John Sparkman, Olin D. Johnston, William Fulbright, the Yarboroughs of Texas, or the late Estes Kefauver. In the 1960 campaign the conservative image seriously victimized Lyndon B. Johnson, who started in politics as a vigorous New Dealer and later maneuvered through the Senate the first civil rights legislation since Reconstruction.

The infinite variety of Southern mythology could be catalogued and analyzed endlessly. A suggestive list would include the Proslavery South; the Confederate South; the Demagogic South; the State Rights South; the Fighting South; the Lazy South; the Folklore South; the South of jazz and the blues; the Booster South; the Rapacious South running away with Northern industries; the Liberal South of the interracial movement; the White Supremacy South of racial segregation, which seems to be for some

[22] Arthur S. Link, "The South and the 'New Freedom': An Interpretation," *American Scholar*, XX (Summer, 1951), 314–24.
[23] A. G. Hopkins to Sam Rayburn, July 29, 1932; Rayburn to J. Andrew West, October 26, 1932, in Sam Rayburn Library, Bonham, Texas.

the all-encompassing "Southern way of life"; the Anglo-Saxon (or was it the Scotch-Irish?) South, the most American of all regions because of its native population; or the Internationalist South, a mainstay of the Wilson, Roosevelt, and Truman foreign policies.

The South, then, has been the seedbed for a proliferation of paradoxical myths, all of which have some basis in empirical fact and all of which doubtlessly have, or have had, their true believers. The result has been, in David Potter's words, that the South has become an enigma, "a kind of Sphinx on the American land."[24] What is really the answer to the riddle, what is at bottom the foundation of Southern distinctiveness has never been established with finality, but the quest for a central theme of Southern history has repeatedly engaged the region's historians. Like Frederick Jackson Turner, who extracted the essential West in his frontier thesis, Southern historians have sought to distill the quintessence of the South into some kind of central theme.

In a recent survey of these efforts David L. Smiley of Wake Forest College has concluded that they turn upon two basic lines of thought: "the causal effects of environment, and the development of certain acquired characteristics of the people called Southern."[25] The distinctive climate and weather of the South, it has been argued, slowed the pace of life, tempered the speech of the South, dictated the system of staple crops and Negro slavery—in short, predetermined the plantation economy. The more persuasive suggestions have resulted from concentration upon human factors and causation. The best known is that set forth by U. B. Phillips. The quintessence of Southernism, he wrote in 1928, was "a common resolve indomitably maintained" that the South "shall be and remain a white man's country." Whether "expressed with the frenzy of a demagogue or maintained with a patrician's quietude," this was "the cardinal test of a Southerner and the central theme of Southern history."[26] Other historians have pointed to the rural nature of Southern society as the basic conditioning factor, to the prevalence of the country gentleman ideal imported from England, to the experience of the South as a conscious minority unified by criticism and attack from outside, to the fundamental piety of the Bible Belt, and to various other factors. It has even been suggested by one writer that a chart of the mule population would determine the boundaries of the South.

More recently, two historians have attempted new explanations. In his

[24] Potter, "The Enigma of the South," p. 142.

[25] David L. Smiley, "The Quest for the Central Theme in Southern History," paper read before the Southern Historical Association, Miami Beach, Florida, November 8, 1962, p. 2.

[26] Ulrich B. Phillips, "The Central Theme of Southern History," in E. Merton Coulter (ed.), *The Course of the South to Secession* (New York, 1939), p. 152.

search for a Southern identity, C. Vann Woodward advances several crucial factors: the experience of poverty in a land of plenty; failure and defeat
in a land that glorifies success; sin and guilt amid the legend of American
innocence; and a sense of place and belonging among a people given to
abstraction.[27] David M. Potter, probing the enigma of the South, has found
the key to the riddle in the prevalence of a folk society. "This folk culture,
we know, was far from being ideal or utopian," he writes, "and was in fact
full of inequality and wrong, but if the nostalgia persists was it because
even the inequality and wrong were parts of a life that still had a relatedness and meaning which our more bountiful life in the mass culture seems
to lack?"[28]

It is significant that both explanations are expressed largely in the past
tense, Potter's explicitly in terms of nostalgia. They recognize, by implica-
tion at least, still another image—that of the Dynamic or the Changing
South. The image may be rather nebulous and the ultimate ends unclear,
but the fact of change is written inescapably across the Southern scene. The
consciousness of change has been present so long as to become in itself
one of the abiding facts of Southern life. Surely, it was a part of the inspiration for the symposium that resulted in this volume. As far back as the
twenties it was the consciousness of change that quickened the imaginations
of a cultivated and sensitive minority, giving us the Southern renaissance
in literature. The peculiar historical consciousness of the Southern writer,
Allen Tate has suggested, "made possible the curious burst of intelligence
that we get at a crossing of the ways, not unlike, on an infinitesmal scale,
the outburst of poetic genius at the end of the sixteenth century when commercial England had already begun to crush feudal England."[29] Trace it
through modern Southern writing, and at the center—in Ellen Glasgow, in
Faulkner, Wolfe, Caldwell, the Fugitive-Agrarian poets, and all the others
—there is the consciousness of change, of suspension between two worlds, a
double focus looking both backward and forward.

The Southerner of the present generation has seen the old landmarks
crumble with great rapidity: the one-crop agriculture and the very pre-
dominance of agriculture itself, the one-party system, the white primary,
the poll tax, racial segregation, the poor white (at least in his classic connotations), the provincial isolation—virtually all the foundations of the
established order. Yet, sometimes, the old traditions endure in surprising
new forms. Southern folkways have been carried even into the factory,

---

[27] C. Vann Woodward, "The Search for a Southern Identity," in *The Burden of
Southern History* (Baton Rouge, 1960), pp. 3–25.

[28] Potter, "The Enigma of the South," p. 151.

[29] Allen Tate, "The New Provincialism," *Virginia Quarterly Review,* XXI (Spring,
1945), 272.

and the Bible Belt has revealed resources undreamed of in Mencken's philosophy—but who, in the twenties, could have anticipated Martin Luther King?

One wonders what new images, what new myths, might be nurtured by the emerging South. Some, like Harry Ashmore, have merely written *An Epitaph for Dixie*. It is the conclusion of two Southern sociologists, John M. Maclachlan and Joe S. Floyd, Jr., that present trends "might well hasten the day when the South, once perhaps the most distinctively 'different' American region, will have become . . . virtually indistinguishable from the other urban-industrial areas of the nation."[30] U. B. Phillips long ago suggested that the disappearance of race as a major issue would end Southern distinctiveness. One may wonder if Southern distinctiveness might even be preserved in new conditions entirely antithetic to his image. Charles L. Black, Jr., another *émigré* Southerner (at Yale Law School) has confessed to a fantastic dream that Southern whites and Negroes, bound in a special bond of common tragedy, may come to recognize their kinship. There is not the slightest warrant for it, he admits, in history, sociology, or common sense. But if it should come to pass, he suggests, "The South, which has always felt itself reserved for a high destiny, would have found it, and would have come to flower at last. And the fragrance of it would spread, beyond calculation, over the world."[31]

Despite the consciousness of change, perhaps even more because of it, Southerners still feel a persistent pull toward identification with their native region as a ground for belief and loyalty. Is there not yet something more than nostalgia to the idea of the South? Is there not some living heritage with which the modern Southerner can identify? Is there not, in short, a viable myth of the South? The quest for myth has been a powerful factor in recent Southern literature, and the suspicion is strong that it will irresistibly affect any historian's quest for the central theme of Southern history. It has all too clearly happened before—in the climatic theory, for example, which operated through its geographical determinism to justify the social order of the plantation, or the Phillips thesis of white supremacy, which has become almost a touchstone of the historian's attitude toward the whole contemporary issue of race. "To elaborate a central theme," David L. Smiley has asserted, is "but to reduce a multi-faceted story to a single aspect, and its result . . . but to find new footnotes to confirm revealed truths and prescribed views."[32] The trouble is that the quest for the central

[30] John M. Maclachlan and Joe S. Floyd, Jr., *This Changing South* (Gainesville, Fla., 1956), p. 151.

[31] Charles L. Black, Jr., "Paths to Desegregation," *New Republic,* CXXXVII (October 21, 1957), 15.

[32] Smiley, "The Quest for the Central Theme in Southern History," p. 1.

theme, like Turner's frontier thesis, becomes absorbed willy-nilly into the process of myth making.

To pursue the Turner analogy a little further, the conviction grows that the frontier thesis, with all its elaborations and critiques, has been exhausted (and in part exploded) as a source of new historical insight. It is no derogation of insights already gained to suggest that the same thing has happened to the quest for the central theme, and that the historian, *as historian,* may be better able to illuminate our understanding of the South now by turning to a new focus upon the regional mythology.

To undertake the analysis of mythology will no longer require him to venture into uncharted wilderness. A substantial conceptual framework of mythology has already been developed by anthropologists, philosophers, psychologists, theologians, and literary critics. The historian, while his field has always been closely related to mythology, has come only lately to the critique of it. But there now exists a considerable body of historical literature on the American national mythology and the related subject of the national character, and Smith's stimulating *Virgin Land* suggests the trails that may be followed into the idea of the South.

Several trails, in fact, have already been blazed. Nearly forty years ago, Francis Pendleton Gaines successfully traced the rise and progress of the plantation myth, and two recent authors have belatedly taken to the same trail. Howard R. Floan has considerably increased our knowledge of the abolitionist version in his study of Northern writers, *The South in Northern Eyes,* while William R. Taylor has approached the subject from an entirely new perspective in his *Cavalier and Yankee.* Shields McIlwaine has traced the literary image of the poor white, while Stanley Elkins' *Slavery* has broken sharply from established concepts on both sides of that controversial question.[33] One foray into the New South has been made in Paul Gaston's "The New South Creed, 1865–1900." Yet many important areas —the Confederate and Reconstruction myths, for example—still remain almost untouched.

Some of the basic questions that need to be answered have been attacked in these studies; some have not. It is significant that students of literature have led the way and have pointed up the value of even third-rate creative literature in the critique of myth. The historian, however, should be able to contribute other perspectives. With his peculiar time perspective he can seek to unravel the tangled genealogy of myth that runs back from the modern Changing South to Jefferson's yeoman and Kennedy's plantation.

[33] Howard R. Floan, *The South in Northern Eyes, 1831–1860* (Austin, 1958); William R. Taylor, *Cavalier and Yankee: The Old South and American National Character* (New York, 1961); Shields McIlwaine, *The Southern Poor White from Lubberland to Tobacco Road* (Norman, Okla., 1939); Stanley M. Elkins, *Slavery: A Problem in American Institutional and Intellectual Life* (Chicago, 1959).

Along the way he should investigate the possibility that some obscure dialectic may be at work in the pairing of obverse images: the two versions of the plantation, New South and Old, Cavalier and Yankee, genteel and savage, regionalist and agrarian, nativist and internationalist.

What, the historian may ask, have been the historical origins and functions of the myths? The plantation myth, according to Gaines and Floan, was born in the controversy and emotion of the struggle over slavery. It had polemical uses for both sides. Taylor, on the other hand, finds it origin in the psychological need, both North and South, to find a corrective for the grasping, materialistic, rootless society symbolized by the image of the Yankee. Vann Woodward and Gaston have noted its later psychological uses in bolstering the morale of the New South. The image of the Savage South has obvious polemical uses, but has it not others? Has it not served the function of national catharsis? Has it not created for many Americans a convenient scapegoat upon which the sins of all may be symbolically laid and thereby expiated—a most convenient escape from problem solving?[34] To what extent, indeed, has the mythology of the South in general welled up from the subconscious depths? Taylor, especially, has emphasized this question, but the skeptical historian will also be concerned with the degree to which it has been the product or the device of deliberate manipulation by propagandists and vested interests seeking identification with the "real" South.

Certainly any effort to delineate the unique character of a people must take into account its mythology. "Poets," James G. Randall suggested, "have done better in expressing this oneness of the South than historians in explaining it."[35] Can it be that the historians have been looking in the wrong places, that they have failed to seek the key to the enigma where the poets have so readily found it—in the mythology that has had so much to do with shaping character, unifying society, developing a sense of community, of common ideals and shared goals, making the region conscious of its distinctiveness?[36] Perhaps by turning to different and untrodden paths we shall encounter the central theme of Southern history at last on the new frontier of mythology.

[34] "In a sense, the southern writer has been a scapegoat for his fellow Americans, for in taking his guilt upon himself and dramatizing it he has borne the sins of us all." C. Hugh Holman, "The Southerner as American Writer," in Charles Grier Sellers, Jr. (ed.), *The Southerner as American* (Chapel Hill, 1960), p. 199.

[35] James G. Randall, *The Civil War and Reconstruction* (Boston, 1937), pp. 3–4.

[36] Josiah Royce's definition of a "province" is pertinent here: "... any one part of a national domain which is geographically and socially sufficiently unified to have a true consciousness of its own ideals and customs and to possess a sense of its distinction from other parts of the country." Quoted in Frederick Jackson Turner, *The Significance of Sections in American History* (New York, 1932), p. 45.

2

The New South Creed:
A Study in Southern Mythmaking

Paul M. Gaston

The term "New South" has been variously defined as both a doctrine and a period of time. In either case, it is said to have been
the means by which the South "redeemed" its heritage. It marked
an escape from the backlog of frustration and defeat dating from
the Civil War, and launched the region into new realms of power
and prestige. The New South, in short, is purported to have
brought with it a multiple endowment: economic abundance, an
equitable settlement of the racial issue (to be duly canonized by
the "separate but equal" prescription of *Plessy* v. *Ferguson* in
1896), and political redemption. Indeed, by the late nineteenth
and early twentieth centuries, it is said that the South had at last
sampled the American Dream. But economic fulfillment, racial
justice, and political parity with the North, though critical elements
of a developing New South Creed, scarcely materialized in succeeding decades. As argued by Paul M. Gaston of the University of
Virginia, perpetual dreams of an emerging "new" South, though
sharply etched in the southern imagination, have since fit rather
poorly with the facts of southern experience. Nearly every facet
of the New South Creed has proven to be a mirage—tantalizing
yet elusive. Its major dividend has been mismanagement and decay
for the region's physical and human resources. All too often race
relations, economic opportunity, and political progress have suffered
from benign neglect and served as little more than convenient
slogans. Perhaps as striking, Professor Gaston maintains, was the

compatability which the New South found with the Old; images
of an Old South Creed were marshaled to support the New. What
The South achieved, in the end, was simply the acquisition of new
volumes for its growing library of sacred beliefs.

One of the ironies of Southern history lies in the simultaneous rise during
the 1880's of both the New South creed and the mythic image of the Old
South. Sweet "syrup of romanticism," to use Professor Woodward's term,
flowed over the Old South in the same decade that the New South spokesmen's ideal of a bustling, rich, and reconstructed South captured the
American imagination. Joel Chandler Harris introduced Uncle Remus to
the general public in 1880 and Thomas Nelson Page's idyllic old Virginia
became a national treasure after the publication of "Marse Chan" in 1884.[1]
[Henry] Grady's landmark address before the New England Society of New
York was only two years later. To compound the irony, most of the New
South spokesmen accepted the mythic view of the past, rarely failing to
preface a New South pronouncement with warm praise and nostalgic sighs
for the golden age that had passed. While Old South idolaters such as
Charles Colcock Jones, Jr., shuddered with horror at the mention of the New
South, its spokesmen showed no such single-mindedness, and the warm
reception they gave the emerging legend further emphasizes the attempt
to relate their movement to the values and aspirations of the past.

The legend of an Old South whose character was shaped by a noble
plantation regime did not, of course, emerge unheralded in the 1880's. Its
origins are in the antebellum period itself. In his illuminating study,
Cavalier and Yankee, William R. Taylor shows that the mythmaking
first appeared shortly after the War of 1812. William Wirt's biography of
Patrick Henry, published in 1818, was the most notable precursor of the
later tradition. "It was a utopia set in the past," Taylor writes.[2] Wirt "con-
structed for himself exactly the kind of legendary Southern past into which
successive generations of Southerners were to retreat in full flight from
the problems of the present."[3] Wirt's preliminary work was overshadowed
in importance in the thirty years before the war by polemics and novels,
reflecting the increasing alienation of Southern thought from dominant

[1] Joel Chandler Harris, *Uncle Remus: His Songs and His Sayings* (New York,
1881 [i.e., 1880]); Thomas Nelson Page, "Marse Chan," *Century Magazine,* XXVII
(April 1884), 932–42.
[2] William R. Taylor, *Cavalier and Yankee: The Old South and American National Character* (New York, 1961), p. 82.
[3] *Ibid.,* p. 92.

American values and ideals. From Thomas Roderick Dew in the early
'thirties to George Fitzhugh in the mid-'fifties, Southern pro-slavery
theorists lauded a stratified agrarian society in terms which they thought
the ancient Greeks might have understood.[4] In fiction, John Pendleton
Kennedy inaugurated the plantation tradition in 1832 by idealizing his own
times and by presenting much of plantation life at its best.[5] "Doing so,"
remarks one historian of the plantation in literature, "he gave matter and
method for a literary tradition."[6] The tradition was amply exploited by a
host of other writers in the next thirty years.

The intensity of the abolition controversy led both defenders and opponents of slavery to enlarge and perpetuate the myth. The defenders, for
obvious reasons, exaggerated the grandeur of their civilization, while the
abolitionist assault had the ironic outcome of adding credibility to the
myth. In drawing pictures of the horror of Southern society, abolitionists
invariably had their dramas of exploitation played on enormous estates
presided over by wealthy planters who lived life on the grand scale. The
contrast between the opulence of the planter and the misery of the slave
no doubt served the abolitionist purpose, but it also contributed to one
of the rare points of agreement between Southerners and Northerners. As
Francis Pendleton Gaines observes, the opponents in the slavery controversy "agreed concerning certain picturesque elements of plantation life
and joined hands to set the conception unforgettably in public consciousness."[7] A half-century after Harriet Beecher Stowe outraged the South
with *Uncle Tom's Cabin,* Joel Chandler Harris took puckish delight in
telling a Northern audience that "all the worthy and beautiful characters
in her book . . . are the products" of a slave society, while the "cruelest
and most brutal character . . . is a Northerner."[8]

When the war came, both sides entered it with rival myths which suc-
cored them during the four years. The North's "Armageddonlike vision,"
Edmund Wilson writes, directed a "holy crusade which was to liberate the

[4] Thomas Roderick Dew, *Review of the Debate in the Virginia Legislature of
1831 and 1832* (Richmond, 1832); George Fitzhugh, *Sociology for the South; or,
the Failure of Free Society* (Richmond, 1854); George Fitzhugh, *Cannibals All! or,
Slaves Without Masters* (Richmond, 1857). The standard monograph on the pro-
slavery philosophy is William S. Jenkins, *Pro-Slavery Thought in the Old South*
(Chapel Hill, 1935).

[5] John Pendleton Kennedy, *Swallow Barn; or, a Sojourn in the Old Dominion*
(Philadelphia, 1832).

[6] Francis Pendleton Gaines, *The Southern Plantation: A Study in the Development and the Accuracy of a Tradition* (New York, 1924), p. 23.

[7] *Ibid.,* p. 30.

[8] Julia Collier Harris, ed., *Joel Chandler Harris, Editor and Essayist: Miscellaneous
Literary, Political, and Social Writings* (Chapel Hill, 1931), pp. 116–17.

slaves and to punish their unrighteous masters." While Northerners saw themselves as acting out the "Will of God," Wilson continues, Southerners undertook the equally noble cause of "rescuing a hallowed ideal of gallantry, aristocratic freedom, fine manners and luxurious living from the materialism and vulgarity of the mercantile Northern society."[9]

Neither myth, of course, died with the conclusion of the war. During the Reconstruction era, the rhetoric of the Northern press and the "bloody shirt" campaigns of victorious Republican politicians kept the vision of a holy crusade alive, although it became hopelessly tarnished as time passed. Curiously, however, Northern novelists began in 1865 to develop a theme of reconciliation that dominated fictional treatments of the war and paved the way for the later emergence of Southern writers on the national scene. Examining the works of fifty-five novelists who produced sixty-four civil war books between 1865 and 1880, Joyce Appleby writes that "for the Northerner who wrote a novel simply to entertain, forgiveness was the order of the day." The plantation romance, as it would appear in the 'eighties, was undeveloped in these works, but all of the later themes of honest misunderstanding, purity of motive, and the integrity of Southern civilization are present.[10]

The sympathetic mood cultivated by the Northern novelists was expanded by the Southern writers of the late 'seventies and 'eighties into a national love feast for the Old South. Southern authors began appearing regularly in the pages of the national periodicals in the mid-'seventies, in the wake of the enthusiasm created by *Scribner's* "Great South" series, a detailed and sympathetic description of the region by Edward King.[11] By 1881, the editor of *Scribner's* was noting that a recent number of the magazine had contained seven contributions by Southerners. Hailing the new contributors, he confidently announced that "a new literary era is dawning upon the South."[12] A decade later the same editor would report

[9] Edmund Wilson, *Patriotic Gore: Studies in the Literature of the American Civil War* (New York, 1962), p. 438.

[10] Joyce Appleby, "Reconciliation and the Northern Novelist, 1865–1880," *Civil War History*, X (June 1964), 117–29. See also Robert A. Lively, *Fiction Fights the Civil War: An Unfinished Chapter in the Literary History of the American People* (Chapel Hill, 1957).

[11] The articles appeared in book form shortly after they were published in the magazine: Edward King, *The Great South: A Record of Journeys* (Hartford, Conn., 1875).

[12] "Southern Literature," *Scribner's Monthly*, XXII (September 1881), 785–6. See also Herbert F. Smith, "Joel Chandler Harris's Contributions to Scribner's Monthly and Century Magazine, 1880–1887," *Georgia Historical Quarterly*, XLVII (June 1963), 169–79; and Charles W. Coleman, Jr., "The Recent Movement in Southern Literature," *Harper's New Monthly Magazine*, LXXIV (May 1887), 837–55.

to Joel Chandler Harris the petulant query of a Northern author, "When are you going to give the North a chance!"[13]

The new development came as no surprise to Albion W. Tourgee, the carpetbag judge of North Carolina whose own fiction had a considerable following in the period. As early as 1865 he had predicted that, within thirty years, "popular sympathy will be with those who upheld the Confederate cause . . . our popular heroes will be Confederate leaders; our fiction will be Southern in its prevailing types and distinctively Southern in its character." Writing in 1888, Tourgee felt that his prediction had been more than borne out, seven years in advance of the deadline. "Our literature has become not only Southern in type," he declared, "but distinctly Confederate in sympathy." Poring over all the popular monthlies of recent issue, Tourgee could not find a single one without a "Southern story" as one of its most "prominent features."[14]

Thus it was that the romantic view of the Southern past achieved what Gaines calls a "complete conquest" in the 'eighties. An enormous number of authors, the most prominent of whom were Harris and Page, "fed to the public fancy some variety of the plantation material."[15] At the same time, the mythic view of the past was achieving the status of an inviolable shibboleth through other means as well. Schoolbooks and educational curricula carefully guarded the old memories. Religious imagery and political rhetoric were built on appeals to former glory. And numerous organizations devoted their full time to perpetuating the correct view of the past. To Jones' Confederate Survivors' Association there were soon added the United Daughters of the Confederacy, for women, and the United Confederate Veterans for men. All basked in the admiration shown them by *The Confederate Veteran,* a reverent journal established in Nashville in 1893 to represent the various memorial groups. One contributor to the *Veteran* stated simply what had now become the orthodox Southern view of the past:

In the eyes of Southern people all Confederate veterans are heroes. It is you [the Confederate veterans] who preserve the traditions and memories of the old-time South—the sunny South, with its beautiful lands and its happy people; the South of chivalrous men and gentle women; the South that will go down in history as the land of plenty and the

[13] R. W. Gilder to Joel Chandler Harris, March 5, 1891, Harris Papers, Emory University.

[14] Albion W. Tourgee, "The South as a Field for Fiction," *The Forum,* VI (December 1888), 404–7.

[15] Gaines, *The Southern Plantation,* p. 82.

home of heroes. This beautiful, plentiful, happy South engendered a spirit of chivalry and gallantry for which its men were noted far and near.[16]

In the mythic image of a chivalric and gallant South there remained no traces of the corrupting influences once imputed by the abolitionists. The descendants of Garrison were ambushed after the war, and by 1880 nothing remained of the abolitionist tradition except the exaggerated accounts of plantation splendor. "Abolitionism was swept from the field," according to Gaines; "it was more than routed, it was tortured, scalped, 'mopped up.' "[17] Remaining was only the enchanting picture of a near-perfect society in which, as Thomas Nelson Page believed, "even the moonlight was richer and mellower . . . than it is now."[18] This rich and mellow moonlight beamed on a country studded with magnolias that offered sweet scents and a becoming background for beautiful maidens. The fathers of the maidens, invariably courtly, noble, and generous, presided over enormous plantations and thousands of lovable, amusing, and devoted slaves. Work was apparently infrequent and leisure was put to constructive and cultivating uses. During the numerous holiday seasons—and especially at Christmastime—the regal splendor of the regime was particularly brilliant, enriching the lives of both white and black. Patriarchal in the extreme— yet underneath wholesomely democratic—the stratified society provided precisely the right niche for each member: each fulfilled his true nature; none was dissatisfied.

The New South prophets had no objection to the beautiful maidens, but their program would amend or replace many other aspects of the civilization cherished in the myth. Whirring cotton mills and crimson blast furnaces were preferred to magnolias and moonlight; the factory with its hired hands was superior to the inefficient plantation; bustle and energy and the ability to "get ahead," rather than a penchant for leisure, should characterize the leadership of the New South. Grady made the difference clear when he told his New York audience: "We have sowed towns and cities in the place of theories, and put business above politics."[19]

Unmindful of paradoxes, the New South spokesmen subscribed with ardor to the mythical conception of the Old South. Grady expressed reverence for the "imperishable knighthood" of the old regime; he admired

[16] Ethel Moore, "Reunion of Tennesseans: Address of Welcome by Miss Ethel Moore," *Confederate Veteran,* VI (October 1898), 482.

[17] Gaines, *The Southern Plantation,* pp. 63–6.

[18] Thomas Nelson Page, *Red Rock: A Chronicle of Reconstruction* (New York, 1898), p. viii.

[19] Joel Chandler Harris, ed., *Life of Henry W. Grady, Including His Writings and Speeches* (New York, 1890), p. 88.

the leisure and wealth which gave to the Old South an "exquisite culture";
he praised the civilization that produced gentle women, honest and devout
citizens—all in that dreamlike time when "money counted least in making
the social status." On another occasion, he referred to the sea-island
plantations of Georgia as "royal homes: . . . principalities in area, duke-
doms in revenue." The man who promised an industrial utopia to his own
generation could say of the past that "the civilization of the old slave
regime in the South has not been surpassed, and perhaps will not be
equaled, among men."[20] The reciprocal love between master and slave, a
basic foundation on which the society rested, was a thing of beauty which
came into glorious blossom during the South's great testing time. Speaking
before a group of Boston merchants, Grady related a "vision" of the war:

> The crisis of battle—a soldier struck, staggering, fallen. I see a slave,
> scuffling through the smoke, winding his black arms about the fallen
> form, reckless of the hurtling death—bending his trusty face to catch
> the words that tremble on the stricken lips, so wrestling meantime with
> agony that he would lay down his life in his master's stead.[21]

[Richard Hathaway] Edmonds, among the most versatile of the New South
leaders, crusaded tirelessly for the industrial order of his day, traced a
continuity of development from the Old to the New South, and urged upon
his fellows the romantic view of the old regime. He would never want
Southerners to forget, he wrote, "to hold in tenderest reverence the memory
of this Southern land; never forget to give all honor to the men and women
of ante-bellum days; remember . . . that the Old South produced a race of
men and women whose virtues and whose attainments are worthy to be
enshrined not only in every Southern, but in every American heart."[22]
Moreover, in the midst of the South's industrial development, he warned
Southerners never to let it be said "that in the struggle for industrial advancement the South has lost aught of the virtues, domestic and public,
aught of the manliness and self-reliance, aught of the charms of her women
and the honor of her men which hallow the memory of the Old South."[23]

By the turn of the century, as these examples suggest, it caused no em-
barrassment for New South prophets to espouse the creeds of both the Old
and the New South. A North Carolina bank president was typical of the
New South accommodation of both creeds when he began an address before the American Bankers' Association by paying reverential homage to

[20] Grady, *New South*, ed. Dyer, pp. 148–60, 260.
[21] Harris, ed., *Grady*, p. 195.
[22] Edmonds, *Old South and New*. p. 11.
[23] Edmonds, *Tasks of Young Men of the South*, p. 12.

the Old South before praising the New. "Prior to the civil war," the talk began, "our Southern land . . . was the home of culture and refinement. With thousands of slaves to cultivate their broad acres, our people lived in ease and plenty."[24]

The allegiance given to the myth of the Old South by the propagandists for the New Order is in itself evidence of the extent to which the romantic view prevailed in the South. Further evidence is found in unsuspected places, the most notable of which is in the writings of Booker T. Washington. Normally, one would not expect the most influential champion of Negro freedom of his generation to contribute to a romanticized view of the slave regime into which he had been born. And, of course, there are many aspects of Washington's picture of the Old South which do not harmonize with the Thomas Nelson Page version. Washington's picture differed from the stereotype in his emphasis on the miserable living conditions of the slaves, the torturous flax shirt, the unpalatable rations, and the absence of the kind of "civilized" living that he was later to champion. Important, too, is his contention that the slaves he knew understood and desired freedom, receiving it first with great jubilation and later with a sobering sense of responsibility.[25]

However, much of Washington's picture resembles the stereotyped version. He stresses the loyalty of the slaves to their masters and insists that it was based on a genuine love. When young "Mars' Billy" died there was great sorrow in the quarters and it "was no sham sorrow but real." There is no sense of resentment, and when emancipation brought hard times to a former master the slaves rallied and stood by him in his adversity. Washington explained that "nothing that the coloured people possess is too good for the son of 'old Mars' Tom' "[26] One is reminded of Irwin Russell's famous lines which began by extolling the virtues of "Mahsr John" and conclude:

> Well, times is changed. De war it come an' sot de niggers free,
> An' now ol' Mahsr John ain't hardly wuf as much as me;
> He had to pay his debts, an' so his lan' is mos'ly gone—
> An' I declar' I's sorry for my pore ol' Mahsr John.[27]

Washington's account of Reconstruction is equally congenial to the romantic version. In his autobiography he includes the standard comic view

[24] Brown, *The New South*, p. 3.
[25] Booker T. Washington, *Up From Slavery* (Garden City, 1901), pp. 1–12.
[26] *Ibid.*, pp. 12–14.
[27] Irwin Russell, *Christmas Night in the Quarters and Other Poems* (New York, 1917), p. 67.

of the newly freed Negro, stating that the principal crazes were for Greek and Latin and public office. He is critical of the precipitous way in which the Negro was pulled up from the bottom rung of society, and he has harsh words to say about Negro preachers, teachers, and politicians. Most important of all is what is not said: nowhere in *Up from Slavery* does one find an indictment of the native white Southerners' behavior during Reconstruction. The Negro suffered in the end, Washington felt, in large part because "there was an element in the North which wanted to punish the Southern white men by forcing the Negro into positions over the heads of Southern whites."[28]

The commitment of both black and white New South prophets to the romantic view of the past was not made without purpose. To some extent, to be sure, there was no alternative for many of them, for their own emotional requirements as well as the need for public acceptance dictated that they operate within the intellectual framework of the time and place in which they lived. But however compelling the emotional and strategic considerations may have been, they were matched in appeal to the New South spokesmen by several concrete, useful functions which the myth of the Old South could perform in the cause of the New South movement. Washington, as will appear in the next chapter, had special reasons for mythmaking. The white leaders in the movement quickly perceived and ably exploited the benefits that the myth offered them. For one thing, they would not have agreed with those later historians who saw the romantic legend exclusively as a source of fruitless ancestor worship and rancorous sectionalism. On the contrary, a close examination shows that it was nationalism rather than sectionalism, an identification rather than a separation, of interests that emerged as benefactors of the myth.

The triumph of the romantic legend in the North in the 'eighties was essential to this result. Once before, in the antebellum period, the Southern mythmakers had found allies in the North, although the Yankee authors of the Southern myth were a distinct and largely uninfluential minority in their society. Several Northern writers, disturbed by a rapid social mobility and an accelerating materialism which produced, in Taylor's words, "glowing optimism and expectations of a secular millennium," consciously cultivated the plantation theme to bare the disquieting developments in their own region. To them, the culture of the South had "many of the things which they felt the North lacked: the vestiges of an old-world aristocracy, a promise of stability and an assurance that gentility—a high sense of honor, a belief in public service and a maintenance of domestic decorum—could be preserved under republican institutions."[29] In the New South era similar

---

[28] Washington, *Up From Slavery*, pp. 80–7.
[29] Taylor, *Cavalier and Yankee*, p. 18.

doubts caused some of the North's finest writers to use the Southern romance to damn the excesses of the Gilded Age. Woodward has recently
called attention to the fact that Herman Melville, Henry Adams, and
Henry James each wrote works which included a Confederate veteran who
"serves as the mouthpiece of the severest stricture upon American society
or, by his actions or character, exposes the worst faults of that society."
These three authors, Woodward writes, detested the "mediocrity, the crass-
ness, and the venality they saw around them," and they found the Southerner "a useful foil for the unlovely present or the symbol of some irrepara-
ble loss."[30]

To most Northern writers and readers of the 'eighties and 'nineties,
however, the commitment to the romantic legend masked few disturbing
social thoughts and stemmed from simple needs. According to Gaines, the
Northerner had a romantic, innate "love of feudalism" and a yearning to
identify vicariously with aristocratic societies. The plantation, "alone
among native institutions," he continues, satisfied "this craving for a system
of caste."[31] Both the craving and the myth that satisfied it continued long
beyond the years of the New South movement. Gunnar Myrdal, noting
the enduring fascination of the American with the romantic legend, wrote
in 1944:

> The North has so few vestiges of feudalism and aristocracy of its own
> that, even though it dislikes them fundamentally and is happy not to
> have them, Yankees are thrilled by them. Northerners apparently cherish
> the idea of having had an aristocracy and of still having a real class
> society—in the South. So it manufactures the myth of the "Old South"
> or has it manufactured by Southern writers working for the Northern
> market.[32]

The complex strands that wove together the myth of the Old South—
alienation of the Southerner from national values and ideals in the antebellum period; alienation of a few Northerners, both before and after the
war, from the strident pace of material progress; innocent love for another,
grander civilization on the part of most—did not obscure for the New
South spokesmen the incalculably valuable service it could perform in the
cause of sectional reconciliation, a basic tenet of the New South creed. If

[30] C. Vann Woodward, "A Southern Critique for the Gilded Age," in *The Burden
of Southern History* (Baton Rouge, 1960), pp. 109–40. The three works discussed
by Woodward are Melville's poem, *Clarel* (1876); Adams's novel, *Democracy* (1880);
and James's novel *The Bostonians* (1886).

[31] Gaines, *The Southern Plantation*, pp. 2–3.

[32] Gunnar Myrdal, *An American Dilemma: The Negro and Modern Democracy*,
2 vols. (New York, 1944), II, 1375.

the myth in antebellum days had bespoken alienation on the part of Southerners from national ways, in the postbellum period it worked in precisely
the opposite direction, uniting the two sections. To the South it gave a
vitally necessary sense of greatness to assuage the bitter wounds of defeat;
to the North it offered a way in which to apologize without sacrificing the
fruits of victory.

Henry Grady has always been regarded as the chief peacemaker among
the New South spokesmen, but Joel Chandler Harris, his friend and col-
league on the Atlanta *Constitution,* served the reconciliation cause in a
more subtle and perhaps more effective manner. Many of Harris's stories
are unmistakable attempts to heal sectional wounds and unite former ene-
mies. While Grady was serving the cause as the ever-available orator, the
shy Harris worked quietly in the background through Uncle Remus.

How Harris served the cause of reconciliation—and, in a larger sense,
how the plantation literature promoted national identification of interests
—is tellingly illustrated in the comparison of two versions of one of Harris's early stories. The original version appeared in the *Constitution* in 1877
under the title "Uncle Remus as a Rebel: How He Saved His Young
Master's Life."[33] The second version, entitled "A Story of the War," appeared in the first of Harris's books, *Uncle Remus: His Songs and His
Sayings,* published late in 1880.[34] The plot is similar in both stories. Uncle
Remus saves his young master from certain death by shooting a Yankee
sniper. In both stories Remus thinks only of his love for his master and
mistress. He knew the Yankee was there to free him, but when he saw
what was going to happen he "des disremembered all 'bout freedom" and
pulled the trigger.[35] In the first version, that intended for relatively local
consumption, the Yankee is killed. In the second telling, however, Harris
is aware of his national audience. Here the sniper loses an arm, but not his
life. He is nursed by Remus and Miss Sally, the plantation belle, regains
his health, and wins the hand of his lovely nurse. Clearly, the second version reveals Harris consciously courting the North, as John Stafford points
out, by demonstrating that "a Yankee is good enough to join the Southern
aristocracy." Moreover, "the North and the South are symbolically wed;
and the North accepts the paternalistic pattern. Thus is the patron flattered
and at the same time the self-respect of the South retained."[36]

---

[33] The text is available in Robert Lemuel Wiggins, *The Life of Joel Chandler
Harris: From Obscurity in Boyhood to Fame in Early Manhood, with Short Stories
and Other Early Literary Work not Heretofore Published in Book Form* (Nashville,
1918), pp. 263–8.

[34] Harris, *Uncle Remus: His Songs and His Sayings,* pp. 175–85.

[35] *Ibid.,* p. 184; Wiggins, *Harris,* p. 267.

[36] John Stafford, "Patterns of Meaning in *Nights With Uncle Remus,*" *American
Literature,* XVIII (May 1946), 94–5.

The intersectional marriage, symbol of reconciliation, was a standard device used by Southern writers of the period. Harris used it to good effect again in "Aunt Fountain's Prisoner." Aunt Fountain, the plantation mammy, says of the Yankee bridegroom: "He ain' b'long ter we-all folks, no furder dan he my young mistiss ole man, but dee ain' no finer w'ite man dan him. No, suh; dee ain'." Cheered by this judgment, New South readers both North and South must have been pleased also to read that this Yankee revived the sagging fortunes of the old plantation by a stern application of "vim and vigor," New South qualities *par excellence*.[37] Thus, as Harris would have it, the marriage of a Yankee to a Southern belle, lovely flower of the old regime, excited Northern sympathy and admiration for the honorable qualities of Southern life and, at the same time, showed Southerners that their future would be prosperous if new concepts of work and organization were accepted.

The role of the Negro and of race relations was of special importance in the romantic legend and, in persuading the North to view the "quaint darky" through Southern eyes, the mythmakers accomplished at least two important results. First, by convincing Northern readers that relations between the races were kindly and mutually beneficial a principal obstacle in the way of sectional harmony was removed. The North had doubted this point, but on the authority of Harris and others it came to accept the Southern point of view.[38] Second, the acquiescence by the North in the Southern scheme of race relations permitted the South to deal with (or to fail to deal with) its race problems unmolested.

Humor was a standard and effective device used by Southern writers to mollify the Northern conscience, for, as Sterling Brown caustically observes, "if the Negro could be shown as perpetually mirthful, his state could not be so wretched."[39] In a more sophisticated vein, Stafford comments that Harris's use of ironic comedy invariably produced the "understanding laugh" which gave emotional release from doubts and guilt feelings and induced whites to tolerate what otherwise would appear to be an evil situation. The "pure humor" of Uncle Remus, then, won "acceptance for the existing class harmony."[40] To humor there was added the element of the essential difference between white and black, the image of the Negro as an exotic primitive, as

[37] Joel Chandler Harris, *Free Joe and Other Georgian Sketches* (New York, 1887), pp. 72–98.

[38] See Stafford, "Patterns of Meaning," p. 97; Paul H. Buck, *The Road to Reunion, 1865–1900* (Boston, 1937), chap. 8; and John Donald Wade, "Profits and Losses in the Life of Joel Chandler Harris," *American Review,* I (April 1933), 28–9.

[39] Sterling A. Brown, "Negro Character as Seen by White Authors," *Journal of Negro Education,* II (April 1933), 188.

[40] Stafford, "Patterns of Meaning," 98–103, 108.

> Original in act and thought,
> Because unlearned and untaught.[41]

To make the ideal of blissful race relations a convincing one, the humorous and primitive Negro is, in hundreds of contemporary stories, the guardian of the old memories and traditions. Far from resenting his life under slavery he finds freedom uncongenial—"I wants ter git shet er dis heah freedom," exclaims a Negro who was freed by his master before the war[42]—or at least not as satisfactory as the "old days," and to every passer-by he recounts the glories of yesteryear. Tourgee designated this stereotype the "poor 'nigger' to whom liberty has brought only misfortune, and who is relieved by the disinterested friendship of some white man whose property he once was."[43] In Page's "Marse Chan" and "Unc' Edinburg's Drowndin'," two of the Virginian's most famous tales, it is the former slave who tells the story, glorifies the past, and laments its passing.[44] In one of Harry Stillwell Edwards's stories the old mammy lives out her years in sight of the grave of her mistress, where she may better preserve the memory of happier days.[45] The longing for the past is everywhere expressed. Old Sam, the faithful body servant in "Marse Chan," declares "Dem was good ole times, marster—de bes' Sam ever see."[46] Chad, the loyal servant in Francis Hopkinson Smith's novel of the Virginia gentleman, feels likewise: "Dem was high times. We ain't neber seed no time like dat since de war."[47] And, in one of the poems of Miss Howard Weeden, the old Negro feels that

> I ought to think 'bout Canaan, but
> It's Ole Times crowds my mind,
> An' maybe when I gits to Heaben
> It's Ole Times dat I'll find![48]

Behind the façade of this pleasant fable of Negro happiness and devotion in the regime of slavery there were, of course, harsh realities. Tourgee ad-

---

[41] The lines are from Irwin Russell's "Christmas Night in the Quarters," the text of which may be found in his *Christmas Night in the Quarters*, pp. 3–24.

[42] Virginia Frazer Boyle, "A Kingdom for Micajah," *Harper's New Monthly Magazine*, C (March 1900), 35.

[43] Tourgee, "South as a Field for Fiction," 409.

[44] Thomas Nelson Page, *In Ole Virginia; or, Marse Chan and Other Stories* (New York, 1887), pp. 1–38, 39–77.

[45] Harry Stillwell Edwards, "'Ole Miss' and Sweetheart," *Harper's New Monthly Magazine*, LXXVII (July 1888), 288–96.

[46] Page, *In Ole Virginia*, p. 10.

[47] Francis Hopkinson Smith, *Colonel Carter of Cartersville* (Boston, 1891), p. 61.

[48] Howard Weeden, *Bandanna Ballads* (New York, 1899), p. 10.

mitted that there were some real examples upon which the stereotype was built, "but they are not so numerous as to destroy the charm of novelty." About the Negro "as a man, with hopes, fears, and aspirations like other men," he wrote, "our literature is very nearly silent."[49] Moreover, as John M. Webb observes, "the fable applies only to the house slaves who had intimate contact with the whites."[50] But, as the legend would have it, the pleasant state of affairs was a general, not a particular or isolated, characteristic of antebellum life.

The generality of the situation, of course, was meant to apply to the postwar years as well as to the slavery regime. In addition to promoting sectional reconciliation and, in further removing the North from agitation of the race question, the image of the happy Negro helped to destroy one of the burdensome obstacles in the way of Northern investments in the South. Northern capitalists constantly complained of the unsettling conditions in the South stemming from racial friction. To the New South spokesmen it semed clear that friction would disappear and capital come rolling in once the race question were left entirely up to Southern determination. This is what Tompkins meant when he wrote that "an excess of zeal in the cause of freedom" on the part of Northerners could serve no useful purpose and was, in the long run, to the disadvantage of the Northern capitalists themselves.[51] The myth of the Old South, with its charming picture of the lovable and loving Negro, served well to jettison the zeal which Tompkins felt was rocking the boat.

Finally, in the South itself the romance of the past was used to underwrite the materialism of the present. The names and signatures of Confederate generals were everywhere in demand by railroad companies and corporations, for the New South prophets were well aware that the blessing of a "colonel" (if there were no generals handy) would do as much to float bonds and raise subscriptions as a dozen columns of optimistic statistics in the *Manufacturers' Record*. In *Colonel Carter of Cartersville*, a successful third-rate novel of the period, one of the characters observes wisely that "in a sagging market the colonel would be better than a war boom."[52] The marriage of the gentle life of the past and the bustling era of the present was perhaps nowhere better symbolized than in the advertising columns of that journal of worship, *The Confederate Veteran*. There one learned that Confederate flags could be purchased from a New York firm and the aspiring capitalist found notices of potentially prosperous factories up for sale.[53]

[49] Tourgee, "South as a Field for Fiction," 409.
[50] John M. Webb, "Militant Majorities and Racial Minorities," *Sewanee Review,* LXV (Spring 1957), 335.
[51] Tompkins, *Manufactures*, p. 22.
[52] Smith, *Colonel Carter*, p. 99.
[53] See, for example, *Confederate Veteran*, VI (October 1898), 493–8.

The several specific uses to which the mythic conception of the Old South were put to serve the needs of the New South movement help to make intelligible the paradoxical commitment of the New South prophets to the legendary romance. Professor Woodward, in his skeptical assessment of the movement, feels that the "bitter mixture of recantation and heresy" which infused the New South creed "could never have been swallowed so readily had it not been dissolved in the syrup of romanticism."[54] But the sugar coating of the pill of the New Departure, important though it was, does not fully account for the phenomenon of mythmaking. More profound, more universal and less tangible forces were at work as well. Henry James suggested some of these when he wrote:

> The collapse of the old order, the humiliation of defeat, the bereavement and bankruptcy involved, represented, with its obscure miseries and tragedies, the social revolution the most unrecorded and undepicted, in proportion to its magnitude, that ever was; so that this reversion of the starved spirit to the things of the heroic age, the four epic years, is a definite soothing salve.[55]

That there were deep wounds whose treatment required a soothing salve is abundantly clear. The South had so irrevocably committed its soul to the war that when defeat came it was more than a surrender of ambitions for independence; it was a crippling blow to the most basic assumptions upon which life in the region was lived. Pride and hope were destroyed by defeat, and humiliation was added by the Reconstruction. Under the circumstances, the search for self-confidence and a return of pride quite naturally involved more than a program of building on the ashes. Somehow the ashes themselves had to be ennobled. The myth worked powerfully to achieve this purpose: it gave back those very things which the Yankee had tried to take away—the knowledge of a proud past and a noble heritage. Without that knowledge, Grady once remarked, "the New South would be dumb and motionless."[56]

The search for a noble past, like the attempt to discover a heritage of nationalism and industrialism, engaged Southerners in an emotional and intellectual quest common to other people in other times. Nations that have been either victimized or blessed by profound social upheaval have commonly undergone, in one way or another, the experience of replanting the bared roots to the past; of developing the mythmaking process to satisfy collective needs. And for Southerners of the New South era, should they be charged with distortion of the past, their reply might be, with the Vir-

[54] Woodward, *Origins of the New South*, p. 158.
[55] Quoted in *ibid.*, p. 157.
[56] Grady, *New South*, ed. Dyer, p. 147.

ginia novelist James Branch Cabell, that "no history is a matter of record; it is a matter of faith."[57]

Allegiance to both the myth of the Old South and the dream of a New South was but one of several contradictions imbedded in the New South creed. There were many others: an institutional explanation of industrial backwardness in the Old South coupled with the faith that natural resources could not help but assure industrialization in the New; an elaborate propaganda campaign to attract immigrants into the region negated by hostility to the immigration pool easiest to tap; a gospel of economic interdependence and reconciliation with the North as part of a campaign for independence and domination; a lauding of freedom for the Negro in a politics of white supremacy; dreams of equal treatment of allegedly unequal races in separate societies devoted to mutual progress—these are among the most obvious.

Rich in paradoxes, the New South creed also had an ironic outcome. Designed to lead the region out of poverty, it made converts by the thousands in all parts of the country of men who looked forward confidently to a South of abundance. Instead, the expectations were unrealized and the South remained the poorest and economically least progressive section of the nation. The plans for regional and personal success, the restoration of self-confidence, and a position of influence and respect in the nation likewise fired the imagination and gained legions of adherents, but they too were largely unfulfilled and at the end of the New South crusade the region found itself in the uncomfortable, if familiar, role of a colonial dependent. Rid of many of the humiliating frustrations of the early postwar years, it was saddled with new ones that had greater staying power. Finally, the dream of a just and practical solution to the race question appealed to former abolitionists and radicals as well as to longtime racists because it promised that justice and practicality could be balanced, that Southerners themselves could do what Yankee reformers had failed to do, and that a harmonious biracial society would emerge and permit Americans to forget about injustice to the black man. Instead, violence increased in the 'eighties, and disfranchisement and rigid segregation followed later as the Negro reached the nadir of his history as a free man.

Unable to bequeath to the next generation of Southerners a legacy of solid achievement, the New South spokesmen gave them instead a solidly propounded and widely spread image of its success, a mythic view of their own times that was as removed from objective reality as the myth of the Old South. In creating the myth of the New South, they compounded all of the contradictions originally built into their creed, added others, and crowned their professions of realism with a flight of fantasy.

[57] Cabell, *Let Me Lie,* p. 74.

3

The Enigma of the South

David M. Potter

To a considerable degree the idea of a South segregated from
national cultural and political patterns, and the cluster of images
supporting that proposition, produced civil war in 1861. But despite
the cathartic nature of the war experience, notions of southern
distinctiveness continued to find sanction in the postbellum decades.
Fascination with the South's legacy of agrarianism, for example,
remained a southern predisposition long after the war itself had
passed into historical memory. Countering the opinions of some
historians and important segments of the southern literary establishment, David M. Potter, late of Stanford University, attests that
the tempting equation of southernism and agrarianism is a myth.
Though apparently stemming from the tradition of the southern
sage Thomas Jefferson, and crystalized in the image of the antebellum cavalier, agrarianism has proven an arid formula for explaining the essence and nature of southernism. The "true South,"
Professor Potter concludes, is an enigma—both elusive and deeply
paradoxical. The "concrete realities of the land" seem rather to
yield a South predicated upon a distinct folk culture. What such
a historical dissection suggests, of course, is yet additional irony
in the southern past. The agrarian-industrial dichotomy, which
Mr. Potter identifies as the core of the southern enigma, was to
prove itself the major tension and dialectic of the New South era.
Truly, the New South's "abandonment" of agrarianism could
hardly have existed, since the South as an agrarian society had
never been more than "an illusion, nourished by a wish."

Among the many flourishing branches of American historical study during the last half-century, one of the most robust has been the history of the South. Fifty years ago, there was already one large body of literature on the Southern Confederacy, especially in its military aspects, and another on the local history of various Southern states, but the history of the South as a region—of the whole vast area below the Potomac, viewed as a single entity for the whole time from the settlement of Jamestown to the present —is largely a product of the last five decades. Today, a multivolume history, a number of college textbooks, a quarterly journal, and a substantial library of monographic studies all serve as measures of the extent of the development in this field.

Anyone who seeks an explanation for this interest in Southern history must take account of several factors. To begin with, the study of American regions is a general phenomenon, embracing not only the South but also New England, the Middle West, and the great physiographic provinces beyond the Mississippi. In a nation as vast and as diverse as ours, there is really no level higher than the regional level at which one can come to grips with the concrete realities of the land. But apart from this regional aspect, the Southern theme has held an unusual appeal for the people of the South because of their peculiarly strong and sentimental loyalty to Dixie as their native land, and for Americans outside the South because of the exotic quality of the place and because it bears the aura of a Lost Cause. Union generals, for some reason, have never held the romantic interest that attached to Stonewall Jackson, Jeb Stuart, George Pickett, Bedford Forrest, and, of course, Robert E. Lee. Today, the predilection of Yankee children for caps, flags, and toys displaying the Rebel insignia bears further witness to the enduring truth that lost causes have a fascination even for those who did not lose them.

But it seems unlikely that either the South as an American region, or the South as Dixieland, or the South as a Lost Cause could hold so much scholarly and popular attention in focus if the South were not also an enigma. To writers for more than half a century the South has been a kind of sphinx on the American land.

To some who viewed it, this sphinx has seemed a great insensate monolith, a vast artifact of the past with no meaning behind its inscrutable expression. Its domain has been just what H. L. Mencken said it was—a cultural desert, a Sahara of the Bozart. But to others this sphinx' has seemed to hold a secret, an answer to the riddle of American life.

To many people today, who think of the South in terms of Freedom Riders and lunch-counter sit-ins, of Tobacco Road and Central High School in Little Rock, of robed Klansmen and burning crosses, and perhaps of a Monkey Trial at Dayton, Tennessee, it may seem hard to believe that not long ago the South was regarded by many thoughtful and liberal-minded people as a kind of sanctuary of the American democratic tradition. What is now deplored as the "benighted South," or the "sick South," was, until recently, regarded by many liberals as the birthplace and the natural bulwark of the Jeffersonian ideal—a region where agrarian democracy still struggled to survive, fighting a gallant rearguard action against the commercialism and the industrial capitalism of the Northeast.

It would be a major undertaking to trace the evolution of this concept. The general idea that American democracy is essentially frontier democracy—which closely resembles agrarian democracy—is forever linked with Frederick Jackson Turner, but Turner gave it a Western rather than a Southern orientation. Certainly one of the earliest writers to apply it to the South was William E. Dodd. In 1911, when Dodd had been but recently appointed to the University of Chicago, and twenty-two years before Franklin Roosevelt sent him as our unswervingly democratic ambassador to Hitler's Berlin, he wrote a sketchy little book, now largely forgotten, entitled *Statesmen of the Old South,* with the significant subtitle, *From Radicalism to Conservative Revolt.* The statesmen whom he treated were Jefferson, Calhoun, and Jefferson Davis, and the theme which he developed was that the democratic or radical South of Thomas Jefferson—an equalitarian South of small subsistence farmers—had been subverted by the increasingly aristocratic and hierarchical South of the great slaveholders whose property interests found embodiment in Calhoun and Davis.

In three brief and seemingly artless chapters, Dodd achieved two very subtle effects. First, he defined to suit himself what may be called a normative South—the South of Thomas Jefferson—and thus established an arbitrary basis for identifying all future developments of a Jeffersonian tenor as truly or intrinsically Southern, and for rejecting all conservative or hierarchical developments as aberrations of Southernism. Using this device, he then proceeded to dispose of the whole conservative, slaveholding South of antebellum fame as a kind of deviation or detour in the true course of Southern history. Thus he finessed the basic question whether the true and realistic image of the South might not be a dualism, with as much of Calhoun as of Jefferson in it, or even whether the true South, historically, is not hierarchical and conservative rather than radical and equalitarian.

In justice to Dodd, one must recognize that his version of Southernism was by no means without foundations. Jeffersonianism, as well as Jefferson, did have distinctively Southern origins, and at almost every decisive turning point in the advancement of American democracy—whether at the time of Jackson, or Bryan, or Wilson, or Franklin Roosevelt—the South has thrown crucial weight on the democratic side. Still, there was something of a tour de force about the way in which Dodd reconciled his love for his native South and his commitment to democracy, and, with very little disclosure of the wishful thinking which was involved, identified the land he loved with the values he cherished.

Whether later writers were directly influenced by Dodd or not, the theme of agrarianism has persisted ever since in the literature of the South, sometimes with the most startling implications. Thus when Charles and Mary Beard came to write about the Civil War in their *The Rise of American Civilization* (1927), they pictured it as a conflict between Southern agrarianism and Northern industrialism; in this way, the defenders of slavery were transmuted into democrats, more or less, since agrarianism was, in the Beards' lexicon, by definition democratic, and industrialism was anti-democratic. Again, at the hands of the Beards and of the late Howard K. Beale, in his *The Critical Years,* published in 1930, Reconstruction was not primarily a contest over the rights of Negro freedmen, but rather a series of coups by industrial capitalism to consolidate its ascendancy and to retain its wartime gains, consisting of tariffs, subsidies, and a monetary system favorable to creditors. The Fourteenth Amendment was not a Magna Carta of freedmen's rights, but rather a bulwark for property interests, disguised as a Negro rights measure in order to catch votes. Again, the implications were ironic: for instance, under this formula Andrew Johnson, a onetime slave-owner and an obdurate foe of Negro rights, appeared as a champion of democracy against the predatory capitalists. Thus Johnson received ecstatic praise in a biography (1929) by that archliberal attorney Lloyd Paul Stryker, who later became a crusading spokesman for Negro rights.

Through all of these treatments there runs a persistent implied affirmation of Dodd's cleverly articulated premise: that which is agrarian in the South is truly Southern; anything not in the agrarian tradition is somehow extraneous—a cowbird's egg in the Southern nest. Almost automatically, this formula reduced the factor of biracialism and caste to secondary importance, or even kept it out of sight altogether. Again, some interesting results follow in the literature. For instance, when Howard W. Odum and his associates at Chapel Hill prepared their great compendium *Southern Regions of the United States* (1936), they deployed no less than six hundred maps and charts to show that the agricultural South, despite its rich natural resources, was worse off in almost every measurable respect than the rest of the country. That is, they mapped, measured, and charted the plight of the agricultural South. But not one graph, map, or chart showed the relatively worse plight of the Negroes within the South. In other words, the most careful reader of this encyclopedic survey of Southern economic and social conditions could almost have overlooked the fact that a biracial system prevailed in the South and that under this system the Negroes experienced adverse differentials in almost every respect. No doubt Odum and his associates chose this presentation deliberately, and certainly not because of any blind agrarianism, for they advocated economic diversification for the South. Their purpose may even have been to avoid dulling the concern of white Southerners about differentials by admitting that these differentials fell more heavily upon the Negro than upon the white component in the Southern population. Or, they may have wished to treat Negroes and whites indiscriminately alike as being handicapped by regional differentials. But in any case, their survey of Southern problems left out the greatest problem of all. Like the doctrinal agrarians with whom they disagreed, they presented an image of the South which emphasized the plight of farmers rather than the plight of Negroes.

In quite a different way, the agrarian premise shows itself also in many of the writings of C. Vann Woodward, the foremost historian of the modern South. In Woodward's biography of Tom Watson (1938), for instance, the protagonist of the drama is Watson the agrarian, and the antagonists are the Bourbon Democrats who have betrayed the interests of the South to the forces of industrial capitalism. Or alternatively, one could say, the protagonist is the earlier Watson, who championed Populism and defended Negro rights, while the antagonist is the later Watson, a reactionary racist who betrayed the ideals of his youth. Though Woodward's treatment is deeply subtle and sensitive to complexities, while Dodd's was superficial and grossly oversimplified, both are alike in regarding the agrarian South as, almost a priori, the true South, and any force within the South which runs counter to it as an aberration. This is, of course, quite a different thing from merely favoring the agrarian cause.

Although a whole generation of writers have made this tempting equation between Southernism and agrarianism, it requires only a limited analysis to see that in many respects the Southern economy and the Southern society have not been agrarian at all—in fact, have embodied almost the antithesis of agrarianism. Agrarianism implies an escape from the commercialism of the money economy, but Southern cotton and tobacco and sugar cultivators have consistently been agricultural businessmen producing for market and for cash income. Agrarianism implies production for use rather than production for sale, and therefore diversification rather than specialization, but the Southern agriculturist stuck to his one-crop system in the past as tenaciously as he clings to segregation at the present. It implies the independence of a husbandman who looks to no one else either for his access to the land or for the necessities of his living, but the Southern cultivator has been historically either a slave or a sharecropper, without land and often without opportunity even to grow his own turnip greens in a garden patch. Meanwhile the Southern landowner, whether an absentee planter or a mortgage-holding bank, frequently failed to follow the ennobling agrarian practice of laboring in the earth. To one who is impressed by these aspects, it may seem realistic to regard Calhoun rather than Jefferson as the typical leader of the South; the plantation producing raw materials for the textile industry, rather than the subsistence farm producing for use, as the typical economic unit; hierarchy rather than equality as the typical social condition; and conservatism rather than radicalism as the typical mode of thought.

One man who was long the leading historian of the South saw the region to some extent in these terms. This was Ulrich B. Phillips, who began his career around the turn of the century with studies of Southern political history and the history of Southern transportation. But wherever his investigations began, they always led him, as he himself said, back to one feature of life in the South which was constant both before emancipation and after, namely the presence of Negroes and whites whose destinies were inextricably intertwined but whose paths in life were separated by a biracial system. Accordingly, Phillips gave only slight attention to the agrarian theme. Instead he concentrated on the staple-crop economy with its plantation units and its slave labor. With supreme thoroughness in research, he made what remains the basic study of slavery as a system of labor (*American Negro Slavery*, 1918). Later he developed an artistry in writing which matched his soundness in research, and he achieved a felicitous conjunction of both talents in a study of the society and economy of the antebellum period (*Life and Labor in the Old South*, 1929).

When Phillips looked at the Southern economy, the image which seemed visible to him was not an independent husbandman laboring in the soil, but a Negro field hand picking cotton. The persistence of this figure, either as a slave or as a sharecropper, and the persistence of the system which kept him in his subordinate role led Phillips, five years before his death in 1934, to write an essay, "The Central Theme of Southern History," in which he stated what he had found at the core of distinctive Southernism. This was not some agrarian ideal, but rather a fixed purpose on the part of the Southern whites to preserve biracialism, or, as he said, in unvarnished terms, to assure that the South "shall be and remain a white man's country."

Although Phillips' stature is still recognized even by his critics, liberal historians have been reluctant to accept his views. Kenneth Stampp has written a new account of slavery (*The Peculiar Institution*, 1956) which emphasizes, as Phillips never did, the harsh and exploitative aspects of the system; Richard Hofstadter has criticized Phillips for giving too much attention to the plantation, and not enough to the slaves held in small holdings; and at least two writers have questioned the "Central Theme."

It is in some ways ironical for liberals, concerned as they are with the "sick South," to reject a formula which explains so cogently the chronic nature of the illness. But what they found fault with was not in fact the accuracy of Phillips' conclusion; it was rather the lack of moral indignation

in his statement of it. By asserting that the policy of biracialism is and
will continue to be a central aspect of Southernism, without personally
repudiating this policy, he made it difficult for liberals to identify with him.
When Harry Ashmore, more recently, said in *An Epitaph for Dixie* (1958)
that the South will cease to be the South when it ceases to be segregated,
the statement was almost identical with that of Phillips, but liberals could
accept Ashmore's because he expects the South, in the old sense, to vanish
(hence "an epitaph"), whereas they could not accept Phillips', because
he seemingly expected the South to survive, with the implied corollary that
efforts at integration must fail. Moreover, in the case of liberals who want
to love the South, as some do, but who find it psychologically impossible
to love an embodiment of biracialism, the only recourse is a resort to
Dodd's original formula: dispose of the factor which is troublesome (in
this case the biracialism) by treating it as a great aberration. Here even
so excellent a book as Vann Woodward's *Strange Career of Jim Crow*
(1955) is a case in point, for though it was intended to emphasize a
thoroughly valid observation—namely, that the patterns of biracialism
have varied and are not immutable—it lends itself to being read as a statement that caste does not have very deep roots in the South. The preface
to the paperback edition (1957) showed that Woodward was himself concerned that his work had been taken too much in this way.

When one considers the degree of hardheadedness and realism which
went into Phillips' view that biracialism lay at the core of Southernism,
and the vulnerability of the doctrine that agrarianism was the heart of the
matter, it seems strange that writers have been so abstinent in accepting
the former and so addicted to the latter. Clearly, the agrarian interpretation has drawn its strength from something other than the sheer weight
of evidence, and it is worth pondering what the real basis of its acceptance
is. In the purely historical literature, this basis is hard to detect, for the
historian purports merely to be describing the agrarianism which he finds
in the past—not to be advocating it. But in 1930 agrarianism enjoyed
open advocacy at the hands of a group of writers, all centered at Vanderbilt University, in the famous manifesto entitled *I'll Take My Stand*. The
twelve Southerners who joined in this profession of faith categorically
rejected the industrial way of life, which they regarded as the prevailing
or American way, and with equal conviction they subscribed to an agrarian
way, which they identified as a Southern way. They hoped to carry this
Southern way to the nation through "a national agrarian movement."

In the extensive and often heated discussion which followed, attention
was focused very heavily upon the operative practicability of their proposals. They were accused of medievalism, and of quixotically renouncing
all the benefits of modern science and technology. They were also accused,
with somewhat more justice, of being in disagreement among themselves

as to whether agrarianism was designed to provide a livelihood for dirt farmers or to restore cultural amenities for the landed gentry. Whether they advocated populism or élitism no one could quite make out. While controversy raged between them and their assailants, not much attention was given to the ideological implications of agrarianism, nor to the question why this particular line of thought had appeared at this particular time. Indeed, the historical significance of agrarian thought has still never been adequately analyzed.

But it is clearly evident that agrarianism appealed to many liberals, both before and after the Nashville group, partly because they were looking for an alternative to the prevailing American way of life. Some writers, like Charles A. Beard, used agrarianism so enthusiastically as a stick with which to beat capitalism that it had some of the appearance of a disguised Marxism. But its real significance lay in the fact that it offered an alternative to Marxism. Here, in fact, was a way in which a man could renounce industrial capitalism and all its works without becoming a Marxist. This is perhaps why the agrarian ideal held so much attraction for such a large number of social thinkers. It gave them a chance to express their dissent from the prevailing system without going outside the American tradition in order to do so.

Another significant feature in making agrarianism attractive was its affirmation that the South had something of value in its tradition to offer to the nation. The Nashville group really felt convinced that the Southern sphinx did have an answer to the riddle, if not of the universe, at least of American life. Their affirmation came at a time when it was being asserted by critics like Mencken that the Southern tradition amounted to little more than a sterile, backward-looking form of ancestor worship. Now suddenly men were saying in a fresh and arresting way that the Southern tradition was not merely a pressed flower in the nation's scrapbook of memories, but rather an urgent message which Americans, deafened by the roar of progress, had failed to hear. To Southerners who yearned to believe that there was some element of vitality in the history of their region, this idea seemed immensely appealing.

The continued acceleration of industrial growth and the failure of the Nashville group to rally a popular following soon showed that agrarianism had no future, but it was still widely believed to have a past, and historians continued to apply it to the interpretation of American history. Henry Bamford Parkes made brilliant use of it in his *The American Experience* (1947), and as recently as 1949, Frank L. Owsley, in his *Plain Folk of the Old South,* delineated the structure of antebellum society in terms in which large slaveholders and plain farmers were practically indistinguishable. In these and many other writings, a number of time-honored propositions continued to find acceptance: that American democracy has been nourished primarily from agrarian roots; that agrarian attitudes are inherently democratic; and that the South peculiarly embodies the agrarian tradition.

But of late the first two of these propositions have come under criticism, and the agrarian view has been attacked, for the first time, at its foundations. As long ago as 1945, Arthur Schlesinger, Jr., in his *The Age of Jackson,* offered the then heretical view that Jacksonian democracy owed more to the East and to class-conscious urban workingmen than to the frontier and its coonskin equality. More recently, Richard Hofstadter, in his *Age of Reform* (1955), has gone even further by arguing that Populism had little affinity with liberal democracy, and was in fact a seedbed for such illiberal manifestations as prohibition, nativism, immigration restriction, Red-baiting, and the like. Thus, according to Schlesinger, democracy was not agrarian, and according to Hofstadter, agrarianism was not democratic.

In literal form, the agrarian formula fitted the South remarkably badly. It envisioned a subsistence economy, agricultural diversification, a wide distribution of small landholdings, a large class of independent husbandmen, and an unstratified society. The cold fact is that none of these features has ever been dominant in the South. In the light of these flaws, as well as of recent criticisms, the whole idea of the South as an agrarian society now seems more and more an illusion, nourished by a wish. But once it is discarded, the question reverts to the enigma of the South. All theory aside, is the South, at a purely descriptive level, distinguishable? And if it is, does the distinction lie in anything more than the fact that biracialism takes a form in the South differing from the form it takes elsewhere?

This is a question which the literature of the future will perhaps explore further. Vann Woodward, in *The Burden of Southern History* (1960), has already moved in this direction with incisive and fertile arguments that certain distinctive experiences of the South have put their mark upon the Southern people: the experience of defeat and frustration, in an America of monotonous, taken-for-granted success; the experience of guilt because of the Negro, in an America with a cult of Adamic innocence; the experience of poverty, in an America with abundance which has caused people to confuse life with a standard of living. But though Woodward discusses these factors as experiences impinging upon the Southern culture, we still need a dissection of the culture itself upon which they impinge.

On the face of it, it seems a matter of observation and not of theory to say that the culture of the folk survived in the South long after it succumbed to the onslaught of urban-industrial culture elsewhere. It was an aspect of this culture that the relation between the land and the people remained more direct and more primal in the South than in other parts of the country. (This may be more true for the Negroes than for the whites, but then there is also a question whether the Negroes may not have embodied the distinctive qualities of the Southern character even more than the whites.) Even in the most exploitative economic situations, this culture retained a personalism in the relations of man to man which the industrial culture lacks. Even for those whose lives were narrowest, it offered a relationship of man to nature in which there was a certain fulfillment of personality. Every culture is, among other things, a system of relationships among an aggregate of people, and as cultures differ, the systems of relationship vary. In the folk culture of the South, it may be that the relation of people to one another imparted a distinctive texture as well as a distinctive tempo to their lives.

An explanation of the South in terms of a folk culture would not have the ideological implications which have made the explanation in terms of agrarianism so tempting and at the same time so treacherous. But on the other hand, it would not be inconsistent with some of the realities of Southern society, such as biracialism and hierarchy, whereas agrarianism is inconsistent with these realities. The enigma remains, and the historian must still ask what distinctive quality it was in the life of the South for which Southerners have felt such a persistent, haunting nostalgia and to which even the Yankee has responded with a poignant impulse. We must now doubt that this nostalgia was the yearning of men for an ideal agrarian utopia which never existed in reality. But if it was not that, was it perhaps the yearning of men in a mass culture for the life of a folk culture which did really exist? This folk culture, we know, was far from being ideal or utopian, and was in fact full of inequality and wrong, but if the nostalgia persists was it because even the inequality and wrong were parts of a life that still had a relatedness and meaning which our more bountiful life in the mass culture seems to lack?

4

The Northern Origins of Southern Mythology

Patrick Gerster and Nicholas Cords

While many explanations for the rise of southern mythology have been offered—ranging from the South's physical landscape to the distorted passions aroused by sectionalism, race relations, and civil conflict—the subject of its northern origins has seldom been given more than passing attention. Indeed, a fairly complete canvassing of relevant historical literature on the question of southern mythology's northern origins discloses some rather interesting results. As argued by the editors of this volume, Patrick Gerster and Nicholas Cords, northerners such as Harriet Beecher Stowe, Stephen C. Foster, Daniel Decatur Emmett, Winslow Homer, Charles Francis Adams, Edgar Lee Masters, and F. Scott Fitzgerald all contributed to creating a romantic and mythical image of Dixie in the American consciousness. The South according to its own devices enjoyed sufficient materials and surely the imagination to shape fictitious mental constructs of its history and thereby fashion a usable past to which southerners could relate as if it were true. But, in addition, regions to the north of the Mason-Dixon line had an important hand in these legendary creations. The formulation and execution of southern mythology is clearly national as well as regional in character. Any view that continues to see the origins of southern legend as a strictly regional prerogative must overlook the attraction of southern mythology for northern artists and writers, the North's romantic fascination with aristocracy and lost causes, the national

From the *Journal of Southern History,* 43 (November 1977) 567–82. Copyright 1977 by the Southern Historical Association. Reprinted by permission of the Managing Editor, with minor editorial changes.

appeal of the agrarian myth, and the South's supposed personification of that ideal, as well as the persistent use of the South in the
peregrinations of northern racial mythology. Southern mythology
stands as testimony to the durable value of seeing the "southerner as
American," even as it bears an indelible regional birthmark.

Though America long has been a haven for myth, the American South,
more than any other region of the country, has taken hold of the nation's
mythic imagination. In fact, it seems scarcely necessary to argue any
longer the relevance of myth to the study of the southern past. Most have
come to share David M. Potter's view that "southern history, more than
most branches of historical study, seems to point up the anomalous
relationships between the past, or our image or legend of the past, and
the present, or our image of the present."[1] It is therefore appropriate to
ask, What are those historical factors which explain the penchant of
southerners and "other Americans" for romance and myth in their view
of southern history?

Particularly since George B. Tindall's seminal essay . . . "Mythology: A New Frontier in Southern History," various studies utilizing
mythology as a focal point have offered new levels of insight into topics
such as the southern lady, the plantation overseer, the Underground
Railroad, the Lost Cause, and the New South creed.[2] These, in conjunction with earlier published efforts, have informed us that southern
mythology is the product of many forces. It seems possible to argue, for
example, that a psychological frame of reference for myth was provided
the South through the utopia-saturated age of its discovery, colonization, and settlement. Or perhaps, as Wilbur Cash has suggested, it was
the South's physical landscape which helped to shape "a sort of cosmic
conspiracy against reality in favor of romance." It is plausible as well
that the growth of southern mythology is related to the passions aroused
by sectionalism, race relations, and civil conflict. And finally, one must

[1]David M. Potter, *History and American Society: Essays of David M. Potter,* ed. Don
E. Fehrenbacher (New York, 1973), p. 150.

[2] George B. Tindall, "Mythology: A New Frontier in Southern History," in Frank E.
Vandiver, ed., *The Idea of the South: Pursuit of a Central Theme* (Chicago, 1964); see
also Anne Firor Scott, *The Southern Lady: From Pedestal to Politics, 1830–1930*
(Chicago and London, 1970); William K. Scarborough, *The Overseer: Plantation
Management in the Old South* (Baton Rouge, 1966); Larry Gara, *The Liberty Line: The
Legend of the Underground Railroad* (Lexington, Ky., 1961); Rollin G. Osterweis, *The
Myth of the Lost Cause, 1865–1900* (Hamden, Conn., 1973); Paul M. Gaston, *The New
South Creed: A Study in Southern Mythmaking* (New York, 1970).

not forget the role played by southern literature in transcribing and perpetuating the region's mythology.[3]

While additional explanations for the rise of southern mythology have been offered, the subject of its northern origins and acceptance has seldom been given more than passing attention. Though widely noted, it has never been given the focused study it deserves.[4] Perhaps because of a long-standing desire to discover a "central theme" for southern history, historians have not cultivated enough of a national perspective on the role the Yankee has played in both the original creation and the tenacious adherence to the South's legendary past. One recent review of a relatively new attempt to explain "The Myth of the Lost Cause," for example, offers the critique that it fails to "throw any new light on how a regional myth attracted such a national audience."[5] Any fairly thorough canvassing of historical literature on the question of southern mythology's northern origins discloses some rather interesting results. Many students of the South have already seen this subject as a rich and worthy challenge for their talents, and their findings, collectively, deserve greater emphasis.

The South enjoyed sufficient sources and imagination to shape fictitious images of its history and thereby fashion a usable past to which southerners could relate as if it were true. But it is worth recalling with Henry Steele Commager that "the most familiar of southern symbols came from the North: Harriet Beecher Stowe of New England gave us Uncle Tom and Little Eva and Topsy and Eliza, while it was Stephen Foster of Pittsburgh who sentimentalized the Old South, and even

[3] For representative examples see Louis B. Wright, *The Colonial Search for a Southern Eden* (University, Ala., 1953); Wilbur J. Cash, *The Mind of the South* (New York, 1941), p. 46; T. Harry Williams, *Romance and Realism in Southern Politics* (Athens, Ga., 1961); and F. Garvin Davenport, Jr., *The Myth of Southern History: Historical Consciousness in Twentieth-Century Southern Literature* (Nashville, 1970).

[4] Over three decades ago Gunnar Myrdal issued a call for scholars "to investigate in further detail the role of . . . [the Yankee] in the original creation and the tenacious upholding of the myth of the 'Old South.' . . ." Myrdal, *An American Dilemma: The Negro Problem and Modern Democracy*, 2 vols. (New York and Evanston, 1962), II, 1376. More recently C. Vann Woodward has reiterated the point: "The South has been almost as essential to the North and North to the South in the shaping of national character and mythology as the Afro-American to Southern-American and vice versa. North and South have used each other, or various images and stereotypes of each other, for many puposes . . . There is need for a history of North-South images and stereotypes, of when and how and why they were developed, the shape they took, the uses that have been made of them and how they have been employed from time to time in regional defense, self-flattery, and polemics." Woodward, *American Counterpoint: Slavery and Racism in the North-South Dialogue* (Boston, 1971), pp. 6,7.

[5] Major L. Wilson's review of Rollin G. Osterweis, *The Myth of the Lost Cause, 1865–1900,* in *Journal of Southern History,* XL (February 1974), 148.

'Dixie' had northern origins."[6] Indeed, the efforts of northern artists—literary, musical, and pictorial—have contributed substantially to the national credibility of southern mythology.

Connecticut Yankee Mrs. Stowe, for example, basing her impressions of the South on extremely limited firsthand experience, worked to implant the "faithful darkey" (Sambo) image of blacks. She also graphically portrayed a stereotyped version of the plantation overseer, who, interestingly enough, uniquely symbolized the acquiescence of the North in southern myth by his Yankee origin: Simon Legree was a Vermonter. And in the process she obliquely gave vitality to the complementary images of semifeudal Cavaliers and virtuous belles.[7] While these distorted characterizations no doubt contributed to the book's emotional appeal and phenomenal sales, they also contributed their share of myth to the nation's understanding of slave conditions in the Old South.

Three years after the appearance of Harriet Beecher Stowe's faithful old Tom, suffering Eliza, and sadistic Simon Legree, another northerner gave additional weight to the developing myth of southern antebellum luxury. In 1855 David Christy of Ohio published his book *Cotton Is King* and in the process touched off a great deal of discussion both in America and Europe about the industrial world's dependence upon the raw cotton of the South. The effect of the book was to obscure the realities of the South's diversified economy and create the impression that Dixie was an empire of plantations and slaveholders. Less than a decade later, the South itself came to rely much too heavily on the fetching idea of King Cotton in formulating its Civil War foreign policy. The literary efforts of Christy in the years before the conflict had helped to instill the idea nationally that the large cotton plantation, caressed by the fragrance of magnolia blossoms, was the principal habitat of the "typical" southerner.

Stephen C. Foster reinforced synthetic southern stereotypes in "Susanna" (1847) and "Old Folks at Home" (1851), composed prior to a one-month excursion into the South in 1852, after which he published "Massa's in de Cold Ground" (1852), "My Old Kentucky Home" (1852), and "Old Black Joe" (1860).[8] These songs, as one scholar has suggested, "nostalgically describe a 'longing for the old plantation' " and along with the novels of John Pendleton Kennedy and William Alexander

[6] Commager, *The Search for a Usable Past and Other Essays in Historiography* (New York, 1967), p. 26.

[7] Tindall, "Mythology," p. 5.

[8] Gilbert Chase, *America's Music* (New York, Toronto, and London, 1955), pp. 291–294.

Caruthers helped to fix the "Plantation Illusion" in the American mind.[9] For decades they continued to feed the nation's romantic imagination trite and charming renditions of antebellum splendor.

Another fact on Foster's myth-building concerns one of the tourist showplaces of Kentucky—Federal Hill near Bardstown—where the composer purportedly wrote "My Old Kentucky Home." Local Kentuckians' efforts to feed the nation's nostalgic taste for the Old South notwithstanding, no evidence exists that Foster ever visited the estate, much less that he wrote his famous song there. According to a letter of Stephen's brother, Morrison Foster, "lyrics and songs including 'My Old Kentucky Home' were composed at Stephen's home in Allegheny County, Pennsylvania."[10] Undeniably, his plantation songs and the notoriety they have received through the efforts of Bardstown residents have had a legend-creating impact on the popular mind of both the North and South as they offer succeeding generations easily evoked versions of an ideal life in the sunny South before the war.

Even considering the influence of Harriet Beecher Stowe, David Christy, and Stephen C. Foster, however, perhaps nothing has captured the flavor of southernism with greater emotional impact than the song "Dixie." Symbolic of the southern way of life, it was written in New York City by an Ohioan, Daniel Decatur Emmett, in 1859.[11] Though used as a marching tune by both Union and Confederate forces during the Civil War, it soon became the unofficial national anthem of the South and has remained one of the most important sentimental expressions of southern regional feeling ever since. As Jefferson Davis and Alexander H. Stephens assumed the leadership of the Confederate States of America, the Emmett-inspired romance had already begun to work its magic. Clement Eaton has described the scene in this fashion: "On February 18, 1861, they were inaugurated in the state capitol at Montgomery, and at the ceremonies a band played the new song 'Dixie,' with its pervading nostalgia. Like the cradles, coffins, patent medicines, tall silk hats, plow—indeed, most manufactured articles used in the South—the song that was destined to become the unofficial anthem of the Confederacy was also an import from the Yankees. . . ."[12]

For succeeding generations the pervading nostalgia of "Dixie" has carried an emotional impact described by the northern novelist F. Scott Fitzgerald in "The Ice Palace" (1920). On a visit to the North, Fitzgerald's

9 Everett Carter, "Cultural History Written with Lightning: The Significance of *The Birth of a Nation*," *American Quarterly*, XII (Fall 1960), 350.

10 Harvey Einbinder, *The Myth of the Britannica* (New York, and London, 1964), p. 361.

11 Chase, *America's Music*, pp. 272–277.

12 Eaton, *A History of the Old South* (New York and London, 1966), p. 511.

heroine, the Georgia belle Sally Carrol Happer, attends a vaudeville performance which concludes with the playing of "Dixie." Fitzgerald describes her as immediately responding to its strong and enduring strains: "To the spirited throb of the violins and the inspiring beat of the kettledrums her own ghosts were marching by and on into the darkness, and as fifes whistled and sighed in the low encore they seemed so nearly out of sight that she could have waved good-by."[13]

The efforts of northern artists to romanticize the South are of course not limited to Stowe, Christy, Foster, and Emmett. Francis Pendleton Gaines reveals that northern drama and northern minstrelsy, as well as northern paintings of the South such as Eastman Johnson's *My Old Kentucky Home* (1859) and Winslow Homer's *Sunday Morning in Virginia* (ca. 1870), gave important consideration to mythical plantation materials.[14] William R. Taylor argues that it was the literary energies of the North as well as the South, the work of James Kirke Paulding of New York, for example, that seeded the fictional southern plantation in literature.[15] And not to be forgotten are the numerous sentimental lithographs of Nathaniel Currier of Roxbury, Massachusetts, and James Merritt Ives of New York City, which offered a national audience unblemished images of Americana, both North and South. Collectively, northern works of art from Stowe and Foster to Currier and Ives did much to effect a national unity of emotion and belief concerning southern history whose verisimilitude was seldom examined by their avid audience. Their creations evoked southern images which were sometimes at odds with fact but of critical importance, nonetheless, to the development of a nationally created regional mythology.

But the questions remain: Why did the North find the myths of the Old South so very comfortable and comforting? What caused this fusion of southern and northern sentiment? How was it that so many northerners were so distinctly of the southern persuasion? Francis Pendleton Gaines was perhaps the first historian to address himself to these questions in a systematic way and to explain the process whereby the South and the North became copartners in the creation of a pseudopast—what the poet Stephen Vincent Benet called "the sick magnolias of the false romance." A form of mythical reciprocity evolved, says Gaines, in that "two opposing sides of the fiercest controversy that ever shook national thought agreed concerning certain picturesque elements of plantation

[13] Fitzgerald, "The Ice Palace," in Malcolm Cowley, ed., *The Stories of F. Scott Fitzgerald* (New York, 1951), p. 76.

[14] Gaines, *The Southern Plantation: A Study in the Development and the Accuracy of a Tradition* (New York, 1925), pp. 12, 95–127.

[15] Taylor, "A Northern Man of Southern Principles," in *Cavalier and Yankee: The Old South and American National Character* (New York, 1961), pp. 225–259.

life and joined hands to set the conception unforgettably in public consciousness."[16] In attempting to explain further this sectional compromise which allowed southern mythmakers to forge an entente with the North, Gaines cited America's latent "love of feudalism" and a "romantic hunger" for "some allegory of aristocracy." The southern plantation, Gaines concludes, "alone among native institutions, satisfies this craving for a system of caste."[17] While a titled aristocracy had long since been declared at odds with the American Creed, the idea of an American aristocracy has never lost its fascination. The Yankee, despite his stated though often superficial differences, liked to fancy himself a Cavalier at heart.

The testimony of the Swedish sociologist Gunnar Myrdal, in his classic study *An American Dilemma* (1944), adds further evidence to the thesis that northern support for southern mythology was a result of "Yankee class romanticism." Noting that the nation has long had a severely distorted mythology about the rank and privilege of European aristocrats, Myrdal maintains that the North was led to fantasize when it came to understanding the "aristocracy" which they thought they knew best—that of the antebellum South. Myrdal could thus explain why southern mythmakers found ready allies in the North for their notions of caste and class: "The North has so few vestiges of feudalism and aristocracy of its own that, even though it dislikes them fundamentally and is happy not to have them, Yankees are thrilled by them. Northerners apparently cherish the idea of having had an aristocracy and of still having a real class society—in the South. So it manufactures the myth of the 'Old South' or has it manufactured by Southern writers working for the Northern Market."[18] Myrdal's point must be understood to be that it was not only "Southern writers working for the Northern market" who portrayed an essentially legendary South, but northern writers joining hands with their southern brethren in allowing myth to parade as history. In line with the earlier findings of Gaines, Myrdal sees that northern regional disaffection and subliminal cravings for the imagined benefits of aristocracy made the province of southern myth a dual domain.

A similar argument about the sustained vitality of the plantation legend in the North has been offered by William R. Taylor. The acceptance of the southern legend among Yankees, claims Taylor, relates to the "age of anxiety," the decade of the 1830s. The so-called Age of the Common Man, based as it was on the ideas of participatory democracy

[16] Gaines, *The Southern Plantation,* p. 30.
[17] *Ibid.,* pp. 2–3.
[18] Myrdal, *An American Dilemma,* II, 1375–1376.

and egalitarianism—though in some ways more imaginary than real—proved threatening to those who wished to salvage remnants of their status which they perceived to be endangered. This crosscurrent of antidemocratic sentiment, says Taylor, produced a "hankering after aristocracy in the North [which] took the form of eulogizing the social system of the South."[19] In short, the social structure of the South came to symbolize for many northerners—James Fenimore Cooper, for example—an important counterpoint, an enviable brand of social stability, when crisis, flux, and anxiety were the order of the day on northern fronts. The strictures and standards of an older order were under fire—or were thought to be—as the nation sought to sustain former republican virtues while also seeking to accommodate itself to far-reaching social and economic change.

Confronted with ambivalence and contradiction growing out of swift change and the social mobility of a new class of expectant capitalists, the North displayed a flirtatious attitude toward stable mythical images then emerging in the South. Many northerners began to cast their eyes southward because it appeared that an Old World aristocracy there had somehow discovered a way of assuring stability and cultivating a sense of gentility and decorum while maintaining a commitment to the public good under a republican form of government. As northern politicians, writers, and social critics attempted to come to terms with the variant and elusive aspects of Jacksonian democracy, conditions precipitated a social imagination in the North conducive to the emergence of a mythmaking frame of mind. And since southerners had already begun to stabilize their own social system through mythology, it was to them that the North turned for guidance and inspiration. C. Vann Woodward has recently summarized this point. The northern zest for southern myth, he observes, owes much to the North's "compensatory dream of aristocracy, the airs of grace and decorum left behind, secretly yearned for but never realized."[20]

According to Wilbur J. Cash, the North's passion for the myth of the Old South was indeed fed by the "imaginary glory" of a mythical aristocracy, but it was also being stirred by a pristine nostalgia for a "purely agricultural past" which the South had come flawlessly to symbolize during the antebellum age.[21] In the Age of Jackson the country was in many ways enamored of the promise of an urbanized and industrialized America, but the United States, according to Richard

[19] Taylor, *Cavalier and Yankee*, pp. 96–97; see also Howard R. Floan, *The South in Northern Eyes, 1831–1861* (Austin, 1958), pp. 89–107.

[20] Woodward, *American Counterpoint*, p. 6.

[21] Cash, *The Mind of the South*, p. 62.

Hofstadter, had been "born in the country" before it "moved to the city."[22] It was thus being drawn by a memory of things past to the imagined glory of its agricultural beginnings and was continuing to view the tillers of the soil as both ideal men and ideal citizens. Accordingly, as the antebellum North seemed to be moving ideologically further and further away from the nation's agricultural origins, the South had taken its stand with the solid values of agrarianism. In the words of Cash, the North "was not only ready but eager to believe in the Southern legend . . . it fell with a certain distinct gladdness on this last purely agricultural land of the West as a sort of projection ground for its own dreams of a vanished golden time."[23] As America came to cherish the notion that agriculture was the most basic of industries and the agriculturist the most virtuous of men, both the North and the South could mutually agree to the plantation legend because of their mutual admiration for the agrarian myth.

While the efforts of artists and a fixation with both aristocracy and the agrarian myth were important contributors to the ready acceptance of Old South mythology, the North seems also to have conspired in southern mythmaking because of its guilt over slavery and its repressed attitudes on race relations. Though it is fairly clear that the South came to defend its "peculiar institution" for reasons of guilt and political survival, it is too easily forgotten that many northerners more than indirectly supported the plantation legend by assuming a posture *opposed* to slavery. C. Vann Woodward has explained that "the North . . . had deeply felt needs of its own to be served by an antislavery myth, needs that were sufficient at all times to keep the legend vital and growing to meet altered demands."[24]

As layers of fantasy and romance came to cloud the historical reality of the northern position on the slavery issue before the Civil War, the revered notion that racial inhumanity was a condition to be found only in the prewar South became a northern exercise in atonement for its own social guilt. Woodward states, "The South has long served the nation in ways still in great demand. It has been a moral lightning rod, a deflector of national guilt, a scapegoat for stricken conscience. It has served the country as much as the Negro has served the white supremacist—as a floor under self-esteem."[25] The resultant idea that the Mason-Dixon

[22] Hofstadter, "The Agrarian Myth and Commercial Realities" in *The Age of Reform from Bryan to FDR* (New York, 1955), pp. 23–59; quotation on p. 23.

[23] Cash, *The Mind of the South,* p. 62.

[24] Woodward, "The Antislavery Myth," *American Scholar,* XXXI (Spring 1962), 312.

[25] Woodward, "From the First Reconstruction to the Second," *Harper's Magazine,* CCXXX (April 1965), 133; see also Stanley M. Elkins, "Slavery and the Intellectual," in

Line divided slavery from freedom in antebellum America was, of course, a historical lie, but "it sprang from . . . [the abolitionists'] laudable impulse to be identified with noble deeds."[26] The antislavery myth did not square with the latent commitment to white supremacy which was a national, not simply a regional, credo. In addition, it fit badly with the subtle forms of de facto segregation encouraging discrimination against northern blacks and with later forms of social control and subordination when the South after Reconstruction "resorted to many of the devices originally developed in the North to keep the Negro in his 'place.'"[27] Only to the degree to which the South could be seen as morally inferior could the North establish its claim to moral superiority. The major props of the myths of antebellum southern society, at least as they related to the question of slavery, demanded political and psychological efforts national in scope. Woodward wryly concludes, "As yet . . . the Yankee remains to be fully emancipated from his own legends of emancipation. Confront him with a given set of symbols and he will set his sense of humor aside, snap to attention and come to a full salute. In the ensuing rigidities of that situation, conversation tends to lag."[28]

The practical impact of this kind of duplicity, of course, was that one brand of mythology energized another. By endorsing the traditional picture of plantation life, northerners were able to hide their own mistreatment of the black man behind the facade of an "antislavery myth." By creating the impression that all Negroes would at last be free if only the institutions and traditions of the South were changed, the North would not have to face up to its own forms of racial inhumanity. The revered notion that race prejudice was a condition to be found exclusively in the prewar South allowed the North to escape its social guilt over the continued existence of discrimination. At its grossest extreme it allowed even some abolitionist organizations to rationalize the exclusion of Negroes. The northern endorsement of the plantation legend in a backhanded way, then, helped support the myth that ideas of white supremacy were to be found only in the Cotton Kingdom. In this way the North found southern mythology useful as a means of stabilizing and perpetuating its own racial mythology well beyond antebellum days. One scholar has concluded that the American South "is a distillation of those traits which are the worst (and a few which are the best) in

Slavery: A Problem in American Institutional and Intellectual Life (Chicago, 1959), pp. 140–222; and William H. Pease and Jane H. Pease, "Antislavery Ambivalence: Immediatism, Expediency, Race," *American Quarterly,* XVII (Winter 1965), 682–695.

[26] Woodward, "The Antislavery Myth," p. 314.

[27] *Ibid.,* p. 318.

[28] *Ibid.,* p. 326.

the national character. . . . And the nation reacts emotionally to the South precisely because it subconsciously recognizes itself there."[29]

The North's racial attitudes seem also to have been a force leading to that region's complicity in the creation of "the tragic legend of Reconstruction." Kenneth M. Stampp has argued that the North functioned as a co-conspirator in the developing mythology of the South following the Civil War:

> Southerners, of course, have contributed much to the legend of Reconstruction, but most northerners have found the legend quite acceptable. Many of the historians who helped to create it were northerners, among them James Ford Rhodes, William A. Dunning, Claude Bowers, and James G. Randall. Thus the legend cannot be explained simply in terms of a southern literary or historiographical conspiracy, satisfying as the legend has been to most white southerners. What we need to know is why it also satisfies northerners — how it became part of the intellectual baggage of so many northern historians. Why, in short, was there for so many years a kind of national, or inter-sectional, consensus that the Civil War was America's glory and reconstruction her disgrace?[30]

Having posed the question of northern involvement in Reconstruction's "tragic legend" and mythology, Stampp demonstrates that feelings of accommodation affected modifications of wartime passions. "Northerners were willing to concede that southerners had fought bravely for a cause that they believed to be just," says Stampp; and "both northerners and southerners agreed that the preservation of the federal Union was essential to the future power of the American people."[31] In even more important ways, however, both North and South could judge Reconstruction to be a "horrid nightmare." Latent and basic racial antipathy toward enfranchised blacks began to find expression after the demise of the Radical Republicans as a reforming force. And outside of Congress changes were occurring which would have the same effect. Northern writers were becoming increasingly "indifferent" to the problems of the freedman, the country began to meet the "threat" of the new immigration with the construction of racial stereotypes, and social scientists supplied national racist thinking an academic rationale supportive of its prejudiced position. As a result, Stampp concludes, "the old middle

---

[29] Howard Zinn, *The Southern Mystique* (New York, 1964), p. 218.
[30] Stampp, *The Era of Reconstruction, 1865–1877* (New York, 1966), p. 13.
[31] *Ibid.*

classes of the North looked with new understanding upon the problems of the beleaguered white men of the South."[32] Just as it had developed the antislavery myth of the antebellum era, the North found it both emotionally and practically convenient after the War for the Union to subscribe for racial reasons to the legend that Reconstruction had been a "tragic era" and a "dreadful decade."

Along with the myths of Reconstruction, the various myths of the Old South continued to enjoy both emotional and strategic appeal in the North after the War for Southern Independence. Indeed, this was true even for those who in other ways saw through the nation's shams and illusions. Particularly during the period that Mark Twain critically labeled the "Gilded Age" — when the smell of scandal and corruption reeked from governmental offices and the boardrooms of industrial corporations — some northern writers began to argue that the social, political, and economic system of the Old South had been in many ways better than the allegedly golden age they saw before them. Thus, in the process of criticizing the shortcomings of Yankee civilization in the 1870s and 1880s, northern writers such as Herman Melville, Henry James, and Henry Adams sought to compare the progress and optimism of the early South with the stagnation and despair of America's "age of excess."[33] The antebellum South, it seemed, had been neither as hypocritical about equality nor as materialistic as the America of Ulysses Simpson Grant, Jay Gould, and "Boss" William Marcy Tweed.

The shortcomings of American Yankee culture in the declining years of the nineteenth century seemed all the more obvious when measured against the seemingly vibrant and charming days when things were different in the South. Post–Civil War America seemed somehow much more vulgar and vain than the South of the Old Regime. The South's longstanding commitments to family, leisured living, honorable conduct, and chivalry seemed to be precisely the values and virtues which America most lacked. In the words of the transplanted southerner Basil Ransom, the leading character of Henry James's novel *The Bostonians* (1886), the "gilded age" which the North had pasted together after the Civil War was "a nervous, hysterical, chattering, canting age, an age of hollow phrases and false delicacy."[34] Though James later admitted to knowing "terribly little" of the kind of life he had attempted to describe, or of the supposed superiority of the South which he offered as an

---

[32] *Ibid.*, p. 19.

[33] These particular writers are discussed in C. Vann Woodward, "A Southern Critique for the Gilded Age," in *The Burden of Southern History* (Baton Rouge, 1960), pp. 109–140.

[34] Quoted, *ibid.*, p. 133.

alternative, he felt comfortable in suggesting that the South's heroic age had much to commend it. Now that slavery had been purged from the southern utopia, one could more easily imagine, through a hindsight conditioned by illusion, that the South of an earlier day had been something very close to the most perfect society American had yet produced. For this reason the North's developing alliance with the South in the creative enterprise of southern mythology worked to unite the sections; for "to the North it offered a way in which to apologize without sacrificing the fruits of victory." Together with forces already at work in Dixie, supporting a legendary view of the southern past, the result could only be "a national love feast for the Old South."[35] The kinship which had eluded the sections through the Civil War period was to be more successfully achieved by means of mythology. On this level they could well communicate, for they were Americans and mythmakers all. They could join hands in a postwar setting for a mutual reacceptance of a southern mythology which had been born decades before, had survived the war years, and was only now at the point of maturing.

In this spirit Henry Adams symbolically suggested the northern fixation for a mythical South in his *Education* (1918). Therein he describes how before the Civil War he (a Boston Yankee) had been a classmate of William Henry Fitzhugh "Roony" Lee at Harvard. In a retrospective on his experiences and his exposure to the symbolic South, Adams writes: "For the first time Adams's education brought him in contact with new types and taught him their values. He saw the New England type measure itself with another, and he was part of the process. . . . This momentary contact with Southern character was a sort of education for its own sake. . . ."[36] Adams's feelings of affinity for the South, personified in his dealings with the son of Robert E. Lee, implied a common ground developing between the regions which would eventually help to effect a concert of interests between the sections.

As the future became the past and southern mythology moved from a nineteenth- to a twentieth-century phenomenon, the North continued to sustain distorted perceptions of the South. The mirage for some continued in the manner of the old romantic school. Thomas Dixon, Jr.'s *The Leopard's Spots,* for example, fed northern audiences his mythical version of Reconstruction history from a New York stage in 1903. Not only did Broadway accept his version of the southern past, but the production was the hit of the theatrical season.[37] Twelve years later David Wark Griffith's cinema classic, *The Birth of a Nation* (1915),

[35] Gaston, *The New South Creed,* p. 179.
[36] Adams, *The Education of Henry Adams* (New York, 1931), pp. 57, 58.
[37] Cash, *The Mind of the South,* p. 197.

adapted Dixon's novel *The Clansman* for the nation's fastest-developing new medium and in the process synthesized the images of the Old South and Reconstruction in "epic" proportions for national consumption. The formidable combination of Dixon's bigotry, Griffith's emotional memories, and the nation's already well developed appetite for the legendary South assured the film monetary success. In this instance at least, as Gunnar Myrdal observed, southerners had discovered the salability of southern mythology on the northern market.[38]

The North's attention to the heroic character of the South also found interesting expression early in the twentieth century through the efforts of a northern-dominated cult of Robert E. Lee. In 1900 General Lee was elected by a nationwide board of electors to the American Hall of Fame. Although he received only 68 votes to General Grant's 93, it was nonetheless a clear prelude to his national canonization.[39] In the succeeding years a northerner, Charles Francis Adams, Jr., became the nation's foremost spokesman in defense of Lee's nobility. Addressing the American Antiquarian Society in 1901 on the topic of "Lee at Appomattox," Adams did his part to assure the acceptance of an entirely positive image for the Confederate leader in northern minds. A high-water mark in Lee's rise from mortal man to an ethereal and heroic ideal, however, came in January 1907 when Adams delivered the Lee Centennial Address at Washington and Lee University. Adams's efforts, in the opinion of one historian, represented the acceptance of Lee as a national symbol and marked "a transition which almost entailed his capture from the South."[40] In the view of the scholar of American heroes, Dixon Wecter, this new stage of Lee hero worship proved "the age of big business felt . . . that it could use a great gentleman in its national pantheon, like a buffalo in a museum of vanishing Americana." The exaggeration and distortion which led to Robert E. Lee's apotheosis may have peaked with the publication in 1926 of Edgar Lee Masters's massive effort, "Lee: A Dramatic Poem."[41] Even as this Chicago lawyer-turned-poet was adding his dash of drama to the burgeoning Lee legend, however, the good general was already suffering the kind of inflation which haunts the memory of most men of historical importance.

[38] F. Garvin Davenport, Jr., "Thomas Dixon's Mythology of Southern History," *Journal of Southern History,* XXXVI (August 1970), 352; Myrdal, *An American Dilemma,* II, 1376.

[39] Thomas L. Connelly, "The Image and the General: Robert E. Lee in American Historiography," *Civil War History,* XIX (March 1973), 61–63; Dixon Wecter, "Lee: The Aristocrat as Hero," in *The Hero in America: A Chronicle of Hero Worship* (Ann Arbor, 1963), pp. 302–304.

[40] Connelly, "The Image and the General," p. 62.

[41] Wecter, *The Hero in America,* pp. 304, 305.

Americans of the 1920s were also exposed to a sympathetic treatment of the imagined glory of the Old South through the literary efforts of Minnesota-born F. Scott Fitzgerald. His southern sensibilities seem to have been garnered in the first place from his father, Edward Fitzgerald, a descendant of old and aristocratic Maryland families, the Scotts and the Keys. "He . . . came from another America," Fitzgerald noted on the occasion of his father's death. Indeed, the elder Fitzgerald "instilled in his son not only beautiful manners, but a sense of honor, an almost eighteenth-century code of decorum. . . . And it was from his father that he 'acquired an extended and showy, if very superficial, knowledge of the Civil War (with an intense southern bias . . .).' It is not surprising, then, to discover that his son saw in that conflict the 'broken link in the continuity of American life.' "[42] Given Fitzgerald's personal testimony, it seems clear that the northern writer firmly believed in the synthetic stereotypes of Cavalier and Yankee and was also willing to accept other features of the Plantation Legend—such as the Southern Belle.

Fitzgerald's romantic attachment to the legendary South was of course stimulated by his personal relationship with Zelda Sayre of Montgomery. She was, in his fanciful imagination at least, "the last of the belles." In her he seems to have found a kindred spirit, as captivated as he with dreams of aristocratic grandeur. Nancy Milford quotes Edmund Wilson to the effect that "if ever there was a pair whose fantasies matched . . . it was Zelda Sayre and Scott Fitzgerald."[43] It was through her, then, that Fitzgerald, in stories such as "The Ice Palace" (1920), drew the nation's attention to what he called the "strange courtliness and chivalry" of "the most beautiful thing in the world—the dead South."[44] Though the setting for the short story is the 1920s, the characters reflect historic sentiments drawn from an earlier day. Neither the Southern Lady nor the Sunny South had changed, apparently, since the golden and legendary days of the Old Regime. His heroine, Sally Carrol, is one of those "gracious, soft-voiced girls, who were brought up on memories instead of money." And the background for her romantic intrigues are "lazy cotton-fields, where even the workers seemed intangible shadows lent by the sun to the earth, not for toil, but to while away some age-old tradition in the golden September fields. And round the drowsy picturesqueness, over the trees and shacks, and muddy rivers, flowed the heat, never hostile, only comforting, like a great warm nourishing bosom for the

---

[42] Nancy Milford, *Zelda: A Biography* (New York, Evanston, and London, 1970), pp. 25–26.

[43] *Ibid.*, p. 25.

[44] Cowley, ed., *Stories of F. Scott Fitzgerald*, p. 66.

infant earth."[45] In his personal affairs and in his fiction—in many ways inseparable—Fitzgerald subscribed to the myth of the Old South. The myth-conditioned South provided him both artistic inspiration and an idyllic mental sanctuary.

It was left to a southerner, however, a contemporary of Fitzgerald's, to most directly capture the flavor of the emotional and strategic appeal which the various myths of the South have had for the North. Nobel laureate William Faulkner, through his character Gavin Stevens in *Intruder in the Dust* (1948), points succinctly to the manner in which northerners have been willing captives of a developing southern mythology. The North, Stevens declares, has displayed a "gullibility: a volitionless, almost helpless capacity and eagerness to believe anything about the South not even provided it be derogatory but merely bizarre enough and strange enough."[46]

The strange career of southern mythology, not unlike that of Jim Crow, saw Dixie "look away" to tap important reservoirs of precedent and support in the nation at large. It would be a mythology forged in the spirit of union, an "all-American" effort to be sure. David M. Potter was surely speaking with measured understatement and pointing only to the most obvious evidence of the South's success at capturing the imagination of its northern neighbor when he observed, "Today, the predilection of Yankee children for caps, flags, and toys displaying the Rebel insignia bears further witness to the enduring truth that lost causes have a fascination even for those who did not lose them."[47] Indeed, it is important to notice that the myths of the South—Old and New—were cultivated by those—North and South—who never owned a slave or planted an acre of cotton. We have heard much of the importance of seeing the "southerner as American"; perhaps we should hear more of the many ways in which "the American" has been distinctly of the southern persuasion, especially when it comes to mythology. For any view which continues to see the creation and perpetuation of southern legend as a regional prerogative would be forced to ignore the attention of northern artists to southern mythology, the North's fascination with aristocracy and lost causes, the national appeal of the agrarian myth, and the South's personification of that ideal, to say nothing of the persistent use of the South in the manipulation of northern racial mythology. All this considered, one trusts that the North and the South will continue to explore the new frontiers of mythology with the same spirit of union they have displayed in the past.

[45] *Ibid.*, pp. 62, 64.

[46] Faulkner, *Intruder in the Dust* (New York, 1948), p. 153.

[47] Potter, "The Enigma of the South," in *The South and the Sectional Conflict* (Baton Rouge, 1968), p. 4.

5

The Progressive Movement
in the South, 1870–1914

Arthur S. Link

Much has been accomplished in the American historical profession
toward arriving at a more valid assessment of the first "ism" to
dominate the twentieth century—progressivism. In making these
judgments, however, the South has traditionally been excluded from
serious consideration. Even at the time, national Progressive leaders
such as Robert M. LaFollette "wrote off" the region because he
considered democracy basically lacking there; later historians seem
to have found it difficult to fit the area into the urban middle-class
model. In this article America's premier Woodrow Wilson scholar,
Princeton historian Arthur S. Link, directs himself to this im-
balance and carefully redresses it. After defining the terms "conservative" and "progressive," Professor Link briefly traces southern
progressivism as it developed out of late nineteenth-century southern radical agrarianism and notes its subtle shift from a rural-eco-
nomic to an urban-political emphasis. In addition, the positive impact
of Woodrow Wilson (a Virginian by birth) on the Progressive movement in the South was significant, as southerners, particularly educators, clergymen, and editors, took up the cause. The article then
goes on to list southern accomplishments as compared to national
progressive goals in areas such as railroad regulation, reform of
party machinery, and corrupt practices legislation. Professor Link
also notes selective achievements in economic and social fields such
as the sixty-hour work week in the textile mills and child labor legislation. If there were southern progressive deficiencies, comparatively

Arthur S. Link, "The Progressive Movement in the South, 1870–1914," *The North
Carolina Historical Review,* 23 (1946), 172–195. Reprinted with permission of the
publisher and author.

they were perhaps no more numerous or gross than those on the national level as a whole—especially since it is now somewhat common to see the entire Progressive movement as complex and laden with paradox. If one can accept imperialism, immigration restriction, and prohibition as "progressive," then certain regressive tendencies in the South (e.g., treatment of the Negro) do not necessarily disqualify that region from the century's first "ism."

Before assessing the nature and extent of progressive democracy in the South, a definition of terms, as they are meant to be understood in this discussion, is necessary.[1] Conservatism, as it is generally understood, connotes a tendency to maintain the status quo and a disposition of hostility to innovations in the political, social, and economic order. Oftentimes the classes that possess a conservative point of view are the wealthy classes, but, of course, this is not always the case. In short, conservatism is usually a reasoned or unreasoned resistance to change.[2] Progressivism, on the other hand, implies a philosophy that welcomes innovations and reforms in the political, economic, and social order. Progressives are usually persons who strive for reforms that alleviate the ills of society, that assure to the people a broader control of their governments, and that look toward affording greater economic, political, and social justice to the people. These progressives are the so-called "liberals," not "radicals"; they have been, as a general rule, essentially conservative insofar as basic property rights and the fundamental capitalistic structure are concerned.[3]

The popular notion that such a thing as progressive democracy in the South was non-existent during the period 1870–1914, or practically so, that the Southern states were ruled by tyrannical political machines, that they were almost unbelievably backward, economically, politically, and socially, has become so persistent that it is hard to down. Most writers ignore the progressive movement in the South altogether; those that do recognize its existence characterize it as a result of Western progressivism. The extremist's view that there was no progressive democracy in the South was expressed by the late Senator Robert M. LaFollette, himself a foremost

[1] Research on this article was made possible by a grant from the Julius Rosenwald Fund.

[2] See *Encyclopaedia of the Social Sciences,* IV, 230–232, for a discussion of conservatism.

[3] For a discussion of this idea see David J. Saposs's provocative article, "The Role of the Middle Class in Social Development, Fascism, Populism, Communism, Socialism," in *Economic Essays in Honor of Wesley Clair Mitchell,* pp. 395–424, especially p. 399.

progressive, in a speech at Saginaw, Michigan, on New Year's day, 1912. He said:

> I don't know of any progressive sentiment or any progressive legislation in the South. . . . A true American believes in democracy. He believes men and women are equal and entitled to an equal chance. But the Democratic party of the South is not by inheritance that sort of organization. All the strength of the party is the aristocracy. The Southern Democrat despises alike the poor white and the negro and that is not the sentiment that makes for popular government.[4]

Despite Senator La Follette's blanket indictment, only his ignorance prevented him from knowing that there was in 1912, and had been for some decades, a far-reaching progressive movement in the South. Basically and primarily it was, before 1900, agrarian in composition and principle, generated by agricultural unrest that came as a result of social, political, and economic causes. Farmers throughout the nation saw control of the national government pass from their hands into the hands of the industrial class after the Civil War. They saw the formation of large combinations in industry, which enabled the industrialists to eliminate competitors and to maintain a monopolistic price level. They saw themselves economically oppressed by the railroads by means of discriminations between persons and places, unjustly high freight rates, pools, and the granting of rebates. They felt themselves economically injured by the national bank system that furthered the interests of the business groups and prevented a free flow of credit to agricultural communities.

The Granger movement was the first attempt by the farmers to strike back at the industrial and railroad giants oppressing them. The economic platform of the Grange is illustrative of this point. It advised farmers to dispense with middlemen and commission agents, expressed violent opposition to monopolies and trusts, demanded regulation of the railroads by the state and national governments in the interests of the producers, and advocated agricultural and industrial education.[5] The year 1871 saw the introduction of the Grange into South Carolina, Mississippi, and Kentucky, and by the end of 1872 the movement had spread widely throughout the South. By the end of that year, for example, South Carolina ranked next to Iowa in the number of granges.[6] The influence of the movement is clearly discernible in the demand for railroad regulation that made headway in the Southern states in the 1870's. There are numerous instances of Granger agitation for

---

[4] *San Antonio Express,* January 2, 1912.
[5] Solon J. Buck, *The Granger Movement,* p. 64.
[6] Buck, *Granger Movement,* pp. 52–55.

railroad regulation in the South. The state grange of Arkansas petitioned the legislature in 1877 for a law establishing maximum rates. In Virginia and Tennessee the state granges were interested in efforts to secure reduced rates by negotiation with the railroad companies. The state grange of South Carolina appealed to the legislature in 1877 and again in 1878 for laws to prevent unjust rates, discrimination, and other railroad malpractices.[7] Obviously the movement for railroad regulation was an early manifestation of the Southern progressive movement. Numerous cooperative stores, banks, manufactories, and insurance companies were also begun by the Grange leaders in the South.[8]

Many causes were responsible for the decline and failure of the Granger movement in the South and in the nation.[9] Even after the passing of the organization as a powerful body, its influence lived on and subsequent agrarian movements became its heirs. The Grangers organized to do battle with the new capitalism—the railroads, the middlemen, the trusts, and the bankers—and, having failed to gain all their objectives, retired from the field.

The Greenback-Labor movement was the successor to the Granger movement, but primarily because it was a third party organization it made little headway in the South. In 1880 a state convention of the Alabama Greenback-Labor party adopted a platform which demanded adequate educational facilities, denounced the convict-lease system, and demanded an equalization of the tax burden.[10] Alabama was the only state in which the party made any headway at all, but in that state "Greenbackism . . . was a significant experiment in political discontent, and gave impetus to Populism as its successor in the state."[11]

The most significant and the largest farmers' organization in the nineteenth century South was the Farmers' Alliance. The Southern Farmers'

[7] Buck, *Granger Movement,* pp. 252–273. See also Francis B. Simkins, *The Tillman Movement in South Carolina,* p. 17.

[8] For Texas, see Ralph A. Smith, "The Grange in Texas, 1873–1900," *Southwestern Historical Quarterly,* XLII (April, 1939), 297–315.

[9] Among the causes for the decline of the Granger movement may be listed the following: (1) The laxness of organization permitted many persons who were not interested in the farmer and his problems to join. For example, it was not uncommon for politicians to use the Grange for their own political advancement. (2) The huge, unwieldy mass within the organization led to dissension within the ranks. (3) The connection of the Grange with a number of political movements led to its decline. (4) The Grange failed to secure permanent and effective railroad regulation. (5) The main cause was the failure of the Granger cooperative endeavors which went to pieces and left a burden of discredit and indebtedness. Buck, *Granger Movement,* pp. 70–74.

[10] John B. Clark, *Populism in Alabama,* p. 25.

[11] Clark, *Populism in Alabama,* p. 28.

Alliance had its origin in a cattlemen's association in Lampasas County, Texas, in the middle 1870's. Within a decade the Texas Alliance had spread throughout the state and under the guidance of its leader, C. W. Macune, began in the late 1880's to absorb similar farmers' organizations in other Southern states. By 1890 the Southern Alliance boasted a membership of over a million and was the most powerful farmers' organization in the country. It was the spearhead of the last great concerted agrarian effort in this country. It and its political successor, the People's party, marked the culmination of the agrarian progressive movement in the South.

When agrarian efforts to liberalize the Democratic party failed, Southern farmers joined their comrades in the West and launched in 1892 the People's party. The platform of the agrarian Democrats and the Populists, as members of the People's party were called, comprehended a broad program of economic and political reforms in the interest of the agrarian and debtor classes. Since the third party was organized in every Southern state, it is possible to see the objectives for which these progressives were fighting. The populistic group in Alabama adopted a platform in 1892 that included the progressive demands of the Democrats and also called for fair elections and a national graduated income tax, and denounced national banks and trusts. A platform of 1894 demanded the removal of convicts from, and prohibition of child labor in, the mines.[12] The Alliance-controlled Democratic party in Tennessee in 1890 demanded free coinage of silver, extension of the public school system, lien laws to protect laborers and mechanics, good roads, and abolition of the convict-lease system.[13] The Democracy in Georgia in 1890, in the control of the Alliance, came out in favor of an enlargement of the powers of the state railroad commission, abolition of the convict-lease system and other prison reforms, revision of the tax system, extension of the public school system, and laws to ensure fair primaries and elections.[14] The 1892 North Carolina Populist platform called for economy in state government, adequate aid to the state educational institutions, reduction of the legal rate of interest to six percent, adequate taxation of the railroads, and a ten-hour day for laborers in mines, factories, and public works.[15]

All of the Southern state parties endorsed the national Populist platform,

[12] Clark, *Populism in Alabama*, pp. 133, 152.

[13] Daniel M. Robison, *Bob Taylor and the Agrarian Revolt in Tennessee*, pp. 144–145.

[14] Alex M. Arnett, *The Populist Movement in Georgia*, pp. 105–106. See also James C. Bonner, "The Alliance Legislature of 1890," in J. C. Bonner and Lucien E. Roberts (eds.), *Studies in Georgia History and Government*, pp. 155–171.

[15] Simeon A. Delap. "The Populist Party in North Carolina," *Historical Papers of the Trinity College Historical Society*, XIV, 52.

but none had so complete a program as did Texas Populism. The 1892 Texas platform reaffirmed the traditional American doctrine of the equality of man and demanded the elimination of certain economic inequalities that weighed heavily upon the farmers. It demanded the recovery of Texas land from railroads and corporations and the prohibition of alien ownership. The Texas Populists advocated, moreover, government construction of railroads, abolition of national banks, free silver, and the issuance by the federal government of legal tender notes to the amount of fifty dollars per capita, while the sub-treasury plan was the means by which the money would be put into circulation. The taxation system and Democratic extravagances in government were criticized. An anti-trust program was endorsed and a labor program which included an eight-hour day, mechanics' lien laws, the establishment of a state board of labor and arbitration, and the abolition of the convict-lease system was adopted. Such political reforms as the direct election of Senators, the President, and the Vice President, proportional representation, and the initiative, referendum, and recall were also endorsed.[16]

The influence of the Alliance and Populist movements in the South was so profound and of such portent to Southern political life that its significance can be understood only when it is realized that it shook the very foundations of Democratic supremacy in the region. Although, with the single exception of North Carolina, the Populists failed to gain control in any Southern state, the agrarians in the Farmers' Alliance seized control of the Democratic party machinery and elected governors and Congressmen in several Southern states. And Populism itself, despite the paucity of its actual gains, had a significant influence on the political life of the South. The movement effected, for the first time since the Civil War, a real cleavage within the Democratic ranks and forced the retirement of many of the old conservative leaders. What is more important, it forced the Southern Democratic party, at least for a time, to become almost as progressive as the Populist party.

An examination of the history of the several Southern states during the 1890's will illustrate this point. In Texas in 1894 the Democrats adopted the Populist program with regard to convict labor. In 1896 they approved the national Populist planks calling for free silver, the issuance of legal tender notes by the federal government, the abolition of national banks as banks of currency issue, the election of United States Senators by the

[16] Roscoe C. Martin, *The People's Party in Texas*, pp. 46–54. This is the best of the state studies on Southern Populism. Again, it should be emphasized that the national Populist platform concerning land, money, and railroad regulation was heartily approved by Southern Populists. It will be remembered, also, that the "sub-treasury" plan was a Southern invention and was one of the chief planks of Southern Populism.

people, and the institution of the income tax. A railroad commission had been established and an alien land law had been passed early in the 1890's by the legislature.[17] The Democrats of Alabama in 1892 adopted a platform demanding free silver, the abolition of the convict-lease system, adequate support for the public school system, primary election laws, and the secret ballot.[18] A farmer-controlled legislature in Tennessee in 1890 and 1891 passed a stringent anti-trust law, drastically raised taxes on corporations, and passed a resolution calling on Tennessee's Congressmen and Senators to support a constitutional amendment for the direct election of United States Senators.[19] By 1896 the Democratic party in that state had become almost completely converted to Populism. Its platform demanded free silver, the abolition of national banks, the repeal of the tax on state bank notes, and a national income tax.[20] In South Carolina Benjamin R. Tillman led the white small farmers to victory in 1890 and subsequently inaugurated a number of reforms, many of which were in the interests of the farmers.[21] In Virginia the conservative Thomas S. Martin organization was forced to take a stand in favor of free silver and the Democratic convention of 1896 was a free-silver carnival.[22]

An Alliance legislature in Georgia in 1890–1891, led by Alliance Governor W. J. Northen, extended the jurisdiction of the state railroad commission, instituted certain reforms in the banking laws of the state, extended the system of state inspection of fertilizers, and established a Negro agricultural and mechanical college.[23] By 1896 the Georgia Democratic convention was demanding free silver, the repeal of the Resumption Act that gave President Cleveland authority to issue United States bonds in order to maintain the gold reserve in the Treasury, the repeal of the federal tax on state bank notes, an income tax amendment, and a revenue tariff.[24] In North Carolina the Farmers' Alliance had captured the legislature by 1890, and in 1891 a state railroad commission was established and en-

[17] Martin, *People's Party in Texas,* pp. 266–267.

[18] Clark, *Populism in Alabama,* p. 132.

[19] Robison, *Bob Taylor,* pp. 152–153.

[20] Robison, *Bob Taylor,* p. 197.

[21] Simkins, *Tillman Movement,* chapters VI, VII, and VIII. Some of the reforms of the Tillman regime were: increased aid to the agricultural college, establishment of a woman's college, reorganization of the insane asylum, raising the valuation of corporation property for taxation purposes, the establishment of a more powerful railroad commission in 1892, a bill limiting the hours of labor in industry, and the dispensary system.

[22] William DuBose Sheldon, *Populism in the Old Dominion,* chapter V.

[23] Bonner, "The Alliance Legislature of 1890," pp. 155–171. See also Arnett, *Populist Movement in Georgia,* p. 121.

[24] Arnett, *Populist Movement in Georgia,* pp. 194–195.

dowed with complete ratemaking authority.[25] In 1895 a fusion Populist-Republican legislature passed an election law aimed a wiping out entirely corruption at the ballot boxes. The election machinery was made completely bipartisan. The people were given the right to elect county commissioners; the legal rate of interest was set at six percent; increased appropriations for public institutions were made, while all corporations which had been exempted from taxation were hereafter to be subject to taxation.[26]

Such were the objectives and achievements of Southern agrarianism and Populism. Of course, the fact that the Populist revolt had forced out the conservative Bourbon leadership within the Democratic party and had necessitated a reorganization and reorientation within the party is not particularly surprising. The movement was nation-wide. It resulted in the expulsion of the Cleveland Democrats of the conservative East from power in party circles in 1896 and the inauguration of the progressive, Bryan-dominated era. Moreover, the return of large numbers of former Populists to the Democratic party upon the fusion of the Populists with the Democrats in 1896 further stimulated the progressive leaven within the Democratic party. The result of a decade of agitation was a much greater emphasis in the South on popular education and social and economic reform. Populistic and agrarian agitation against the railroads and banks resulted in increased regulation of these institutions by the state governments. The activities of state departments of agriculture were expanded and greater emphasis was given to agricultural and vocational education. Significant reforms in the political machinery of the states were effected by the utilization of the party primary instead of the state convention as the method of nominating party candidates, the replacement of the old party ballot with the secret ballot, and the adoption by many Southern cities of the commission form of city government.

Although the Populist revolt caused the downfall of the Bourbon domination, it brought to the fore in Southern political life a new type of leadership, the leadership of the demagogues. Men like Cole L. Blease of South Carolina, Jeff Davis of Arkansas, and Theodore G. Bilbo of Mississippi were typical demagogues who stirred the people to democratic revolt and who rose to power by class agitation and race hatred, but who offered their constituents few measures of progressive legislation.

Throughout the decades of agrarian revolt, class agitation, and conflict, there remained a great number of Democrats who were neither Bourbons nor Populists, but middle-of-the-road progressives. As a general rule, this group found its recruits in the middle classes of the South among the more

[25] John D. Hicks, "The Farmers' Alliance in North Carolina," *North Carolina Historical Review*, II (1925), 174–175.
[26] Delap, "Populist Party in North Carolina," pp. 57–59.

prosperous farmers, small business men, school teachers, editors, and other professional groups. They looked askance alike at the defection of the Populists and the conservatism of the Bourbons. But to a great degree the aims of the Southern progressives—popular education, reforms looking toward greater popular control of the state governments, and the abandonment by the state governments of laissez-faire as a guide for economic and social action—were much the same as those of the Populists. In Virginia the progressives were led by Carter Glass, Andrew J. Montague, and William A. Jones; in North Carolina by Charles B. Aycock, Josephus Daniels, Claude and William Kitchin, and Walter Clark. In Georgia, Hoke Smith and Thomas W. Hardwick; in Florida, Frank L. Mayes; in Alabama, Benjamin B. Comer; in Louisiana, John M. Parker; in Kentucky, Ollie M. James and John C. W. Beckham; in Oklahoma, Robert L. Owen and Thomas P. Gore; and in Texas, James Stephen Hogg, Charles A. Culberson, and Robert L. Henry were representatives of this middle-class progressivism. Indeed, the statement might perhaps be made that no region of the country, in proportion to its population, could boast a greater galaxy of progressive leaders.

After 1900 the Southern progressive movement reveals itself in a somewhat different light from the nineteenth century agrarian radicalism. In the first place, the farmers of the South and of the nation as well entered upon a period of relative prosperity around 1897 which continued with few interruptions until 1920. As money became more plentiful farm prices rose and consequently agrarian demands for extreme financial reforms diminished. In the second place, what was perhaps the farmers' paramount problem—adequate regulation of railroad rates and services—was gradually being taken care of by federal and state action. As a consequence, there was a gradual shift in emphasis in the Southern progressive platform. It ceased to be almost entirely agrarian in outlook, while the leadership of the movement passed from the hands of the farmers to progressive editors, politicians, and other urban groups. The chief issues of the progressive movement in the early part of the twentieth century, from 1900 to 1914, were primarily political. Once again, it should be pointed out that this development within progressive ranks was nation-wide.

The culmination of the Southern progressive movement came as a result of a national development—the Woodrow Wilson presidential campaign both before and after the Baltimore convention of 1912. Even by 1911 Wilson was displacing Bryan as leader of the progressive Democrats and liberal Southerners hastened to join the New Jersey governor's ranks. Wilson's New Freedom philosophy and program had a powerful appeal to certain groups in Southern society. The fact that he had taken the lead in smashing a reactionary political machine in New Jersey won him the support of liberals in every Southern state who were fighting to overthrow conservative political organizations. The most significant fact about the Wilson movement in the South was that these Southern progressives seized upon it as a weapon to use against the conservatives in order to gain control of their own state governments. Wilson's economic philosophy was very much like Bryan's and the New Jersey governor's campaign against the "money trust," big business, and in favor of a revenue tariff naturally won him the support of the old Bryan men. The educational leaders in the South—from the universities and colleges to the country schools—played an important role in the movement. Southern teachers were naturally gratified to see one of their fellows step from college halls to the national political stage and the remarks of anti-Wilson editors which reflected on the candidate because he had been a professor drove thousands of teachers into the Wilson ranks. Wilson was popular, not only with the educators in the South, but also with the college students and the enthusiasm for him which swept through college campuses was phenomenal. As Wilson was supported by Southern educators, so was he likewise supported by many Southern clergymen. Wilson's adherence to and profession of the Christian faith, and his Christian life were reasons enough for thousands of ministers and members of the church to enlist in his cause. The religious press, abandoning its usual hands-off policy in political campaigns, generously supported Wilson in the prenomination campaign of 1912.[27]

If the writer had to single out the group of men that made the greatest contribution to the Wilson movement in the South he would almost inevitably name the Southern editors who heralded the coming of the New Freedom. Their work in presenting the man to the people and in engendering enthusiasm and support for his cause was the foundation stone of Wilson's campaign in the South. It is not strange that many of the strongest Wilson editors—Josephus Daniels, William E. Gonzales, Frank L. Mayes, and Luke Lea—were also devoted followers of William Jennings Bryan. Nor is it strange that most of the anti-Bryan editors were also antagonistic to the New Jersey governor. The powerful leavens of progressivism and conservatism necessitated such an alignment. Many of the Southern editors were also politicians of influence.[28]

[27] See, for example, *Christian Advocate* (Nashville), March 8, 1912; *Birmingham Age-Herald,* August 20, 1912; Raleigh *News and Observer,* April 2, 1912; *Atlanta Constitution,* Febraury 5, 1912; *Atlanta Journal,* April 16 and 26, 1912; *Presbyterian Standard* (Charlotte), March 24, 1911, April 24, and July 17, 1912; *Presbyterian of the South* (Richmond), February 8, 1911.

[28] Daniels and Robert Ewing were national Committeemen, respectively, from North Carolina and Louisiana. Gonzales dominated the progressive faction of the party in South Carolina. Lea and E. B. Stahlman were spokesmen for the progressive Democrats in Tennessee. James R. Gray of the *Atlanta Journal* was allied with the political fortunes of Hoke Smith and the progressive faction of the Georgia Democracy.

The Wilson movement in the South became in effect a struggle for progressive Democracy, and progressive Southern politicians were in the vanguard of the movement. Men who had been Bryan's spokesmen for nearly sixteen years—Daniels, Tillman, Gonzales, Hoke Smith, Frank L. Mayes, Nathan P. Bryan, Braxton B. Comer, Luke Lea, Charles A. Culberson, Robert L. Henry, William H. Murray, and Thomas P. Gore—perhaps realized that the Commoner's day as a presidential candidate had passed and found a new leader in Woodrow Wilson. There were, of course, Bryan men in the South who supported Champ Clark, who was running as a progressive. On the other hand, the consistent opposition of the conservative Southern state organizations came as a result of the liberalism of the Wilson movement.

The Wilson movement was moderately successful in achieving its immediate goal, the winning of the Southern delegations. Wilson won proportionately as much support in the South as in any other section of the country. From the long-range point of view the movement was significant in that it became the spearhead of a great progressive revolt. It brought to the fore important issues which demanded solution; it engendered a tremendous amount of discussion concerning popular government and progressive reform.[29]

So much for the general development of the progressive movement in the South from the Granger movement to the Wilson era. An interrogator might reasonably ask: if the South had such a considerable body of progressives and was so visibly affected by the progressive movement, why did not the region show results by way of progressive reforms? Such a question creates a perplexing problem in the establishment of a yardstick of progressivism. It might be helpful to consider the reform measures that were outstanding during this period and to analyze the accomplishments of the Southern states.

One example of progressive reform in which Southern states were virtual pioneers was the difficult problem of railroad regulation. In the rebuilding of the railroads in the South after the destruction that occurred during the Civil War, Northern capitalists played an influential part. And with the subsequent consolidation of Southern railroads into large systems also came the attendant evils of monopolistic control. The railroads levied fares and freight rates at their pleasure and often to the oppression of the

---

[29] Spatial limitations have required that the writer merely summarize the general characteristics of the Wilson movement in the South. For a fuller discussion, however, see Arthur Link, "The South and the Democratic Campaign of 1912," unpublished Ph.D. dissertation in the library of the University of North Carolina. "The Wilson Movement in Texas, 1910–1912," *Southwestern Historical Quarterly,* XLVIII (October, 1944), 169–185; "The Democratic Pre-Convention Campaign of 1912 in Georgia," *Georgia Historical Quarterly,* XXIX (September, 1945), 143–158.

people, while stock watering, discrimination in rates, the free pass evil, and under-assessment for taxes were frequently practiced evils. The political corruption attendant upon the railroads' suspicious and frequent sorties into politics, as well as the malpractices mentioned above, led soon after the restoration of home rule to a popular demand that the railroads be subjected to public control.

Virginia took the first step and in 1877 the legislature of that state established a state advisory railroad commission on the order of the Massachusetts type.[30] The powers of the Virginia commission were purely supervisory and recommendatory and it was not until 1901 that popular agitation for a commission with power to set rates finally culminated in the establishment of a powerful Corporation Commission with complete administrative, legislative, and judicial powers over railroads and other corporations.[31] A year following the establishment of the first Virginia commission, South Carolina set up an advisory railroad commission modeled after it.[32] Four years later, however, the legislature amended the law so as to endow the commission with full power to set freight and passenger rates.[33]

Georgia was the first Southern state and, along with California, the first state in the country effectively to regulate railroad rates and operations.[34] The Georgia constitution of 1877 made the establishment of a railroad commission by the legislature mandatory and, in compliance with this emphatic directive, the legislature in 1879 established the state commission. The Georgia commission had extraordinary powers to fix and compel fair and uniform rates, to forbid discrimination among persons and places, and to abolish the discrimination inherent in the long-and-short-haul practice. Schedules of rates established by the commission were to be accepted as just and fair by the state courts, while railroad companies were compelled to submit to the commission their records and business files.[35] The Georgia commission was exceedingly effective in bringing the railroads of the state under its control, and it secured reductions

[30] *Acts of the General Assembly of the State of Virginia,* 1876–1877, chapter 254, pp. 254–257.

[31] See the *Virginia Constitution of 1902,* article XII, sections 155–156, in *Acts of the General Assembly of the State of Virginia,* 1902–1903–1904, pp. 31–37.

[32] *Acts and Joint Resolutions of the General Assembly of the State of South Carolina,* 1878, chapter 662, pp. 789–792.

[33] South Carolina, *Acts,* 1881–1882, chapter 595, pp. 791–841.

[34] The earlier legislative efforts of the Midwestern states of Illinois, Minnesota, Wisconsin, and Iowa during the heyday of the Granger movement were ineffective and short-lived.

[35] *Acts and Resolutions of the General Assembly of the State of Georgia,* 1878–1879, chapter 269, pp. 125–131.

in passenger and freight rates of between fifty and sixty percent.[36] In addition to the fact of its successful career, the Georgia commission is significant in that practically all other Southern states subsequently established commissions modeled after it. In 1907, largely due to the persistent efforts of Hoke Smith, leader of the progressive wing of the Democratic party in Georgia and governor of the state in 1907, the legislature reorganized the railroad commission and greatly extended its jurisdiction. It was in reality transformed into a corporation or public utilities commission. The most interesting feature of the new law was a provision which made it the commission's duty to promulgate such rules regarding the issuance of stocks and bonds as would put an end to over-capitalization and guarantee honest values to purchasers of securities.[37]

Kentucky in 1879 established an advisory railroad commission.[38] The commission was, however, deprived of all authority to supervise railroad rates by a decision of the Kentucky Court of Appeals in 1896, but an act of the legislature in 1900 conferred the authority upon the commission to prescribe "reasonable and just" freight and passenger rates.[39] After a prolonged battle with the Louisville and Nashville Railroad the commission's right to prescribe reasonable maximum intrastate rates was confirmed by the Supreme Court of the United States.[40]

The Alabama legislature in 1881 established a railroad commission, but withheld from it the authority to fix rates and fares. The carriers were required to submit to the commission their tariffs of freight and passenger charges for examination and if the commission should find any charge which it deemed unreasonable, it was directed to notify the railroad in question.[41] The provisions of the Alabama law were a decided improvement upon the law establishing the Virginia commission but were obviously inadequate effectively to deal with the problem of railroad regulation. Consequently, in 1883 the legislature gave the commission authority to determine reasonable rates.[42] The Alabama commission was successful in decreasing tariff charges, but there was considerable popular agitation for an act to increase the commission's powers. The leader of the move-

[36] Jim David Cherry, "The Georgia Railroad Commission, 1879–1888," unpublished M.A. thesis in the library of the University of North Carolina.

[37] Georgia, *Acts,* 1907, chapter 223, pp. 72–81.

[38] *Acts of the General Assembly of the Commonwealth of Kentucky,* 1879, chapter 1019, pp. 92–95.

[39] Kentucky, *Acts,* 1900, chapter 2, pp. 5–7.

[40] Maxwell Ferguson, *State Regulation of Railroads in the South,* pp. 123–124. This is the only general work on the subject.

[41] *Acts of the General Assembly of Alabama,* 1880–1881, chapter 91, pp. 84–95.

[42] Alabama, *Acts,* 1882–1883, chapters 103 and 104, pp. 177–178.

ment for more effective regulation after 1900 was Braxton Bragg Comer, who was elected president of the commission in 1904. In 1906 Comer was elected governor on a railroad-regulation platform and in 1907 called upon the legislature to abolish the "debauching lobby" maintained by the railroads at Montgomery and to pass laws providing for thorough railroad regulation.[43] In compliance, the legislature passed a series of acts which extended the jurisdiction of the commission to include most of the public utility companies of the state, reduced the freight rates on one hundred and ten articles of common production, and reduced passenger rates to two and one-half cents a mile.[44] A bitter fight between Governor Comer and the Louisville and Nashville Railroad resulted. In 1913, however, this railroad gave up its fight against the Alabama commission and accepted its schedules.[45]

Tennessee in 1883 established a railroad commission and authorized it to set just and reasonable rates,[46] but the railroads of the state were able to halt the work of the commission by use of judicial injunctions. As a consequence, the commission law of 1883 was repealed in 1885. However, in 1897 a new commission was established and endowed with full authority to regulate rates and tariffs.[47] It was successful in effecting a drastic reduction in transportation charges.[48] The Mississippi legislature in 1884 established a commission[49] which effectively reduced freight rates during 1886 and 1887. Passenger rates, because of the competitive practices of the Mississippi railroads, were already exceedingly low.[50] Florida in 1887 established a commission modeled almost exactly after the Georgia commission of 1879.[51] The Florida legislature, however, abolished the commission in 1891 because it did not approve of the new chairman appointed by the governor and it was not until 1897 that the commission was reestablished.[52] In 1899 the legislature considerably strengthened the

[43] Albert B. Moore, "Braxton Bragg Comer," *Dictionary of American Biography,* IV, 329–330.

[44] *General Laws of the Legislature of Alabama,* 1907, chapter 17, p. 80; chapter 30, p. 104; chapter 31, pp 105–107; chapter 69, pp. 135–166; chapter 329, pp. 404–405.

[45] Ferguson, *State Regulation,* p. 138. For a discussion of Comer's battle with the Louisville and Nashville Railroad see Rupert B. Vance, "Spell-Binders of the New South," unpublished manuscript in possession of Professor Vance.

[46] *Acts of the State of Tennessee,* 1883, chapter 199, pp. 271–279.

[47] Tennessee, *Acts,* 1897, chapter 10, pp. 113–126.

[48] Ferguson, *State Regulation,* pp. 140–146.

[49] *Laws of the State of Mississippi,* 1884, chapter 23, pp. 31–41.

[50] Ferguson, *State Regulation,* pp. 148–151.

[51] *Acts and Resolutions Adopted by the Legislature of Florida,* 1887, chapter 3746, pp. 118–126.

[52] Florida, *Acts,* 1897, chapter 4549, pp. 82–94.

commission's authority by more clearly defining its powers and giving it judicial authority,[53] and in 1901 it promulgated a comprehensive freight rate schedule.[54]

After many years of agitation, the legislature of North Carolina in 1891, dominated by members of the Farmers' Alliance, established a railroad commission based on the Georgia model.[55] Within less than a year's time freight and passenger schedules were promulgated that brought about numerous reductions.[56] In 1899 the railroad commission was transformed into a corporation commission, one of the first of its kind in the United States. The powers and duties of the old railroad commission were transferred to it, but its jurisdiction was extended to cover all carriers, as well as telephone companies, public and private banks, loan and trust companies, and building and loan associations.[57] The North Carolina commission attempted to bring to an end the discriminatory rates levied by the Virginia railroads to favor Virginia cities and to eliminate the discrimination practiced by the north-south lines running through the state.[58]

The Trans-Mississippi Southern states kept well abreast of the Southeastern states in the perplexing and difficult business of railroad regulation. Texas, under the progressive leadership of Governor James Stephen Hogg, in 1891 established a railroad commission to set reasonable rates,[59] and in 1893 the legislature enacted a stock and bond law designed to prevent the railroads from increasing and collecting fictitious debts by means of increasing the rates.[60] In Arkansas a railroad regulation amendment to the state constitution was adopted in 1897, and in 1899 the legislature established a commission. The railroads were required to furnish rate schedules to the commission, to keep rate schedules posted, and to furnish facilities for the care of persons and property transported. Discriminations of any sort, rebates, pooling, and the long-and-short-haul practice were prohibited. The commission was empowered to determine the valuation of the railroads, to conduct hearings, and to regulate freight, express, and passenger rates.[61] In 1907 the commission's jurisdiction was extended to

[53] Florida, *Acts,* 1899, chapter 4700, pp. 76–93.

[54] Ferguson, *State Regulation,* pp. 154–161.

[55] *Laws and Resolutions of the State of North Carolina,* 1891, chapter 320, pp. 275–288.

[56] Martha Frances Bowditch, "The North Carolina Railroad Commission, 1891–1899," unpublished M.A. thesis in the library of the University of North Carolina.

[57] North Carolina, *Laws,* 1899, chapter 164, pp. 291–307.

[58] Ferguson, *State Regulation,* pp. 174–177.

[59] *Revised Civil Statutes of the State of Texas,* 1895, chapter 13, pp. 909–920.

[60] Texas, *Statutes,* 1895, chapter 14, pp. 920–923.

[61] William F. Kirby (ed.), *A Digest of the Statutes of Arkansas,* sections 6788–6826, pp. 1407–1415.

sleeping car companies.[62] A railroad commission was established in Louisiana by a provision of the constitution of 1898. The commission was directed to set reasonable rates and was given authority over sleeping-car, express, telephone, and telegraph companies, and steamboats and other water craft as well as the railroads.[63] The first endeavor of the commission was to put an end to the disastrous competition between the railroads and steamboats, while numerous reductions in freight rates were effected.[64] Oklahoma's progressive constitution of 1907 restricted railroad and corporate activities in many ways. Considerable space was given to expressing the limitations and regulations of railroads and other public corporations which were regulated by a corporation commission of three members.[65]

In concluding this discussion of state railroad regulation in the South, it may reasonably be said that commissions in every Southern state regulated the transportation companies, for the most part, in the public interest and that the movement was successful in bringing benefits to the people in the form of reductions in rates, uniformity of schedules, and increased taxation of the railroads. It is the conclusion of the only authority in the general field that state regulation in the South effectively ended discrimination and reduced freight and passenger rates to an unjustly low level.[66]

The Southern movement for railroad regulation was manifestly a part of the nation-wide movement, and it is interesting to note that Southerners exercised considerable influence in the national movement for railroad reform. It is a well-known fact that John H. Reagan of Texas was regarded as the father of the Interstate Commerce Act of 1887. Robert M. LaFollette, writing years later, declared that "To Reagan of Texas, more than any other man in the House, belongs the credit for the passage of the act."[67] La Follette also wrote that he and his progressive lieutenants in Wisconsin had profited greatly from Reagan's wise advice when they drew up Wisconsin's railroad regulation law.[68] The advocates of national railroad legislation always had the overwhelming support of Southern representatives and Senators, and Senator Ben Tillman of South Carolina gave conspicuous service to the Roosevelt administration when he piloted the Hepburn rate bill through the Senate in 1906.[69]

[62] Charles W. Fornoff, "The Regulation of Public Service Corporations," in David Y. Thomas, *Arkansas and Its People, a History, 1541–1930*, I, 338–341:

[63] *Constitution of the State of Louisiana, 1898*, articles 283–289.

[64] Ferguson, *State Regulation*, pp. 180–184.

[65] *Constitution of the State of Oklahoma*, 1907, article X, sections 2–35.

[66] Ferguson, *State Regulation*, pp. 207–212.

[67] R. M. La Follette, *La Follette's Autobiography*, p. 119.

[68] La Follette, *Autobiography*, pp. 119–120.

[69] Henry F. Pringle, *Theodore Roosevelt*, pp. 420–425; Claude G. Bowers, *Beveridge and the Progressive Era*, pp. 225–226. Tillman received considerable support from Senator Joseph Weldon Bailey of Texas in the fight for the Hepburn bill.

In any discussion of the program of the progressive movement the measures advocated by progressives directed toward the reform of the party machinery loom large. One of the most important of these measures was the direct primary, by means of which reformers hoped to wrest control over the nominating process from the political bosses and to restore it to the people. Under La Follette's leadership, Wisconsin in 1903 adopted the mandatory state-wide direct party primary. Before 1890, however, every county in South Carolina used the primary system for the nomination of local officers and legislators, and in 1896 the state-wide Democratic party primary was inaugurated.[70] As early as 1897 the legislature of Arkansas had legalized primary elections.[71] The Mississippi legislature in 1902 enacted a law requiring that all nominations for state, district, county, and county district officials be made by primary elections.[72] The primary system was in use in Virginia at least by 1905, and in that year the United States senatorial primary was adopted by the Democratic party.[73] The first state-wide primary in Georgia was held on June 7, 1898, and the primary system was used regularly by the Democrats thereafter.[74] In 1902 Alabama Democrats adopted the primary system for nominating their candidates. Following the primary for state officers in 1902, the friends of the primary system began to agitate for a senatorial primary by means of which the voters could instruct the members of the state legislature upon their preference for United States Senator. The system was adopted in 1906.[75] Governor William S. Jennings, elected in 1900, was the last

[70] David D. Wallace, *History of South Carolina*, III, 336, 356. The South Carolina legislature in 1896 enacted a statute to prevent frauds at the primary elections, but the party primary was not made legally mandatory nor brought within the protection of the general election laws. South Carolina, *Acts and Joint Resolutions*, 1896, chapter 25, p. 56.

[71] Kirby (ed.), *Status of Arkansas*, 1904, chapter 57, sects. 2892–2897, pp. 705–706. In 1917 an act adopted by the initiative required primary elections of the major parties. T. D. Crawford and Hamilton Moses (eds.), *Digest of the Statutes of Arkansas, 1919*, chapter 54, sects. 3757–3782, pp. 1075–1083.

[72] Mississippi, *Laws*, 1902, chapter 66, pp. 105–112. Section 18 of this law also provided for the nomination of United States Senators by the senatorial primary.

[73] Robert C. Glass and Carter Glass, Jr., *History of Virginia Democracy*, I, 292. In 1912 the Virginia legislature passed an act "to establish and regulate the holding of primary elections." Virginia, *Acts*, 1912, chapter 307, pp. 611–619.

[74] Walter G. Cooper, *The Story of Georgia*, III, 370. A Georgia law of 1900 provided that primary elections should be held under the regulations prescribed by the party, but also provided that clerks of the superior courts should receive and count the election returns. Georgia, *Acts*, 1900, chapter 117, pp. 40–41.

[75] Albert B. Moore, *History of Alabama*, I, 909–910. In 1903 the Alabama legislature enacted a law which gave legal sanction and protection to all party primaries that might be held in the state. Alabama, *General Laws*, 1903, chapter 417, pp. 356–365.
  In 1911 the legislature made a sweeping revision of the primary act and exempted from its application parties that polled less than 25 per cent of the votes at the general election. Alabama, *General Laws*, 1911, chapter 479, pp. 421–449.

governor of Florida nominated by a political convention. The legislature, early in his administration, enacted the primary system into the body of Florida laws.[76] By 1908, at least, Florida had instituted the senatorial primary.[77] The primary system had been in operation in Tennessee for some time before 1901, for in that year the state legislature enacted a law to legalize and regulate party primaries. All primary elections in the state were to be conducted under the provisions of the general election laws.[78] During the administration of Governor John C. W. Beckham, around 1905, the Kentucky Democratic party adopted the primary system,[79] while Texas[80] and Oklahoma[81] adopted the system in the early years of the twentieth century. Although the primary system had been in use since 1900 in the counties of North Carolina, it was not until 1915 that the legislature made its use mandatory on a state-wide basis.[82] Thus it would appear that the primary election idea was almost indigenous to the South, as far as its use in this country is concerned. It is clearly evident that a good majority of the Southern states were using the system by the time Wisconsin adopted it.

Another measure of reform advocated by progressives in the early part of the twentieth century was corrupt practices legislation, designed to purify the election process. By the end of the Wilson period every Southern state had enacted legislation making it a criminal offense to give bribes to influence a voter, and every Southern state except Florida had enacted severe legislation against the receiving of such bribes. Arkansas, Louisiana, Mississippi, North Carolina, Oklahoma, Tennessee, and Texas prohibited candidates from promising appointments before elections, while Arkansas and Texas had declared it unlawful for candidates to pay for the conveyance of voters to the polls. Alabama, Arkansas, Louisiana, and Mississippi

[76] The Florida law was passed in 1901. It provided for complete state regulation of party primaries. Florida, *Acts,* 1901, chapter 5014, pp. 160–165.

[77] Harry Gardner Cutler, *History of Florida,* I, 179.

[78] Tennessee, *Acts,* 1901, chapter 39, pp. 54–59. The poll tax requirement for voting did not apply in the primary election.

[79] George Lee Willis, *Kentucky Democracy,* I, 391–392. In 1912 the Kentucky legislature instituted the mandatory primary system which included the United States senatorial primary. Kentucky, *Acts,* 1912, chapter 7, pp. 47–77.

[80] A Texas law of 1905 made primary nominations mandatory for all candidates for state, district, and county offices. The law affected at the time, however, only the Democratic party since it applied only to parties polling more than 100,000 votes. Texas, *General Laws,* 1905, chapter 11, pp. 543–565. See also O. Douglas Weeks, "The Texas Primary System," in Frank Carter Adams (ed.), *Texas Democracy,* I, 531–554, especially p. 531.

[81] Oklahoma in 1909 adopted the mandatory primary as the method by which all political parties were to nominate candidates for all state offices. Oklahoma, *Session Laws,* 1909, Senate Bill No. 5, pp. 270–274.

[82] North Carolina, *Public Laws,* 1915, chapter 101, pp. 154–168. See also Robert D. W. Connor, *North Carolina, Rebuilding an Ancient Commonwealth,* II, 481–482.

denied party leaders the right to solicit campaign funds from candidates. By 1919 every Southern state had enacted laws of varying effectiveness and severity prohibiting the intimidation of voters, while Alabama, Texas, Mississippi, Tennessee, Florida, and Kentucky had made it unlawful for employers to intimidate or attempt to influence the voting of their employees. Arkansas, Florida, Kentucky, Oklahoma, Tennessee, and Texas also required employers to give their employees ample time to vote on election day. Tennessee, South Carolina, Oklahoma, Alabama, Georgia, Kentucky, Louisiana, Mississippi, and North Carolina passed legislation prohibiting illegal and unqualified registration, while all of the Southern states endeavored to prevent illegal and fraudulent voting. Kentucky, Louisiana, Mississippi, and Tennessee prohibited distinguishing marks or signs on election ballots, and Louisiana, Tennessee, and Virginia made it unlawful for a person to participate in a primary or convention of a party other than his own. Alabama, Arkansas, Florida, Texas, and Virginia required that political advertisements in newspapers be clearly denoted as such, while North Carolina, Louisiana, Mississippi, Florida, Arkansas, and Alabama required that political posters and advertisements bear the names and addresses of the persons responsible for issuing them. Florida and Virginia made it unlawful for a candidate to purchase editorial support in a political campaign. In the matter of campaign expenditures, Alabama, Arkansas, Florida, Kentucky, Louisiana, North Carolina, Oklahoma, South Carolina, and Virginia limited the amounts a candidate for governor might expend in his campaign for nomination and election. The sums varied from $3,000 in Oklahoma to $10,000 in Alabama. Virginia allowed an expenditure of fifteen cents for every voter who cast his vote for the highest party candidate at the last election. All of the states except Mississippi and Tennessee required candidates to file statements of their campaign expenditures either before or after the primary and election, or both. Alabama, Florida, Georgia, Kentucky, Louisiana, Mississippi, North Carolina, Oklahoma, Tennessee, and Texas attempted either to prohibit or to regulate the contributing by corporations to campaign funds.[83]

Four other political reforms were prominently in vogue in 1912: the presidential preferential primary, the commission form of city government, the direct election of Senators, and the initiative, referendum, and recall. During the presidential prenomination campaign of 1912 the issue of the presidential primary, in which the voters instructed delegates to the national convention to vote for their specified candidate, arose. The system, which supposedly deprived the political bosses of the power to select

[83] This discussion of corrupt-practices legislation in the Southern states is based upon Earl R. Sikes, *State and Federal Corrupt-Practices Legislation*, and is taken directly from the tables in pp. 258–291. It is difficult to determine the effectiveness of the laws. Sikes deals only with the legislation and not with the application of the laws.

presidential candidates, was adopted in the South in 1912 by Florida, Georgia, and Mississippi. In 1913 a preferential primary law was enacted by the Texas legislature.[84]

The commission form of city government originated in Galveston, Texas, in 1900 under extraordinary circumstances.[85] What was begun as an emergency administrative measure proved so effective a method of city government that it was not only retained in Galveston, but spread throughout the country. By 1914 commission government was operative in most of the larger Southern cities—in Galveston, Birmingham, Mobile, Montgomery, Shreveport, New Orleans, Wilmington, Oklahoma City, El Paso, Columbia, Chattanooga, Knoxville, Memphis, Dallas, San Antonio, Fort Worth, Houston, and Austin—and in many of the smaller cities as well.[86] It is interesting to note in this connection that Staunton, Virginia, was the first city in the country to adopt the city manager form of government.[87]

There was, and had been since the days of the agrarian revolt, a widespread demand in the South for the adoption of a constitutional amendment providing for the popular election of United States Senators.[88] As a matter of fact, by the time the amendment went into effect senatorial candidates in every Southern state were first nominated by the people in a party primary. The principles of the initiative, referendum, and recall never found widespread acceptance in the South, although Oklahoma in 1907 and Arkansas in 1909 wrote the reforms into their bodies of law.[89]

[84] Weeks, "The Texas Primary System," p. 532.

[85] In 1900 a great hurricane and flood swept over the city and, in order to facilitate the progress of reconstruction, the citizens of Galveston placed the government and job of rebuilding in the hands of a business commission.

[86] Aside from the cities named above the following places had the commission form of government by 1914: Anthony, Beaumont, Corpus Christi, Denison, Kennedy, Lyford, Marshall, Marble Falls, Palestine, Port Lavaca, Sherman, Waco, and Greenville, Texas; Ardmore, Bartlesville, Duncan, Enid, Miami, McAlester, Muskogee, Sapulpa, Tulsa, and Wagner, Oklahoma; Bristol, Clarkesville, Etowah, and Richmond City, Tennessee.

Commission city government was almost unanimously favored by the press of the South. See, for example, editorials in Raleigh News and Observer, March 15, 16, 17, 1911; Wilmington Morning Star, December 20, 1910, March 14, 15, 1911; Charlotte Daily Observer, November 16, 1911; Pensacola Evening News, January 13, 1912; Columbia State, April 13, 1911; San Antonio Express, January 9, 1911; Mobile Register, December 24, 1910; Petersburg (Va.) Daily Index-Appeal, February 19, 20, 21, 22, 23, 1911; Oklahoma City Daily Oklahoman, March 11, 1911; Birmingham Age-Herald, May 2, 1911.

[87] Benjamin P. DeWitt, The Progressive Movement, pp. 309–310.

[88] See, for example, editorials in Tulsa World, February 25, 1911; New Orleans Times-Democrat, December 19, 1910; Nashville Tennessean and American, December 20, 1910.

[89] Arkansas adopted only the initiative and referendum. Thomas, Arkansas and Its People, I, 320. For Oklahoma, see Grant Foreman, History of Oklahoma, p. 314. For editorials favorable to the initiative referendum, and recall, see: New Orleans Time-Democrat, December 15, 1910; Nashville Tennessean and American, December

Although Southern progressives gave emphasis to the struggle for political reform, they by no means were oblivious of the necessity of reform in the economic and social fields. As early as 1889 the Georgia legislature passed a law limiting work in the textile mills to sixty-six hours a week,[90] and in 1892 South Carolina enacted a similar law.[91] In 1911 both Georgia and North Carolina set the maximum number of hours per week operatives could work in textile factories at sixty.[92] In the matter of child-labor legislation, Southern progressives were likewise active. "There are only a few characteristics of the child labor struggle in the South which differentiate it from the movement in the nation at large, and even in them the difference is largely one of degree rather of kind," writes the authority on this movement.[93] The leader in the struggle of child labor legislation in the South was Edgar Gardner Murphy of Alabama, who was chiefly instrumental in the organization of the National Child Labor Committee.[94] Alexander J. McKelway, a Presbyterian minister of Charlotte, was the executive secretary in the South for the committee and for years carried on a struggle for child labor reform. The advocates of child labor legislation were not successful in accomplishing all of the objectives for which they were striving, but they did secure a number of reform laws in the textile states and presented vividly the child labor problem to the southern people.[95]

It is undoubtedly true that Southern editors led the fight for progressive reforms in the South.[96] Especially was this true in the fight against the notorious convict-lease system and the iniquitous fee system that make crime profitable to sheriffs and constables. The editor of the *Mobile Register,* editors Frank L. Mayes of the *Pensacola Journal,* Fred Seeley of the *Atlanta Georgian,* and Edward W. Barrett of the *Birmingham Age-Herald*

21, 1910; Oklahoma City *Daily Oklahoman,* February 17, 1911; *Mobile Register,* December 30, 1910; Columbia *State,* May 24, 1911; Little Rock *Arkansas Democrat,* December 2, 1910.

[90] Elizabeth H. Davidson, *Child Labor Legislation in the Southern Textile States,* pp. 69–70.

[91] Davidson, *Child Labor Legislation,* p. 90.

[92] Davidson, *Child Labor Legislation,* pp. 163, 206.

[93] Davidson, *Child Labor Legislation,* p. 2.

[94] Davidson, *Child Labor Legislation,* p. 125.

[95] Miss Davidson (*Child Labor Legislation,* pp. 275–278) lists in a table the laws controlling child labor passed by the Southern states.

[96] Among the progressive newspapers in the South during the period after 1900 the following were outstanding: *Mobile Register,* Raleigh *News and Observer,* Petersburg *Daily Index-Appeal,* Columbia *State, Atlanta Georgian, Atlanta Journal, Pensacola Journal, Birmingham Age-Herald, Birmingham News,* Nashville *Tennessean and American,* New Orleans *Times-Democrat,* Little Rock *Arkansas Democrat,* Galveston *Daily News,* Dallas *Morning News, Houston Chronicle, Louisville Post,* Oklahoma City *Daily Oklahoman,* and the Richmond *Times-Dispatch.*

led in the fight against these twin evils.[97] Progressive editors and leaders were also active during this period in an effort to secure adequate public health programs and insurance laws.[98]

Insofar as the foregoing movements for reform were progressive, it can be stated that there was a well organized progressive movement in the South aimed at remedying the ills of the region's social and economic and political order. It, of course, had serious deficiencies. None of the Southern editors, as far as this writer knows, who were agitating for political reforms, gave any consideration to the ominously steady increase in farm tenancy. The perplexing problems of the economic, social, and political development of the Negro likewise escaped serious attention from Southern editors. Although practically all the Southern editors severely condemned lynching, none dared to advocate political rights for the black man. As far as progressive democracy went in the South, it was progressive democracy for the white man.

It is only too apparent to the student of recent Southern history that many Southern institutions and practices were, during this period, antiquated and backward. Bearing this fact in mind, it may none the less be stated with emphasis that there were few sections of the country in which the masses of the people were more powerful than in the South. Certainly many of the dominant Southern political leaders during this period were not representative of the conservative classes. Demagogues like James K. Vardaman of Mississippi, Jeff Davis of Arkansas, or Cole Blease of South Carolina ostensibly represented the lower classes in a very definite class movement against the Bourbon conservatives. Progressives like Hoke Smith of Georgia; Robert L. Owen of Oklahoma; Charles A. Culberson, James S. Hogg, Thomas W. Gregory, and Robert L. Henry of Texas; Andrew J. Montague, William A. Jones, and Carter Glass of Virginia; Ollie M. James and J. C. W. Beckham of Kentucky; Luke Lea of Tennessee; Josephus Daniels, Claude and William W. Kitchin, and Walter Clark of North Carolina; Frank P. Glass and B. B. Comer of Alabama; William E. Gonzales, Ira B. Jones, and Ben R. Tillman of South Carolina; John M. Parker, Arsène Pujo, and Newton Blanchard of Louisiana; or Nathan P. Bryan and Frank L. Mayes of Florida continually fought the reactionaries and conservatives and were in the vanguard of the progressive movement, not only in the South, but in the nation as well.

[97] The following editorial from the *Mobile Register,* October 10, 1911, is characteristic of the anti-convict-lease editorials:

"The Register has constantly fought this leasing system and has shown up its abuses and inhumanity. It is a relic of barbarism which is a stain on Alabama. . . . The leasing system is wrong in principle, unsafe in operation and cruel in effect."

[98] For the early years of the North Carolina public health board, see Hilda Jane Zimmerman, "The Formative Years of the North Carolina Board of Health, 1877–1893," *North Carolina Historical Review,* XXI (1944), 1–34.

6

After Suffrage: Southern Women in the Twenties

Anne Firor Scott

The Southern Lady has always enjoyed a special niche in the inner chambers of the southern mind. Passive, demure, and properly innocent, the fabled southern "belle" assumed the role of indispensable helpmate to the mannered "Southern Gentleman." Indeed, it was together that they fashioned the distinct setting of instinctive ease so long associated with southern life before the Civil War. This mythic profile of Southern Womanhood, this artifact of the South's historic past, survived the war and in fact enjoyed a sustained measure of acceptance in the decades thereafter—even into the twentieth century. Such misty renditions of the Southern Woman, according to Anne Firor Scott, Professor of History at Duke University, cannot withstand the scrutiny of historical scholarship, nor do they meet even minimal standards of reality. This "chivalric nonsense," though long pampered, exquisitely preserved, and although periodically demonstrated false during the late nineteenth century, suffered a strategic setback with the passage of the Nineteenth Amendment. It was at this juncture, and only after earlier abortive attempts at emancipation, that the southern "belle" was at last armed with a legal basis from which she might do battle with her encrusted stereotype. Moving "from pedestal to politics" with greater velocity and vengeance after 1920, southern women staged important forays into general governmental reform. Child welfare, labor conditions, and race relations all served as focal points for southern feminists. As a result, the energies of southern women in the twen-

Anne Firor Scott, "After Suffrage: Southern Women in the Twenties," *Journal of Southern History*, 30 (August 1964), 298–318. Copyright 1964 by the Southern Historical Association. Reprinted by permission of the Managing Editor.

ties, although only selectively successful, did much to question the cult of Southern Womanhood, and also to damage the associated notion that southern politics was invariably nonprogressive and "conservative."

In few parts of the country was the nineteenth amendment awaited with higher expectations than among an earnest group of Southern women. Not unlike the present-day Southern liberal who yearns for a federal civil rights bill because the road to state and local legislation is so long and rocky, Southern women who had labored for state suffrage and for social reform against an opposing tide looked to the federal amendment for help. For them the vote had also become a symbol of something much larger—the image of the "new woman." Long constrained by Southern tradition about woman's place in Southern life, they saw the amendment as a grant of freedom and a new measure of independence.

One of these women remarked in a private letter in 1920 that she was planning a trip to Europe because "once we *really* get into politics (i.e., once the suffrage amendment is ratified) I will never be able to get away."[1]

Another, in North Carolina, thought "the advent of women into political life" would mean "the loosening of a great moral force which will modify and soften the relentlessly selfish economic forces of trade and industry in their relation to government. The ideals of democracy and of social and human welfare will undoubtedly receive a great impetus."[2] For many years these earnest women had organized themselves, talked to legislators, worked for or against congressmen in their home districts, testified at hearings, haunted the polls on election day, cajoled money, written newspaper articles, watched the progress of more advanced Northern and Western women—and now, at last, had the federal help that promised to open the way to substantial achievement.

By 1920 Southern women had come to exert increasing influence in public affairs, but many of the problems that concerned them were still unsolved: the dislocations caused by industrialization, the conditions of work for women and children, the inadequacies of the educational system, the lack of opportunity for many children, prison conditions, the ravages of alcohol and disease, injustice to Negro citizens. To all such problems, and some new ones they would discover along the way, the newly en-

[1] Madeline McDowell Breckinridge to Allie S. Dickson, March 20, 1920, in Breckinridge Family Papers (Manuscript Division, Library of Congress).

[2] Notes for speech in Mary O. Cowper Papers (Mrs. Cowper, Durham, N. C.).

franchised women now addressed themselves with renewed hope. Their successes as well as their failures have tended to vanish—in Vann Woodward's phrase—in that twilight zone between living memory and written history. An examination of what they tried to do, of the goals reached, the obstacles encountered, the failures endured, throws new light on the South in the twenties and upon the springs and motives behind the emancipation of Southern women.

What this record shows will depend upon the questions we ask. If we ask whether woman suffrage led to progress in social reform in the Southern states and to a more active political life for women, the answer is clearly that it did. If we ask in addition whether the broader hope, the dream of a new life for Southern women in which their independence, their right to think for themselves, to work for the things they believed in, to be respected as individuals regardless of sex, was accomplished in the twenties, the answer must be much more qualified.

It may be worth recalling at the outset that early in the nineteenth century the South had adopted a more rigid definition of the role of women than any other part of the country and had elevated that definition to the position of a myth. There were inherent contradictions in the elements of women's role as the culture defined it: women were supposed to be beautiful, gentle, efficient, morally superior, and, at the same time, ready to accept without question the doctrine of male superiority and authority. On matters not domestic they were to be seen and not heard, while in the domestic sphere it was taken for granted that a woman would rule. For those without inherited means, marriage was the only road to economic security (as for inherited wealth, its control passed at marriage into the hands of the husband). For those who did not marry, the only acceptable pattern was to become the pensioner—and often *de facto* servant—of some male relative. Hints that some women felt the contradictory nature of these expectations, and resented them, appeared from time to time before the Civil War. After the war, changes which seemed likely to alter the culture pattern appeared on all sides; but, as part of the comforting glorification of the past with which the South tended to evade present problems, the image of the Southern Lady—whatever the reality—survived relatively unchanged.[3] The force of this culture image was so strong that Southern women had to follow a more devious road to emancipation than those elsewhere. It was only after long apprenticeship in such outwardly safe organizations as church societies and the Woman's Christian Temperance

[3] W. J. Cash goes so far as to argue that woman's role was more rigidly defined after Appomattox and emancipation than before. *The Mind of the South* (New York, 1941), 131. He cites no evidence; and, on the basis of much reading in diaries, letters, newspapers, and church and organization records, I think he overstates his case.

Union that they began to venture into women's clubs and suffrage organizations.[4]

From this process a few women emerged as recognized leaders. These few had in common impressive social standing and family background, intelligence, courage, and a degree of inner security that permitted them to survive criticism. Such were Madeline Breckinridge in Kentucky, Mary Munford in Virginia, Nellie Sommerville in Mississippi, Sallie Cotten in North Carolina, Pattie Jacobs in Alabama—each highly respected in her own state by men as well as women.[5] Now, with the power of the ballot and the new freedom it symbolized, they hoped not only to be more effective in public life but also to modify significantly Southern thought about the proper role of women.[6]

They were well aware that the older image of the Southern Lady, although undergoing modification in a number of ways, was still very much alive in 1920. The image was, of course, made up of a number of components, some external: beauty, gentleness, winning ways. Other components related to appropriate behavior: modesty, domesticity, chastity, and submission to male opinions. It was a lovely image that could be maintained with a minimum of strain whenever the woman in question was lucky enough to be well endowed with the outward qualities (the proportionate number so endowed was doubtless about the same in 1920 as in

[4] Anne Firor Scott, "The 'New Woman' in the New South," *South Atlantic Quarterly,* LXI (Autumn 1962), 473–83.

[5] The obituaries upon Madeline Breckinridge's untimely death in 1920 suggest she was Kentucky's leading citizen as well as its leading woman. Certainly she had a hand in almost every reform movement in that state for twenty years; and, by way of the Lexington, Ky., *Herald,* her voice was widely heard. A close study of her biography reveals all the elements that created the Southern "woman movement." See Sophronisba Preston Breckinridge, *Madeline McDowell Breckinridge, a Leader in the New South* (Chicago, 1921) and Breckinridge Family Papers.

[6] Madeline Breckinridge, for example, regularly advised every woman to read Margaret Fuller, John Stuart Mill, and Olive Shreiner. The private papers of the women upon whom this study is centered reveal their vision of an ideal woman, educated and fully developed and free to undertake the work that interested her most. They were so often criticized for wanting to "be like men" that it is worth pointing out that their ideal human being was not a man but some other woman (Jane Addams, Anna Howard Shaw, Frances Willard, for example) and that they did not think men were doing a very good job with politics and government or in shaping society generally. What they aimed for was not freedom to be like men but freedom to be themselves. Economic independence loomed large in the minds of the pioneers—they had nothing against marriage, and most were married, but they objected to it as an economic necessity. It is interesting to find exactly the same arguments in the most recent comprehensive work on the subject, Simone de Beauvoir, *The Second Sex,* H. M. Parshley, trans. and ed. (New York, 1953). Mary Johnston and Ellen Glasgow were active suffrage women, and their novels are rich in oblique attacks on the existing system. See especially Glasgow, *Virginia* (New York, 1913) and Johnston, *Hagar* (Boston, 1913). Both novels will repay careful reading for anyone interested in the inner springs of the woman movement.

1820). But it was the definition of appropriate behavior that women were most anxious to modify. In earlier years the effective leaders of the movement had had to conform behavior to the image. As a Virginia woman remarked in 1918, "the wise suffrage leaders here have realized . . . that success depends upon showing their cause to be compatible with the essentials of the Virginia tradition of womanliness, and both instinct and judgment have prevented the adoption here of the more aggressive forms of campaigning."[7]

In the twenties, maintaining the ladylike image was still considered to be good politics, but the active women continued to alter behavior remarkably. A few of the more radical wanted to dispense, once and for all, with what they called the "chivalric nonsense" that put woman on a pedestal in order to keep her out of the affairs of the real world. A young North Carolina woman, for example, reflected:

Last year I travelled from one end of our State to another. I saw thousands of women, old and young, mothers and little girls, working in stores and factories ten or eleven or twelve hours a day; or worse, working in the factory all night, and taking care of their homes by day. And I asked, where is this chivalry that so protects women? And I saw working in the fields, hoeing cotton and corn and doing all kinds of hard labor, women and children, white as well as black. And again I asked, whom does chivalry protect? In the last session of the legislature, I heard arguments about a bill which would have raised the amount allowed from the estate to a widow and her children for the first year of widowhood. And many were the jokes made and the slurs slung about mothers who would spend the amount for silk stockings instead of on the care of children. Respect for motherhood, reverence for womanhood, was not the ruling thought when the bill was considered, for it was voted down. It was not the political rights nor any of the deeds of the "new woman" who took the working women from their homes and made them labor as if there was no such thing as chivalry and pedestals. . . . Genesis says that after the Lord had created male and female, he gave them dominion over the earth and then he rested. The two were created to work out welfare for all on earth. Why not go on with the work and stop babbling about chivalry when there is no chivalry except for the small class whose financial conditions prevents their needing it.[8]

[7] Orie Latham Hatcher, "The Virginia Man and the New Era for Women," *Nation*, CVI (June 1, 1918), 651.

[8] Mary O. Cowper, "That Pedestal Again," North Carolina League of Women Voters, *Monthly News*, November 1927. See also the very interesting series of articles by Nell Battle Lewis in Raleigh, N. C., *News and Observer*, May 1926, in which she discusses the question thoroughly and perceptively.

The older ideal of the Southern Lady cropped up in another way when the opponents of reforms for which women worked used it as a weapon. It was hardly politic to argue in public that one believed in child labor or enjoyed the profits that stemmed from women laboring long hours into the night, but—given the Southern frame of reference—it was quite possible to attack the proponents of reform on the ground that they were "unwomanly" and thus to discredit the cause for which they fought. This was done repeatedly, and the cry was often echoed, of course, by other men who feared for their own domestic comforts.

Even before the Nineteenth Amendment was ratified state suffrage organizations began to turn themselves into leagues of women voters with the announced purpose of educating newly enfranchised citizens and working for "needed legislation." Leaders gathered in Chicago for intensive training, organized by a political scientist from the University of Chicago, and went home with instructions to pass along all they had learned. "Citizenship schools" blossomed over the Southern landscape, and courses with reading lists worthy of graduate instruction in political science were found side by side with mundane classes in election law, registration procedures, and How to Mark a Ballot. The troops were receiving basic training.[9]

At the same time every state had its legislative council in which women's groups of the most diverse kinds joined together to work for legislation. The Alabama council was typical; it was made up of sixteen organizations, ranging from the Women's Trade Union League to the Methodist Home Missionary Council. Despite their diverse origins the organized women were in surprising accord on legislative goals.

Whether the goal was a social reform such as the abolition of child labor, or a political one such as the reorganization of the state government, veterans of the suffrage movement were political realists and skilled lobbyists. Their lobbying technique, developed before they had any votes to deliver, was based upon tact and superior information rather than upon threats. Though they were trying to throw off the shackles of chivalry, women voters were not above appealing for chivalric responses in a good cause.

An example of typical methods may be seen in a letter from a Virginia lady of the old school describing her efforts to persuade Congress to adopt a child labor amendment:

I got busy about the child labor amendment and stirred up the Virginia Federation of Labor and the Ministerial Union of Richmond which means all the Protestant clergymen of the city . . . the Federation of

[9] Charles E. Merriam, "The Chicago Citizenship School," *Journal of Social Forces,* I (September 1923), 600.

labor sent official communications to all senators and all congressmen and our papers have given us good notices. . . . I carried your summary of the situation to our leading morning paper and he promised to use it and comment on it editorially.[10]

A favorite device was the publication of complete lists of legislators with their views on various issues presented for the voters' information. Indeed, education of the electorate was a basic technique, and there was always an effort to develop support for their programs among "the people back home." The experience of the suffrage campaign came into play at every turn.

The ideological milieu of the twenties was nowhere conducive to social reform. The Red Scare had affected every part of the country, and programs considered mild in 1912 were now labeled Bolshevik.[11] The reform-minded women in the South were little disturbed at the outset by the fact that many of the causes in which they had long been interested were now termed radical. The president of the Tennessee League of Women Voters remarked mildly,

> Some good souls are pleased to call our ideas socialistic. They are indeed uncomfortable often for some folk. Some timid souls of both sexes are only half converted to the new order . . . [yet] every clear thinking, right feeling and high minded man and woman should consecrate his best talents to the gradual re-organization of society, national and international.[12]

The ink was scarcely dry upon the suffrage amendment before legislatures began to realize that women now expected more respectful attention

[10] Kate Pleasants Minor to Mrs. John J. O'Connor, April 18, 1924, in League of Women Voters of the United States Papers (Manuscript Division, Library of Congress), Virginia file.

[11] Note, for example, the comment of the foremost woman progressive of the day: "Social progress during the decade from 1919 to 1929 was conditioned at every turn by the fact that we were living in the midst of post-war psychology. . . . Any proposed change was suspect, even those efforts that had been considered praiseworthy before the war. To advance new ideas was to be radical, or even a bolshevik. . . . Throughout the decade this fear of change, this tendency to play safe was registered most conspicuously in the fields of politics, but it spread over into other fields as well." Jane Addams, *The Second Twenty Years at Hull House, September 1909 to September 1929, with a Record of a Growing World Consciousness* (New York, 1930), 153. Or this characterization from the center of Southern liberalism: "Besides there is mighty little freedom of opinion anywhere in the old South as you know. . . ." E. C. Branson to R. W. Hogan, Chapel Hill, N. C., December 17, 1922, in Eugene Cunningham Branson Papers (Southern Historical Collection, University of North Carolina Library).

[12] Report of the President, Tennessee League of Women Voters, January 1923, in League of Women Voters Papers, Tennessee file.

than in the past. "The men were scared to death of what the women might do," one North Carolina woman recalled.[13] In that state, as a measure of insurance against reprisal for having rejected the suffrage amendment, the governor and legislature agreed to appoint the president of the Federated Clubs as commissioner of charities and public welfare, one legislator being overheard to remark that she was "pretty, anyway, and won't give us any trouble." The insurance turned out to be inadequate, for in short order North Carolina women, abetted behind the scenes by the same pretty welfare commissioner, were demanding that the Woman's Bureau of the United States Department of Labor be invited to survey the working conditions of women in North Carolina textile mills.

Textile manufacturing was a major economic interest in the state, and working conditions in the mills were frequently bad, wages were low, and many children were employed. The mill-owners reacted strongly. The women were accused of being unwomanly to mix in things about which they knew nothing, of being dangerous radicals or at the very least dupes of Northern manufacturers bent on spoiling the competitive advantage that child labor and cheap female labor gave the South. The YWCA, one of the groups joining in the request for a survey, was threatened with a loss of contributions. The state president of the League of Women Voters was hailed before a self-constituted jury of millmen and lectured severely. The suggestion reached her that her husband's sales of mill machinery would diminish rapidly if she and the league continued their interest in women's working conditions. Families divided as wives argued with husbands about the survey. Textile men brought pressure upon the governor and upon agencies of the state government. In 1926 the governor, while standing firm against allowing "outsiders" to meddle in North Carolina's business, agreed to order his own Child Welfare Department to make the study—but nothing happened. In 1929 when the Gastonia strike became a national issue, the North Carolina League of Women Voters, in publishing an explanation of the strikers' side of the argument, remarked that if the women's request for a survey of working conditions had been granted the problems that had led to a bloody strike might have been ameliorated.[14]

[13] Interview with Mrs. Kate Burr Johnson of Raleigh, N. C., November 1, 1963. See also comment of the Georgia women who drew up a bill in 1921 to remove the civil disabilities of women: "These legislators were so courteous and obliging the women could scarcely believe it was the Georgia Legislature. They gave everything asked for and asked 'is there anything more we can do for you?'" Elizabeth Cady Stanton and others (eds.), *The History of Woman Suffrage* (6 vols., New York, 1881–1922), VI, 142.

[14] The story of the long fight between millmen and North Carolina women's groups is covered in detail in Mary O. Cowper Papers. Mrs. Cowper was executive secretary of the North Carolina League of Women Voters. The outlines as given here are confirmed by Mrs. Kate Burr Johnson, who was commissioner of welfare

North Carolina women were more successful in their efforts to bring about stronger state child labor laws.[15] In every Southern state, in fact, women worked strenuously against the use of child labor. Many of them supported the federal child labor amendment that Congress adopted in 1924 and then went on to work for its ratification by their legislatures. In the meantime, an intensive effort to establish broad programs of child welfare took shape. In Virginia, for example, the women urged the legislature to set up a Children's Code Commission and, having secured it, persuaded the governor to appoint five of their number to it. When the commission brought in twenty-four recommendations for new laws, ranging from a statewide juvenile court system to compulsory education, the women turned their attention once more to the legislature, and as a result of their unceasing toil eighteen of the twenty-four recommendations became law in the 1922 session.[16]

That same year a combination of women's groups in Georgia secured the passage of a children's code, a child-placement bill, and a training school bill but failed when they joined forces with the Federation of Labor for a legislative limitation on hours of work for women. The hearing on this last proposal brought out "every cotton mill man in Georgia," and, while the eloquent testimony of Mrs. Elliott Cheatham persuaded the committee to report the bill, the millowners' influence in the legislature prevented it from being brought to a vote. Two years later efforts to secure ratification of the federal child labor amendment also failed in the Georgia legislature, and women in the state then turned to efforts to strengthen state laws.[17]

Similar issues, all of them demonstrating the increasing influence of women, appeared in the other Southern states. In Arkansas, where as early as 1919 the suffrage organization had come out for minimum wages and maximum hours in all cotton mills, the federal child labor amendment was ratified by the legislature. Credit was given jointly to a woman legislator, the Arkansas Federation of Labor, and the women's organizations. The wife of the man who had led the floor fight against the amendment was

---

during the 1920's and was working behind the scenes with the women's groups. For contemporary analysis, see Nell Battle Lewis, "The University of North Carolina Gets Its Orders," *Nation,* CXXII (February 3, 1926), 114–15. Nora Houston of Virginia who was active in the effort to improve working conditions was also a painter and left at her death a dramatic painting of the Gastonia strike.

[15] North Carolina League of Women Voters, *Monthly News,* 1922–1926.

[16] Adele Clark Papers (Miss Clark, Richmond). Miss Clark helped organize the campaign. See also Eudora Ramsay Richardson, "Liberals in Richmond," *Plain Talk,* VI (February 1930), 213–19.

[17] Mrs. E. B. Chamberlain to Mrs. Solon Jacobs, October 25, 1922, and Report to Director of Southeastern Region, January 10, 1924, in League of Women Voters Papers, Georgia file.

reported to be delighted that he had failed; of her it was said, "she expressed the spirit of Arkansas women in politics."[18]

One result of the growing movement against the exploitation of women and children in the mills was an increasingly close association between Southern women and the labor movement. Lucy Randolph Mason, bluest of Virginia bluebloods, who was to become an organizer for the CIO, noted in 1930: "For a number of years many of us southern women have been concerned over the lack of social control in the development of southern industry. Vast numbers of southern women are becoming more acutely conscious of the need of safeguards, which have already been supplied by most of the states. . . ."[19] Association with labor unions actually had begun during the fight for suffrage when trade unions, along with the Farmers Alliances, were virtually the only male organizations to support woman suffrage. As early as 1910 the Georgia Suffrage Association reported holding its convention in the halls of "the Federation of Labor, *its true friend.*"[20] Now, in the twenties, women's interests were in line with labor concerns, and they not only found a good press in liberal journals such as the *New Republic* but also co-operated with labor unions.[21]

Particularly important in deepening woman's concern for industrial labor was the work of the YWCA. Even before the first World War, the YWCA had undertaken to bring college students in touch with the facts of industrial life, and in the twenties a student-industrial movement flourished. Its legislative program included the abatement of poverty, abolition of child labor, a living wage as a minimum in every industry, an eight-hour day, and protection of workers from the hardships of continued unemployment. Through the YWCA, students at Randolph Macon were studying the problems of coal miners, while those at Converse delved into social legislation, and at Westhampton, unemployment. Girls from these and other colleges served on a regional committee for student-industrial co-operation, seeking, as they put it, to Christianize the social order.[22] Part of this program included a series of summer institutes for factory girls that by 1927 had evolved into the Southern Summer School for Women Workers in Industry, directed and financed by Southern women. The school grew steadily through the twenties and early thirties. The nature of its sympathies was evident in 1928 when strikers from the Marion Manufacturing Company

[18] Miss Earl Chambers to Marguerite Owen, October 2, 1924, *ibid.,* Arkansas file.
[19] Lucy R. Mason to Henry P. Kendall, December 31, 1930, in Lucy Randolph Mason Papers (Manuscripts Collection, Duke University Library, Durham, N. C.).
[20] Stanton and others (eds.), *History of Woman Suffrage,* VI, 125.
[21] There is ample evidence for this in League of Women Voters Papers, state files, and Mary O. Cowper Papers. Common interests made inevitably for co-operation.
[22] Gladys Bryson, student secretary, YWCA, to Lucy Somerville, March 23, 1923, in Somerville Family Papers (Woman's Archives, Radcliffe College Library, Cambridge, Mass.).

were invited to the campus to tell their story and were afterward joined by students and faculty in a march through Marion. It was the opinion of the *Nation* that "This small group of women . . . are playing an important part in the fight against economic slavery in the South."[23]

When unionization became a genuine possibility during the New Deal, a large proportion of the women graduates of the Summer School became active organizers. There is something appealing in the picture of a group of well-to-do Southern women, of ladylike mien, busy training labor organizers. Nor is there the least doubt, from the record, that they knew what they were doing. They were not innocent philanthropists taken in by hard-bitten radicals.[24]

The Southern Council on Women and Children in Industry, organized in 1931 to bring about a shorter working day and an end to night work in all the textile states, was another joint effort growing out of the experience of women in their separate states. The council hired Lucy Mason to organize their campaign. Calling to the colors a few progressive-minded millmen who agreed with her objectives, she then set out to convert some of those who did not agree, recognizing clearly that pressure on the legislatures could not succeed without the support of some of the millowners.[25]

From a national point of view the concern for child welfare was reflected in the passage in 1921, largely due to the work of women over the nation, of the Sheppard-Towner Act for maternal and infant health. Nineteen of twenty-six Southern senators voted for the bill. In the House, 91 of the 279 votes in support of the bill came from the South and only 9 of 39 votes against it.[26] This support for a federal welfare program from Southern members of Congress is less impressive than the enormous amount of follow-up work that Southern women undertook to secure appropriation of the required matching funds from state legislatures and then to report on the actual results of the public health work thus instituted. It is not too much to say that the co-operative state work within the framework of the Sheppard-Towner Act brought about a revolution in maternal and infant health.[27]

In some ways the most intriguing of all the public activities of Southern women in the twenties was their racial work. The roots went back at

[23] Marion Bonner, "Behind the Southern Textile Strikes," *Nation*, CXXIX (October 2, 1929), 352.

[24] See Lucy P. Garner, "An Education Opportunity for Industrial Girls," *Journal of Social Forces,* I (September 1923), 612–13, and Alice M. Baldwin Papers (Manuscripts Collection, Duke University Library).

[25] Lucy Randolph Mason Papers, box 1.

[26] *Congressional Record,* 67 Cong., 1 Sess., 4216, 8036–37.

[27] This story is reflected in detail in League of Women Voters Papers, state files. See especially all the state-by-state reports on the operation of the law and the collection of letters from Texas women who benefited from it. Reports of the Children's Bureau also contain details of the actual workings of the law.

least to 1901 when Miss Belle Bennett encouraged the Woman's Board of Home Missions of the Methodist Episcopal Church, South, to undertake work among Negro girls and offered a personal contribution to that end. From that year forward the board annually appropriated money in behalf of work among Negroes. In 1910 another Methodist, Mary DeBardelben of Alabama, volunteered for missionary service, not in far-off lands but among Southern Negroes. In 1915 yet another Southern Methodist, Mrs. Lily H. Hammond, published a pathbreaking book in which she pleaded for a permanent burial of the "old Negro mammy" and some sensible attention to the needs of Mammy's daughters.[28]

The real breakthrough came in 1920 at an extraordinary meeting of Southern churchwomen in Memphis at which four Negro women spoke forthrightly of the needs of Southern Negroes. One of them told of having been forcibly removed by twelve white men from a Pullman car while on her way to Memphis. In the emotional stir of the moment, the ninety-odd white women, representing a number of churches, agreed that talk was not enough and constituted themselves the Woman's Department of the Commission on Inter-racial Cooperation. Headed by Mrs. Luke Johnson of Griffin, Georgia, and supported by leading women in every state, units of this organization set up interracial committees to attack common social and economic problems.

When the National League of Women Voters decided in 1924 to establish a Committee on Negro Problems with membership from every state that had more than fifteen per cent Negro population, members from eight Southern states accepted appointment. Many of these women had been active in their local interracial committees, of which there were eventually some eight hundred functioning in the South. In Tennessee white women organized a special citizenship school for Negro women. Many of the committeewomen took personal responsibility for their Negro fellow citizens, as did Mary Cooke Branch Munford of Richmond, who made a room of her house permanently available to Negroes for public meetings, or a busy doctor's wife in Alabama who waged a one-woman campaign for better Negro education. When the Richmond city council considered a segregation statute in 1929, it was Lucy Randolph Mason, almost singlehandedly, who brought about its defeat.[29]

The most spectacular work in this field began in the thirties. It started

---

[28] Noreen Dunn Tatum, *A Crown of Service: A Story of Woman's Work in the Methodist Episcopal Church, South, from 1878–1940* (Nashville, 1960), 32, 65, 234; Lily Hardy Hammond, *In Black and White: An Interpretation of Southern Life* (New York, 1914). See also Wilma Dykeman and James Stokely, *Seeds of Southern Change: The Life of Will Alexander* (Chicago, 1961), 82–96.

[29] Norfolk *Journal and Guide*, February 2, 1929. See also Katherine Du Pre Lumpkin, *The Making of a Southerner* (New York, 1947) for evidence of the significance of the YWCA in breaking through traditional racial barriers.

with the organization in 1930, under the imaginative leadership of Jessie Daniel Ames, a Texas woman who had been active in a dozen reform movements, of the Association of Southern Women for the Prevention of Lynching. At its peak this organization had 40,000 small-town and rural churchwomen enrolled in an effort to put an end to the most spectacularly disgraceful aspect of the Southern race problem. While the federal anti-lynching law was blocked in the United States Senate, this band of Southern women took upon themselves the sometimes heroic responsibility of opposing any specific threat of a lynching in their own towns or counties.

The crusade against lynching was the most dramatic aspect of women's interracial work. Less visible, but of great significance, was the way in which groups of white and Negro women in the twenties were sitting down together to tackle common problems in an atmosphere of forthright discussion. Though a few Negro women were careful publicly to eschew any desire for social equality, most of them hammered away on equal rights in court, an end to segregation and discrimination in transportation, the Negro's need for the ballot, and every other sensitive issue that stood between whites and blacks in the South during this period of the resurgent Ku Klux Klan.[30]

Although women's interests tended to center upon measures that had a humanitarian element, especially those affecting disadvantaged groups and children, they devoted much time to more strictly political questions. After learning the mechanics of government, they turned their efforts to the improvement of governmental organizations. Studies of local and state governmental structure were published and used in schools and by other organizations. In Virginia in 1922 women's groups worked for an executive budget and improved election laws. A year later the state legislative chairman of the Virginia League of Women Voters reported that she was in daily attendance at budget hearings.[31] In 1924 her organization concentrated its attention on the improvement of tax administration and reported it had won an initial skirmish in the legislature by securing active consideration of the question despite orders from the Democratic machine that the subject was not to be raised. In the same legislature Virginia women voters worked for a bill to create a uniform fiscal year and were successful in their effort.[32] The League had also supported bills, that failed to pass,

[30] The story of women's interracial work is in Jessie Daniel Ames Papers (Mrs. Ames, Tryon, N. C.). Mrs. Ames pioneered the antilynching group and was for twelve years executive secretary of the Woman's Department of the Inter-Racial Commission. What is given here is a mere glimpse into a complex and fascinating story that deserves a chapter or a book all to itself.

[31] Nora Houston to Maud Wood Park, December 12, 1923, in League of Women Voters Papers, Virginia file.

[32] Miss M. E. Pidgeon to Belle Sherwin, 1924, *ibid.*

for civil service, creation of a conservation department, county government reform, and reforms in the state educational machinery.

Similar interests and similar campaigns developed in other states. Women in Georgia and Tennessee, after initial forays into the question of more efficient government, became convinced that the supreme obstacle lay in outmoded state constitutions; and in both states campaigns for constitutional reform were launched in the twenties and were eventually successful.[33] Kentucky women in 1937 began to work for home rule for cities, improvements in local charters, and the adoption of city manager government.

To an interest in the structure of government was added a concern for making government more democratic. Because of their long exclusion from politics, women were sensitive to the implications of "consent of the governed." It was they who invented the now commonplace idea of "getting out the vote." In some places women's work led to spectacular increases in the percentage of qualified voters going to the polls. In Alabama 54.4% of the qualified voters went to the polls in 1924 after women sponsored a get-out-the-vote campaign, compared to less than 30% in 1920. One county, where the women had been particularly active, got out 84.1% of its qualified voters.[34] Florida in the same year reported a 65.9% increase over 1920 in the qualified voters going to the polls.[35]

The poll tax was the subject of dual concern. Women's groups opposed the tax, but in the meantime they set out to collect money for the payment of poll taxes in order to increase the number of qualified voters. In 1925 Louisiana women collected $30,000 to this end. The work of North Carolina women for the Australian ballot, that finally succeeded in 1929, was part of the same interest in making the operation of government more democratic.

Close to home, yet a long way from women's traditional concerns, were two other political issues that developed strength in Southern women's groups in the twenties: government ownership of Muscle Shoals and the regulation of utility rates. Interest in both these questions developed from studies of the cost of living, and women in Alabama and Tennessee became enthusiastic supporters of what was to become the Tennessee Valley Authority. On these as on other questions the politically active women seem to have taken a pragmatic view without much concern for traditional free enterprise arguments.

In all their enterprises, political or social, women knew that the main

[33] *Ibid.,* Georgia and Tennessee files.

[34] Report on the Get Out the Vote Campaign, November 29, 1924, *ibid.,* Alabama file.

[35] Mrs. J. B. O'Hara to Ann Webster, September 2, 1924, *ibid.,* Florida file.

road to influence lay through political parties. Interest in partisan politics antedated suffrage, and unofficially some women had long taken an interest in party fortunes. It had been the accepted doctrine that the national suffrage organization should be nonpartisan since it hoped to get support from both parties for the national amendment. That this principle was occasionally honored in the breach is made clear when we find Jane Addams trying to recruit Jean Gordon of Louisiana for the Progressive party in 1912 or discover Mrs. Breckinridge on a speaking tour for the Democrats in 1916. A keen interest in party methods and organization had been one of the by-products of the highly organized national suffrage campaign.[36] Carrie Chapman Catt, the commanding general of the final suffrage drive, was intent that women should find their way not just to the outskirts but to the center of power in the political parties. At the Victory Convention in Chicago in 1920 she had told them:

> The next battle is going to be inside the parties, and we are not going to stay outside and let all the reactionaries have their way on the inside! Within every party there is a struggle between progressive and reactionary elements. Candidates are a compromise between these extremes. You will be disillusioned, you will find yourselves in the political penumbra where most of the men are. They will be glad to see you, you will be flattered. But if you stay long enough you will discover a little denser thing which is the umbra of the political party—the people who are picking the candidates, doing the real work that you and the men sanction at the polls. You won't be welcome, but there is the place to go. You will see the real thing in the center with the door locked tight. You will have a hard fight before you get inside . . . but you must move right up to the center.[37]

At the outset, a considerable number of Southern women set out to become active in party politics. Party organizations welcomed them, if not with enthusiasm at least with a realistic appreciation of their potential voting power. Some states began at once the custom that has since become standard of appointing a woman as vice-chairman of the state party committee. A considerable number of Southern women showed interest in running for elective office; and, though numerous obstacles lay between almost any woman and nomination, enough persisted so that by 1930 only Louisiana had yet to have women in the state legislature. But only a few, a

[36] See Carrie Chapman Catt and Nettie Rogers Shuler, *Woman Suffrage and Politics: The Inner Story of the Suffrage Movement* (New York, 1924) and Maud Wood Park, *Front Door Lobby,* Edna Lamprey Stantial, ed. (Boston, 1960).

[37] Mary Gray Peck, *Carrie Chapman Catt, a Biography* (New York, 1944), 325–26.

very few, Southern women seem to have made their way to that mysterious center of power to which Mrs. Catt had directed them.

One of these was Mrs. Nellie Nugent Somerville of Greenville, Mississippi, whose political influence preceded the Nineteenth Amendment. As soon as it was legal to do so she ran for the state legislature in a campaign that was a model of thorough organization and was elected. She had been observing party organization long enough to know the ropes, and she hoped the newly enfranchised women would be similarly observant. She advised them to be certain they had a hand in choosing county committees and reminded them: "It now becomes the duty of women voters to take lively interests in the details of political machinery. When any meeting or election is ordered by your political party be sure you take part in it."[38]

The chief obstacle to following such advice was the unwillingness of male politicians to promote women of independent mind and political skill. They preferred more amenable females, and hence the forthright and well-trained suffrage veterans often found themselves at odds with the entrenched politicians.[39] Mrs. Somerville herself managed to surmount the obstacles, and in 1924 Mississippi Democrats were divided into Somerville and Percy factions. At the showdown, hers won. She also served as a member of the committee on permanent organization of the 1924 Democratic National Convention and marshaled William G. McAdoo supporters in imposing array.[40] Her record in the legislature suggests that she understood the effective use of political power. When a bill she had initiated failed to pass, the fact was reported as news—as a rule anything she offered did pass—and her colleagues were frequently quoted in praise of her hard work and effectiveness as a lawmaker.[41]

Another politically minded woman who reached a position of genuine power in the party was Sue Shelton White of Tennessee, an independent court reporter, secretary to members of the Tennessee Supreme Court, and from 1920 to 1926 secretary to Senator Kenneth McKellar. In 1915 she drafted the first mother's pension law to be presented to the Tennessee legislature, finally passed in 1920. She went from Senator McKellar's office to practice law in Jackson, Tennessee, and was sufficiently effective in Democratic politics to be invited to work for the Democratic National

[38] Article in Jackson, Miss., *Woman Voter,* November 19, 1923. For the details of Mrs. Sommerville's campaign, see letters of her daughter, September 1923, in Somerville Family Papers.

[39] See analysis of first woman vice chairman of the Democratic National Committee, Emily Newell Blair, "Women in the Political Parties," American Academy of Political and Social Science, *Annals,* CXLIII (May 1929), 217–29.

[40] Clippings and note in Sommerville Family Papers.

[41] *Ibid.,* clippings. She had the additional distinction of providing the state with another successful woman politician, her daughter Lucy who followed her in the legislature in the 1930's and ultimately became a federal judge.

Committee. With Nellie Davis (Tayloe) Ross she helped lay the groundwork for the extensive women's program of the party during the early Franklin D. Roosevelt years. A fellow lawyer, who was general counsel of the Federal Social Security Board, said at her death:

> Sue knew politics from the inside and from the outside. Politics were more than a game to her, though I think she relished the intricacies of the game. She used her political acumen as an instrument for the promotion of the general welfare. And she wielded the instrument with a grace and effectiveness that delighted the wise and distressed the stupid.[42]

Mrs. Somerville and Miss White were exceptional rather than typical, but women in politics ranged from those who were effective politicians in their own right to those who blamed the men for not permitting them to gain nomination. The success stories make good reading, but the overall picture of women's efforts to exercise real influence in the political parties, South or North, was not one to gladden Mrs. Catt's heart. Sue White analyzed the Southern situation in 1928 in a letter to Mary Dewson of the Democratic National Committee:

> Women have been discouraged by the rank and file of the party organization. . . . We still have the old anti-suffrage attitude in the south, women have been indifferent, and their indifference has been preached to them, aided, abetted and encouraged. They have viewed politics as something they should stay away from. They have been told so and have believed it and the few feminists who have tried to push in have been slapped in the face. . . . And the few women who have been artificially reared up as leaders are not leaders of women and have been reared not to lead women but to fool them.[43]

Miss White's analysis was confirmed by Emily Newell Blair, the national vice-chairman of the Democratic party in the twenties. In Mrs. Blair's view, at the very beginning, competent women—the genuine leaders—had essayed party politics, but when they showed themselves unwilling to be rubber stamps they were replaced by women more willing to be led. These were the artificial leaders to whom Miss White referred.[44]

An increasing number of Southern women did undertake simple party work of the doorbell-ringing and envelope-stuffing variety—a trend that

[42] Jack Tate in Sue Shelton White Papers (Woman's Archives, Radcliffe College Library).

[43] Sue Shelton White to Mary Dewson, November 23, 1928, *ibid.*

[44] Blair, "Women in the Political Parties."

still continues. And whether they helped make policy or not, women voters affected the outcome of elections. Women claimed to have defeated James E. Ferguson and elected William P. Hobby governor of Texas in 1920. In Mississippi Henry L. Whitfield, former president of Mississippi State College for Women, was elected governor in 1923, largely through the efforts of alumnae of the college. South Carolina women thought they had a large hand in the defeat of Cole Blease. One South Carolina woman who worked through the whole campaign remarked innocently, "We made no partisan stand, we merely got out the vote." Tennessee Democrats, perhaps looking for a scapegoat, blamed the women for the Republican victory in Tennessee in the 1920 election. The women themselves claimed credit for the return of Cordell Hull to Congress three years later.[45]

Evidence of the increasing effectiveness of women voters may be deduced from the vituperative attacks leveled at them. In addition to the accusations that they were being used by Northern manufacturers, they were accused of being radical, unfeminine, of organizing Negro women, and of using "illegitimate pressure" to put across the measures of a "feminist block." David Clark, perhaps the South's bitterest enemy of child labor regulation, went so far as to claim that more babies died after the Sheppard-Towner Act was in operation than before. His *Textile Bulletin* attacked women harshly. The Associated Industries of Kentucky circulated a condemnation of "political women" reprinted from the Dearborn, Michigan, *Independent*. The Louisville *Herald* suggested the reason: "As we have said, the woman voter is making herself felt in ways not chartered for her. We will not go to the length of saying she is always welcome in these channels, but there are times when one may gauge the need of one's activity and curiosity by the ungracious manner of one's reception."[46]

Many of the women who undertook a more active role in Southern politics in the twenties had encountered this ungracious reception. But their motivation was deeply rooted. Those who had been trained during the two or three decades before suffrage were eager to move into a more active and effective political role in 1920. By then their goals had been formulated. Their underlying motivation is complex, but at least two main drives seem clear: first, the drive to assert themselves as individual human beings with minds and capacities that could be used; and, second, the drive to improve the world in which they lived. The balance of these motives varied from person to person. Some, like Lucy Mason, were primarily interested in social reform:

[45] These claims appear in letters and reports to the National Office of the League of Women Voters in League of Women Voters Papers. The information about Governor Whitfield is contained in Lucy Somerville Howorth to author, February 5, 1964.

[46] Louisville, Ky., *Herald,* May 9, 1923.

When I was fourteen, a missionary's sermon made me want to be a missionary myself. Later I recognized that religion can be put to work right in one's own community. It was this belief that took me into the Equal Suffrage League, and later the League of Women Voters, both of which were interested in labor and social legislation.[47]

Others thoroughly enjoyed the game of politics and the feeling of power that might occasionally go with it. Nearly all felt that significant reforms would be more easily achieved with women's help.

The Nineteenth Amendment changed a good many things, but it brought only a partial modification in the Southern culture pattern, and the difficulties in the way of women's full participation in public life were considerable. One major obstacle, in addition to the demands of home and family, was the flat opposition of many men. Equally important was the unwillingness of many women to assume and carry through large responsibilities. From the record it seems that numbers of women had a vague desire to "do something" but needed leadership in finding what to do and how to do it, and the leaders were never sufficiently numerous to tap all the potential resources. A good example, no doubt an extreme one, was a Virginia town of which it was reported that when a certain Miss Terry was at home the town was jumping with women's political activities but when she went to Europe all was quiet.

Around the handful of leaders there gathered a slowly growing number of supporters and workers, and when this support was effectively channeled specific goals were achieved. In almost every instance groups of men were working to the same ends, and frequently there was co-operation. It is impossible to say what would have happened without the women's efforts, but it does seem clear that in the two areas of race relations and factory regulation much less would have been accomplished without them.

Through it all the outward aspect of the Southern Lady was normally maintained as the necessary precondition of securing a hearing. For some women, this was a perfectly compatible role, so long as they could change its behavioral aspects. Others impatiently called for an end to pedestals, but even they found it more effective to operate within the ladylike tradition. The other side of the coin was that the image of the proper Southern Lady was used effectively as a weapon by those who objected to the substantive goals for which women were working, hoping thus to discredit the goals themselves.

No one would argue that the Southern states became a progressive paradise in the twenties, but it is impossible to study the history of the

[47] Lucy Randolph Mason, *To Win These Rights: A Personal Story of the CIO in the South* (New York, 1952), 4.

welfare movements of the time without being surprised by the degree to which the spirit of progressivism was still in flower, and the amount of hopeful optimism about the future of reform that animated women in the face of the general spirit of reaction which is said to have permeated political life. Professor George B. Tindall has adumbrated the "business progressivism" of Southern state governments in the twenties.[48] To the picture he drew must now be added the decided growth through the decade of the conception of state responsibility for public welfare, not in the old custodial sense, but in the newer sense of ameliorating the underlying conditions that created serious human problems. To the growth of this idea and its application in law, Southern women made a considerable contribution.

When all this has been said we are left with the most troublesome questions still unanswered. In spite of the impressive record of accomplishment, the high expectations of the women who had led the suffrage movement did not come to pass. What happened to the verve and enthusiasm with which the suffrage veterans set about to reorganize society? That it did not all vanish is evident from the Southern scene today, but that it did not lead to a clear-cut image of a New Woman to replace the Southern Lady is also evident. The numbers of women in public life, in proportion to the population, are probably no more today than in 1925. While the number of women in labor force climbs—some say alarmingly— the number of women in responsible jobs of leadership, policymaking, or in the professions is still not large. To these difficult and intriguing questions historians of women must now begin to turn their attention.

[48] George B. Tindall, "Business Progressivism: Southern Politics in the Twenties," *South Atlantic Quarterly*, LXII (Winter 1963), 92–106.

7

The Great Confrontation: The South and the Problem of Change

John Hope Franklin

Man has invariably found his past experience and present condition somewhat less perfect than he imagined it might be. Undaunted, however, he usually has sought a state of faultless excellence through the psychological manipulation of the past or the future. He has found it possible, then, to extrapolate visions of individual and social perfection from the imagined glories of the historic past or to suggest that utopia stands on the verge of becoming. Americans are no strangers to such a process, having developed a particular ideological bias in support of such mythical ventures and fictions. In a variation on this theme, and unlike many societies which consistently point to the far horizon as the abode of utopian dreams, the American South has long been convinced that it indeed discovered, and for a time savored, a golden age of perfection. Such a time, when things were *different,* was the South of antebellum days. It is just such a preserved memory that John Hope Franklin, James B. Duke Professor of History at Duke University, here attempts to analyze. By artfully controlling its legendary past, and summarily announcing that the pure and perfect society had already arrived, the South's fund of historical experience has served as a convenient touchstone. The region's greatest energies have thus been expended in preserving, as a historical antique, her gilded past. As a result, Professor Franklin contends that the South has too often failed to

John Hope Franklin, "The Great Confrontation: The South and the Problem of Change," *Journal of Southern History,* 38 (February 1972), 3–20. Copyright 1972 by the Southern Historical Association. Reprinted by permission of the Managing Editor.

accommodate itself to fundamental change—as reflected by the correlated experience of women and blacks. As both groups can attest, the South has been more a believer in civil and human *rites* than rights. And though such imitations of grandeur may at times be appealing—in the words of Wilbur Cash, "perpetually suspended in the great haze of memory . . . colossal, shining, and incomparably lovely"—they fail to take due account of the myths and fallacies which serve as the substructure of the South's supposed perfection. Both the South's past and present stand frustrated and obscured by its myths.

The vision of the New World as the utopia of their dreams—or as the challenge to create one—seized all Europeans who decided to cast their lot with what was, perhaps, the most remarkable overseas venture in the history of mankind.[1] Not every New World settler came of his own volition, of course. There were the kidnapped orphans and derelicts from Britain's streets and tippling houses, the debtors from scores of Europe's jails, and the hapless Africans whose "most sacred rights of life & liberty" were violated by a "cruel war against human nature itself."[2] Regardless of their background or antecedents, all who came were soon caught up, in one way or another, in the relentless drive to find or create an Eden that would completely satisfy the aspirations of its people. Indeed, many would project "visions of liberation and perfection in the vacant spaces of the New World."[3]

The search for the perfect society was everywhere. New Englanders believed that they were approaching utopia as they developed a set of religious and economic institutions whose centralized control tolerated neither variations nor aberrations. Those in the Middle Atlantic area saw in their very diversity the key to a prosperous and peaceful future. In the South the remarkable success of a staple economy built on a reliable and durable labor system gave white settlers the opportunity to establish and maintain a social order free of the anxieties that plagued some of their neighbors to the North. It appeared to most of those in authority and

[1] The view of the New World as a liberating and regenerating force has been discussed by many writers. See the summary statement in David Brion Davis, *The Problem of Slavery in Western Culture* (Ithaca, 1966), 4–7.

[2] This was among the indictments against the king that did not appear in the final draft of the Declaration of Independence. Carl L. Becker, *The Declaration of Independence: A Study in the History of Political Ideas* (New York, 1942), 180–81.

[3] Davis, *Problem of Slavery,* 4.

leadership that only the refinements were necessary to forge a state of existence that would be lasting and satisfying.

But utopia was not quickly or easily attained—not for everybody or, indeed, for anybody. Soon, religious misfits were challenging authority in New England, stimulating in due course a whole body of restless souls who would expand into new areas to attempt what they had failed to accomplish in their first New World homes. Pennsylvanians and New Yorkers soon discovered that their vaunted pluralism was not entirely satisfactory; and they also began the westward trek. Even residents in the South, unhappy with limited profits or unable to compete in a slave economy, looked beyond the mountains to the new Southwest for new worlds to conquer. Those remaining behind seemed no happier after the dissidents departed than before. They continued to seek some new arrangement in their economy, some modification in their religious practices or in their relationships with their fellows that would be more satisfying. In some areas they began to industrialize, to embrace or at least witness the emergence of new religions, and even to free their slaves.

These new arrangements created as many problems as they solved. Industrialization required capital that was not always available. The former slaves of the "free" states, although not overwhelming in numbers, were new competitors in the free labor markets and their troublesome presence raised questions about their place in the social order. The new religions and the modernization of the old religions caused anxious moments of soul-searching and raised doubts regarding the stability of human and even divine institutions. The quest for the perfect society seemed never ending.

There was, however, one region—the South—where, thirty years before the Civil War, the search for utopia came to a grinding halt. If the quest of all southerners for perfection had been less vigorous, it was nevertheless more fortuitous; for they had discovered what they regarded as the components of a perfect civilization. In due course they became the zealous guardians of what they had discovered.

It was in the context of the sectional controversy that white southerners sharpened their conception of the perfect society; and by the time they defined it they discovered that they had achieved it. In the North the Transcendentalists advanced the idea of the perfectibility of man, but the emphasis was on how imperfect the social order was. In the South there was rather general agreement on the depravity of man, but the real emphasis was on how perfect the social order was. In a dozen areas the northern reformers sought to bring about change. They called for equal rights for women, the recognition of labor as an equal partner with management or capital in the economy, democratization of the schools, and above all, the abolition of slavery. Some were quite specific about such things as prison reform, pacifism, and religious pluralism, while others registered no confidence in the social order by retreating into communitarian settlements such as Icaria in Iowa or Zoar in Ohio.

In the South things could hardly have been better. The economic system was, for all practical purposes, perfect. As one writer claimed, slavery was the force that "beautifully blends, harmonizes, and makes them [capital and labor] as one. . . . This union of labour and capital in the same hands, counteracts . . . all those social, moral, material, and political evils which afflict the North and Western Europe."[4] Observed from any angle—whether it be the perfect distribution of labor by means of the slave system or the inevitable cooperation of the indolent with the industrious or the most effective utilization of the soil and other resources—the South's economic system was as close to perfection as one could hope for or even want.

The South's political system was, in the eyes of white southerners, a remarkable achievement. White men, relieved of the cares and the drudgery of manual toil, were free to give their attention to the problem of governance. It was, as James Henry Hammond put it, a harmony of the South's political and social institutions. "This harmony gives her a frame of society, the best in the world, and an extent of political freedom, combined with entire security, such as no other people ever enjoyed upon the face of the earth."[5] It was sheer folly, the slavocracy insisted, to argue that the essential element of a republic was the perfect political equality of all persons. On the contrary, Representative Thomas L. Clingman insisted, inequality was a significant element of the constitutional republican form.[6] As far as slavery was concerned, the Constitution itself recognized slavery and the inequality of persons. That fact was extremely important to the southern position. As William Pinkney pointedly asked in 1820, "if it be true that all the men in a republican Government must help to wield its power, and be equal in rights . . . why not all the *women*?"[7] No, the South's political system was the ideal system, even if it did not, and perhaps *because* it did not, extend equality to blacks or to women!

The role of the white woman in southern life was defined with a precision that made it almost legal. There were, of course, some legal restrictions on women such as their inability to sue or be sued alone or to own. property separate from their husbands or to dispose of property they

---

[4] "American Slavery in 1857," *Southern Literary Messenger*, XXV (August 1857), 85.

[5] *Congressional Globe*, 35 Cong., I Sess., 961–62 (March 4, 1858).

[6] *Ibid.*, 30 Cong., 1 Sess., Appendix, 43–44 (December 22, 1847).

[7] *Annals of Congress*, 16 Cong., 1 Sess., 414 (February 15, 1820).

owned before marriage without the permission of their husbands.[8] But the southern woman's role as defined by custom and tradition was one infinitely more exacting than the requirements of the law. For she had to fulfill the queenly role in what Anne Firor Scott has called "The Image," while having to perform the dozens of tasks in the rather unattractive everyday life that was "The Reality." Thus "She was timid and modest, beautiful and graceful," she was " 'the most fascinating being in creation . . . the delight and charm of every circle she moves in.' " But she was also a submissive creature "whose reason for being was to love, honor, obey, and occasionally amuse her husband, to bring up his children and manage his household."[9] It could be a grim and drab business, especially when isolation from friends and insulation from many of her husband's activities doomed her to an accommodation that made the image supremely difficult to live up to.

One facet of the insulation must have been extremely painful; and that was the manner in which her lord and master, by his own conduct, defined the role of the black woman. The nocturnal visit—or, for that matter, the emboldened daytime visit—to the slave cabin, the regular trips to Charleston or Mobile or New Orleans when it was "not convenient" to have other members of the family accompany him, and the regular appearance of mulatto babies on the plantation took their toll in the capacity of the mistress to live up to expectations. But the other woman's lot must have been at least as difficult. "When she is fourteen or fifteen," one of them said, "her owner, or his sons, or the overseer, or perhaps all of them, begin to bribe her with presents. If these fail to accomplish their purpose, she is whipped or starved into submission to their will."[10]

When Frederick Law Olmsted visited Richmond in the autumn of 1855 he was "surprised at the number of fine-looking mulattoes, or nearly white colored persons" that he saw. "Many of the colored ladies were dressed not only expensively, but with good taste and effect, after the latest Parisian mode." About a fourth of those whom Olmsted observed "seemed . . . to have lost all distinguishingly African peculiarity of feature, and to have acquired, in place of it, a good deal of that voluptuousness of expression which characterizes many of the women of the south of Europe."[11] The

[8] Guion Griffis Johnson, "The Changing Status of the Southern Woman," in John C. McKinney and Edgar T. Thompson, eds., *The South in Continuity and Change* (Durham, 1965), 421.

[9] Scott, *The Southern Lady: From Pedestal to Politics, 1830–1930* (Chicago and London, 1970), 4.

[10] [Harriet B. Jacobs], *Incidents in the Life of a Slave Girl,* edited by Lydia Maria Child (Boston, 1861), 79.

[11] Olmsted, *A Journey in the Seaboard Slave States* (New York, 1856), 18, 28.

wife of one planter "found it impossible to long keep a maid . . . for none could escape the licentious passions of her husband, who was the father of about one-fourth of the slaves on his plantation, by his slave women."[12] Another "watched her husband with unceasing vigilance; but he was well practised in means to evade it."[13] Small wonder one mistress was beside herself with rage, when a visitor mistook one of the girl servants for a member of the slaveholder's family and addressed her with appropriate familiarity.[14] But the half million mulattoes in the United States by 1860 were an integral part of the perfect society to which the white southerner had become so attached and committed.[15]

The white southerner's social order was one in which his own sense of superiority was constantly nurtured by the subordination to which he subjected all blacks. It mattered not whether the blacks were slave or free— although their natural lot was, of course, as slaves—they existed for the sole purpose of gratifying the needs, desires, even the ego, of the whites. It was so important to the white elite to maintain the southern social order that they enlisted every white, regardless of economic or social status, in its support.[16] Color became the badge of distinction, and every white man could be proud of his own racial distinction. "We have among us," Judge Abel P. Upshur declared, "but one great class, and all who belong to it have a necessary sympathy with one another; we have but one great interest, and all who possess it are equally ready to maintain and protect it."[17]

A sense of racial superiority became at once a principal defense of slavery and an obsession with it as the "cornerstone" of southern civilization. "[P]ublic liberty and domestic slavery were cradled together," Robert Toombs declared.[18] This view complemented James Henry Hammond's argument that Africans had the requisite vigor, docility, and fidelity to perform the "drudgery of life" while the whites preoccupied themselves with "progress, civilization, and refinement."[19] Others, in large numbers, lent their philosophical speculations and their scientific "findings" to further

[12] John Thompson, *The Life of John Thompson, a Fugitive Slave* (Worcester, 1856), 31.

[13] [Jacobs], *Incidents,* 49.

[14] Lewis and Milton Clarke, *Narratives of the Sufferings of Lewis and Milton Clarke* (Boston, 1846), 20.

[15] U.S. Bureau of the Census, *Negro Population, 1790–1915* (Washington, 1918), 208.

[16] See, for example, James D. B. De Bow, *The Interest in Slavery of the Southern Non-Slaveholder* (Charleston, 1860).

[17] Upshur, "Domestic Slavery," *Southern Literary Messenger,* V (October 1839), 685.

[18] Quoted in William S. Jenkins, *Pro-Slavery Thought in the Old South* (Chapel Hill, 1935), 291.

[19] *Cong. Globe,* 35 Cong., 1 Sess., Appendix, 71 (March 4, 1858).

justification of the inevitable lot of Negroes as slaves. Physiologically they were inferior, emotionally they were juvenile, and intellectually they were hopelessly retarded. Fortunately for them, the argument went, they were the chattel of an aristocracy characterized by talent, virtue, generosity, and courage.[20]

The fact that more than one-tenth of all Negroes in the United States were free and that some of them were most accomplished in the economic and intellectual spheres did not shake the confidence of white southerners in their perfect society that refused to recognize blacks as persons worthy of any respectable social status. Free Negroes were pariahs, and the whites enacted laws to confirm it. The fact that the annual crop of runaways was regularly increasing created an apprehension that whites successfully concealed. A slave who ran away was afflicted with a disease called "drapetomania," which could be cured by flogging; or he was the victim of the evil designs of abolitionists, which could be dispelled by more stringent laws and direct action.[21] The fact that there were slave revolts and rumors of them merely confirmed the demented and immoral character of some of the slaves which could best be dealt with by constant surveillance. In any case, slavery was a great missionary institution, "one arranged by God." As Bishop Stephen Elliott of Georgia put it, "we are working out God's purposes, whose consummation we are quite willing to leave in his hands."[22]

White southerners did not leave such matters altogether in God's hands. If their religious institutions were ordained by God, they were, in turn, built and managed by man and with a view toward refining and sustaining the perfect society. In forging what one observer has called "a southern religion" the whites made certain that the orthodoxy of their churches, regardless of denomination, was in perfect harmony with the southern social order.[23] The churches condemned all signs of social instability such as intemperance, gambling, divorce, and dancing. Indeed, some religious groups objected to any and all programs of reform, holding to the view that their mission was to save souls rather than rehabilitate society.

Under the circumstances this was a better stance, even if some idealists preferred to advocate social change. As the leading politicians and planters

[20] William Stanton, *The Leopard's Spots: Scientific Attitudes Toward Race in America, 1815–59* (Chicago, 1960); and Jenkins, *Pro-Slavery Thought*.

[21] S. A. Cartwright, "Diseases and Peculiarities of the Negro," in James D. B. De Bow, ed., *The Industrial Resources, etc., of the Southern and Western States* (3 vols., New Orleans and Washington, 1853–1856), II, 322.

[22] Quoted in Jenkins, *Pro-Slavery Thought,* 217–18.

[23] Joseph H. Fichter and George L. Maddox, "Religion in the South, Old and New," in McKinney and Thompson, eds., *The South in Continuity and Change,* 359–60.

would look with suspicion if not scorn on those who criticized things as they were, it was scarcely prudent to challenge them. Better still, it proved to be the better part of wisdom to speak out for the status quo. Thus, the leading clergymen not only rationalized slavery as an institution whose severity was mitigated by the influence of Christianity, but some of them defended it with incomparable zeal. Slavery was not a sin, they told its critics, for it conformed to the highest code known to man and was based on divine revelation.[24] Indeed, it was the abolitionists who were sinful, for they refused to recognize the explicit sanctions of slavery in the Scriptures.[25] In the course of the slave controversy the southern clergy did not fail to provide their political leaders with every conceivable moral and religious defense of the institution that they could possibly use.

Thus, southerners, believing that their social system was the best that had evolved, must have been immensely pleased by the actions of their religious leaders in breaking off from their northern brethren. By 1845, when southern Baptists followed the example of the Presbyterians and Methodists in setting up their own sectional denominations, slavery had become as much a part of the religious orthodoxy of the South as the Creation in the Book of Genesis or Armageddon in the Book of Revelations. The work of promoting and defending slavery, when entrusted to the southern clergy, could not have been in safer hands. It was left for James Henley Thornwell, the brilliant Presbyterian minister and philosopher, to put the matter succinctly when he said that slavery was "one of the conditions in which God is conducting the moral probation of man—a condition not incompatible with the highest moral freedom, the true glory of the race, and, therefore, not unfit for the moral and spiritual discipline which Christianity has instituted."[26]

By 1860 it was sheer folly to criticize the social order that the white southerners had developed. They had succeeded where others had failed; and they were unwilling to countenance any suggestion for change. They insisted that it was the North that needed to change. Yet, it was the North that was pressing for change in the South. With his characteristic sneer, George Fitzhugh observed that the "invention and use of the word Sociology in free society, and of the science of which it treats, and the absence of such word and science in slave society, shows that the former is afflicted with disease, the latter healthy."[27] The North's radical movements, such as communism, socialism, and anarchism, were a clear indica-

[24] A classic statement of the case is in Thorton Stringfellow, "The Bible Argument: or, Slavery in the Light of Divine Revelation," in E. N. Elliott, ed., *Cotton Is King, and Pro-Slavery Arguments* (Augusta, Ga., 1860), 459–521.

[25] *Ibid.,* 461, 496–97.

[26] Thornwell, *The Rights and the Duties of Masters* (Charleston, 1850), 43–44.

[27] Fitzhugh, *Sociology for the South, or the Failure of Free Society* (Richmond, 1854), 222.

tion of its failure. If slavery was more widely accepted, man would not need to resort "to the unnatural remedies of woman's rights, limited marriages, voluntary divorces, and free love, as proposed by the abolitionists."[28]

If the South was unwilling to make any significant concessions toward change during the antebellum years, it saw no reason why defeat at the hands of the North during a bloody Civil War should justify or provide any reason for change. To be sure, the slaves had been set free, the Confederacy had collapsed, and southern agrarianism had proved no match for the northern industrial juggernaut. But that was sheer might, which was not necessarily right. "They say *right* always triumphs," Emma LeConte wailed in 1865, "but what cause could have been more just than ours?"[29] Such southerners were not prepared to accept the changes that came in the wake of the Civil War.

Emma LeConte apparently spoke for many. While white southerners were compelled to recognize the most obvious results of the war, such as the end of the legalized institution of slavery, they were willing to make few concessions regarding the place of blacks in the social order or, indeed, the existence of a new social and political order. The attempts to nullify the effects of the Reconstruction amendments and the moves at the first opportunity—in 1865 and again at the time of the overthrow—are clear indications that they would resist change with all the resources at their command. The hue and cry over the importance of preserving the integrity of the South's political institutions was never so loud as when whites were vowing to keep blacks from holding office, regardless of ability, training, or experience. By the end of the century the virtually total disfranchisement of blacks indicated how successfully southern whites had resisted change.

That the postwar readjustments were essentially a realignment to prevent revolutionary or even significant change can be seen in the superficial adjustments that white southerners made to the "new order." They would accept the former slaves as free agricultural workers, but only on terms that made a mockery of freedom. Sharecropping and peonage made it possible for the leaders of the old order to subject masses of poor whites to a new form of degradation and to keep most Negroes in a state of involuntary servitude.[30] They would accept industrialization, but only on their own terms. This would assure them that the new industry would operate

[28] Fitzhugh, *Cannibals All! or, Slaves Without Masters* (Richmond, 1857), 97–99.
[29] LeConte, *When the World Ended: The Diary of Emma LeConte*, edited by Earl S. Miers (New York, 1957), 90.
[30] The convict lease system and peonage are among the forms of involuntary servitude discussed in C. Vann Woodward, *Origins of the New South, 1877–1913* ([Baton Rouge], 1951), 212–15; George B. Tindall, *The Emergence of the New South, 1913–1945* ([Baton Rouge], 1967), 212–13; and Stetson Kennedy, *Southern Exposure* (Garden City, N.Y., 1946), 48–77.

along lines that were strikingly similar to the plantation system. The new factories were largely if not exclusively for whites; and when blacks were employed, they would have their "place" on the lowest rung on the employment ladder, with no hope of climbing up. The Negro factory worker, who could not even approach the pay window to receive his inferior wage until all whites had been paid, knew that whites would stop at nothing in their determination to degrade him.[31]

We now know that the romantic picture of woman's role in the antebellum South was more imaginary than real. In the years following the war more southern white women everywhere openly played the role that many had covertly played before the war.[32] The census continued to describe them as "keeping home" while, in fact, they were managing farms and plantations, teaching in the local schools, working in factories, and entering numerous service occupations.[33] Meanwhile, their black counterparts shared the lot consigned to all former slaves, happily with some lessening in the exploitation of them as mistresses or concubines.

Regardless of race or color, the gallant men of the South did not greet the changing role of women with enthusiasm. Some regarded it as an affront to their own masculinity, while others were certain that it was an advance herald of the doom of their way of life. If women persisted in their quest for equality, they would undermine some of the most important foundations of civilization. Only men, said Georgia's Senator Joseph E. Brown, could deal with "the active and sterner duties of life," such as farming, road building, attending public assemblages, and voting.[34] Leave such matters as voting to men, and the future of society would be in safe hands. Furthermore, if white women gained the franchise, black women voters would follow in their wake, and such a calamity was too terrible to contemplate. Surely, this must have been in the minds of some of the women who themselves opposed their own enfranchisement.[35]

And during the antebellum years the southern churches had learned their role well, so well in fact that they continued to function as principal bulwarks against change in the postwar years. Southern clergymen remained vigorous and vocal proponents of the Confederate cause, while their "churches became centers of conservative political sentiment and of resistance both to the invasion of northern culture and to the doctrine of the New South."[36] They did much to insulate the South from social as well

[31] J. C. Wood to J. O. Wilson, secretary, American Colonization Society, February 9, 1903, American Colonization Society Records, Series I, Vol. 292 (Manuscript Division, Library of Congress, Washington, D. C.).

[32] Woodward, *Origins of the New South*, 226–27.

[33] Scott, *Southern Lady*, 106–33.

[34] *Congressional Record*, 49 Cong., 2 Sess., 980 (January 25, 1887).

[35] Scott, *Southern Lady*, 169–70.

[36] Fichter and Maddox, "Religion in the South," 360.

as religious change by opposing church unity, a liberal theology, and a new role for religious institutions in the social order.

Southern churches could differ, almost violently, over such matters as immersion as opposed to other forms of religious induction, but they were not in conflict over the prime role of the church in preparing its children of God for the next world. Not only should its members be content with the world as it was, but they should be aggressive defenders of the social order as God ordained it. "Organized religion in the South became," as Hodding Carter put it, "the mighty fortress of the *status quo* . . ."[37] It seems fruitless to argue that the churches merely reflected the views of their communicants or even that they shaped the views of their communicants. What is important is that the conflict between the position of the church on religious and social questions was indistinguishable from the position of other southern institutions. It stood against change as firmly as any other.

It was in the area of race relations that the South of the postwar years was more committed to stability—a euphemism for the status quo—than in any other area. And since the threat of change appeared to be greater, what with Radicals enfranchising the freedmen and enacting civil rights laws, the active, vehement resistance to change was greater. That is why southern whites became active in 1865 in defining the place of Negroes in southern life and continued to do so until the definition had extended to every conceivable aspect of life. The way to make absolutely certain that the status of blacks would not change was to institutionalize and legalize their subordinate and degraded place in southern life.

If the place of blacks was to be subordinate, whites argued, they must not be permitted to participate in the affairs of government. The move that began in 1865, only to be rather mildly interrupted for a few years during Reconstruction, was resumed in the 1870s and virtually completed by the end of the century.[38] If their place was to be degraded, whites reasoned, they must be separated on all means of transportation, in all places of public accommodation, in schools, churches, hospitals, orphanages, poorhouses, jails, penitentiaries, and cemeteries.[39] They were to receive no address of courtesy but were always to extend it to whites of any age or status. Their oath in the court was to be taken on a separate

[37] Carter, *Southern Legacy* (Baton Rouge, 1950), 30.

[38] William A. Mabry, *Studies in the Disfranchisement of the Negro in the South* (Durham, 1938); Vernon L. Wharton, *The Negro in Mississippi, 1865–1890* (Chapel Hill, 1947); and Paul Lewinson, *Race, Class, & Party* (London, New York, and other cities, 1932) are among the many works that deal with the new legal status of Negroes in the postwar years.

[39] John Hope Franklin, "History of Racial Segregation in the United States," American Academy of Political and Social Science, *Annals,* CCCIV (March 1956), 1–9; and Charles S. Johnson, *Patterns of Negro Segregation* (New York and London, 1943).

Bible, and they were never to challenge the claims or assertions of whites.[40] The enforcement of these laws and customs was the responsibility of all whites, who could resort to violence with impunity to prevent any breach whatsoever.

As the South entered the twentieth century it was as deeply committed to its social order as it had ever been; and it was as determined to resist change as it had been a half century earlier. But the resistance would be more difficult, for the forces of change were everywhere, and they seemed to be sweeping everything before them. If the forces were all powerful and all pervasive, then the South would perhaps be forced to adopt what Wilbur J. Cash called a "revolution in tactics," without yielding significant ground on important matters.[41] It would thus be in a position to force the new dispensation to accommodate itself to the South's social order, rather than the other way around.

When progressivism called for a greater role for government in the regulation of many aspects of life, the South's leaders responded with their own special brand of progressivism. Indeed they took the initiative in the promotion of direct primary elections, but they made certain that the increased democracy would be for whites only.[42] The great movement to extend education swept over most of the South, but the widespread practice of discriminating against Negroes in the expenditure of public funds detracted from the movement as a truly progressive one.[43] In more than one state the reform movement was carried forward on a wave of race-baiting and race-hating, with the clear understanding that the benefits of reform, whether they were political or economic, would not breach the line that separated the races.

One of the most effective obstacles to the success of women's suffrage was the specter of race. There were, of course, the expected arguments in 1917 and 1918 that the proposed constitutional amendment permitting women to vote was "against the civilization of the South."[44] And there were some courageous southern suffragettes who *demanded* the vote. But by 1917 no leading southern member of the House of Representatives and no southern member of the Senate had declared for women's suffrage.

[40] Bertram W. Doyle, *The Etiquette of Race Relations in the South: A Study in Social Control* (Chicago, 1937).

[41] Cash, *The Mind of the South* (New York, 1941), 183.

[42] Woodward, *Origins of the New South*, 372–73.

[43] Louis R. Harlan, *Separate and Unequal: Public School Campaigns and Racism in the Southern Seaboard States, 1901–1915* (Chapel Hill, 1958), 248–69.

[44] See the communication from Caroline Patterson, president of the Georgia Association Opposed to Woman Suffrage, to Frank Clark, January 4, 1918, U. S. Congress, House of Representatives, Committee on Woman Suffrage, 65 Cong., 2 Sess., *Extending the Right of Suffrage to Women: Hearings on H. J. Res. 200, Jan. 3–7, 1918* (Washington, 1918), 327.

There persisted the argument, developed in the previous century, that the suffrage amendment would open the door to voting by Negro women and, perhaps, even Negro men. "Remember that *woman suffrage*," one southerner cried, "means a reopening of the entire *negro suffrage* question, loss of State rights, and another period of reconstruction horrors, which will introduce a set of female carpetbaggers as bad as their male prototypes of the sixties."[45] Indeed, the connection in the minds of many southerners between race and women's suffrage was so strong that the suffragists themselves devoted much attention to the task of dispelling the connection. They did so by assuring southern whites that if they enfranchised women they could continue to disfranchise blacks![46]

Despite fierce opposition by many southerners, including some women, to the changing role of women, the march toward freeing southern women from some of the trammels of the nineteenth century seemed inexorable. In time they would sit in a few seats of power such as the governor's chair in Texas, in one Arkansas seat in the United States Senate, and on the North Carolina Supreme Court. Some of them would reject the tired and largely false claim that blacks had been lynched to protect their virtue and would call for civilized conduct to replace the barbarism of the rope and faggot.[47] But as the status of southern women improved, there remained the lag between blacks and whites of the so-called weaker sex; and few raised their voices in the effort to close the gap in wages, in educational opportunities, and in the general esteem of southern chivalry.

The secularization of life in general tended to undermine the effectiveness of southern organized religion and to challenge age-old orthodoxies and fundamentalist doctrines. It would be incorrect, however, to assume that the conservative character of southern religion disappeared altogether or that southern churches were easily adjusting to social and economic change. All too often Protestant churches in the South became centers of refuge for the most conservative social and political forces and, as in earlier years, led the resistance to change.[48]

Nowhere was the resistance to change more pronounced than in the opposition of southern religious groups to theories that challenged the literal interpretation of the Holy Scriptures. They vigorously opposed the

[45] Quoted in A. Elizabeth Taylor, *The Woman Suffrage Movement in Tennessee* (New York, 1957), 112.

[46] Elizabeth C. Stanton *et al.,* eds., *History of Woman Suffrage* (6 vols., New York and other cities, 1881–1922), V, 463.

[47] Wilma Dykeman and James Stokely, *Seeds of Southern Change: The Life of Will Alexander* (Chicago, 1962), 143–52.

[48] The conservative character of southern churches is discussed in Kenneth K. Bailey, *Southern White Protestantism in the Twentieth Century* (New York, Evanston, and London, 1964), 1–24. For a discussion of the southern churches and race see David M. Reimers, *White Protestantism and the Negro* (New York, 1965), 25–50.

teaching of what they called atheism, agnosticism, and Darwinism.[49] In Texas Governor Miriam A. Ferguson, in denouncing Darwinism, said that she would not let "that kind of rot go into Texas text-books."[50] In Tennessee a young high school teacher was found guilty of teaching evolution and was saved from punishment only by a technicality. In several states in the 1920s the Bible Crusaders put up a vigorous, if unsuccessful, fight to eliminate Darwinism from the public schools.[51] In all these efforts southern religious groups manifested a fierce and fearsome hostility to change.

In the antebellum years the fight for the freedom of the slaves was spearheaded by northern white abolitionists, although both slaves and free Negroes did much more for freedom than has generally been conceded.[52] In the post-Reconstruction years the fight for racial equality and human dignity was waged largely by blacks, with only an infrequent assist by whites. In the twentieth century the struggle to destroy every vestige of racial distinction passed through several stages, with whites—largely in the North—giving greater assistance on some occasions than on others.

In their struggle for complete equality blacks, whether in the South or in the North, could be fairly certain to receive northern white assistance in matters of transportation, voting, education in general, and in the enjoyment of places of public accommodation. They could not be nearly as certain of such support in matters of employment, housing, security in their persons, and equal education in the urban ghetto. In that sense the resistance to significant change in race relations could be as vigorous in the North as in the South.[53]

But if northern whites could react crudely and even violently to the pressures of the new masses of blacks in the urban ghettoes, they were merely catching up with a problem that southerners had faced for centuries. They were less prepared to meet it, for although they had always consigned Negroes to an inferior place in their society, they had been smug in their satisfaction that the numbers were insignificant and the "problem" correspondingly minor.[54] They had much to learn, and they became apt,

[49] Tindall, *Emergence of the New South,* 204.

[50] Quoted in Maynard Shipley, *The War on Modern Science: A Short History of the Fundamentalist Attacks on Evolution and Modernism* (New York and London, 1927), 174.

[51] The fight is summarized in Bailey, *Southern White Protestantism,* 72–91.

[52] Benjamin Quarles, *Black Abolitionists* (London, Oxford, and New York, 1969).

[53] Gilbert Osofsky, *Harlem: The Making of a Ghetto: Negro New York, 1890–1930* (New York, 1966) and Allan H. Spear, *Black Chicago: The Making of a Negro Ghetto, 1890–1920* (Chicago and London, 1967) deal with white resistance to change in two northern cities.

[54] Gilbert Osofsky, "The Enduring Ghetto," *Journal of American History,* LV (September 1968), 243–55.

even eager students of the southern method of dealing with the problem of race.

Even as Negroes left the South in increasing numbers between 1910 and 1950 white southerners discovered that the nationalizing of the race problem did not relieve them of having to confront the significantly changing status of those blacks who remained. Negroes wanted better jobs and equal pay. They wanted to vote and hold office. They wanted to desegregate public transportation and the schools. They wanted to eradicate every vestige of second-class citizenship, and they insisted that there could be no compromise with the high principles that were the birthright of *all* Americans.[55]

For white southerners this was the most serious challenge to their social order since the Civil War. They had always conceived of their "perfect society" in terms of the subordination of Negroes. Now that it was once again challenged, they would respond characteristically by that remarkable combination of praising things as they were and resisting the change that they abhorred. The South had devoted centuries to building its civilization, they insisted. Except for a few malcontents and those exposed to outside subversive influences, Negroes in the South were not only better off than elsewhere but were happy with their condition. "Go down South where I live," John E. Rankin told the House of Representatives in 1948. That is "where more Negroes are employed than anywhere else in the country, where they enjoy more happiness, more peace, more prosperity, more security and protection than they ever enjoyed in all history."[56]

But change was taking place so rapidly that there was scarcely time to celebrate the old order. Two world wars and a New Deal had facilitated the South's industrial revolution. Government, federal and state, had introduced social controls and social programs that poverty and privation forced the South to accept. The successful drive of southern women to liberate themselves from their long entrapment was greatly accelerated by changes and reforms in the political and economic spheres. Even religious institutions felt the winds of change and responded with various forms of accommodation. And in all these changes white southerners asked the age-old question, "How will it affect the blacks?" It was an affirmation of V. O. Key's assertion that "Whatever phase of the southern . . . process one seeks to understand, sooner or later the trail of inquiry leads to the Negro."[57]

Not only were these numerous developments affecting the blacks in a

[55] Rayford W. Logan, ed., *What the Negro Wants* (Chapel Hill, 1944). See also the "Publisher's Introduction" by W. T. Couch, in which he expressed disagreement with most of the contributors to the volume.

[56] *Cong. Record*, 80 Cong., 2 Sess., 4543 (April 15, 1948).

[57] V. O. Key, Jr., *Southern Politics in State and Nation* (New York, 1949), 5.

dozen different ways, but specific developments in the area of race relations overshadowed other disquieting events. Some southern white leaders observed what was happening on the racial front in utter disbelief, while others regarded it as their greatest challenge that must be confronted and combated. In the process some of their responses were as graceless as they were reprehensible.

When President Harry S. Truman issued executive orders and recommended legislation to protect Negroes in their enjoyment of civil rights, Senator Richard B. Russell, Jr., of Georgia condemned the moves as steering this country toward a "police state" and threatened to introduce legislation looking toward the removal of blacks from the South.[58] In 1947 a federal district court judge, J. Waties Waring, ruled that the Democratic primary of South Carolina could not exclude Negroes from participating in its elections. Immediately, a South Carolina member of the House of Representatives, W. J. Bryan Dorn, wailed that it opened the way for Communists to vote in the Democratic primary.[59] Another representative from South Carolina, L. Mendel Rivers, predicted that the decision would cause bloodshed, and he seriously considered the possibility of instituting impeachment proceedings against Judge Waring.[60] The return of Harry Truman to the White House in 1948 and the refusal of the United States Supreme Court to review the Waring decision effectively subdued the confrontation that Russell and Rivers and company sought to bring about.

White southerners all across the region attempted to meet the changes that blacks sought in the field of education by launching a massive program to equalize the facilities and programs in white and Negro schools. If they approached success in this ploy, it was effectively undermined by the Supreme Court decision in 1954 that declared legally segregated schools unconstitutional. The South's response was varied, but the major response was rejection of the law of the land. Its leading members of the United States Congress—more than one hundred of them—signed a manifesto that praised the "separate but equal" decision of 1896 as "founded on elemental humanity and commonsense" and condemned the 1954 decision as an "unwarranted exercise of power by the Court" that "planted hatred and suspicion where there has been heretofore friendship and understanding."[61]

The signatories of this "Declaration of Constitutional Principles" were

[58] Atlanta *Constitution,* July 27, 1948; Charleston *News and Courier,* July 28, 1948.

[59] *Cong. Record,* 80 Cong., 2 Sess., Appendix, 4654–55 (July 27, 1948).

[60] Charleston *News and Courier,* August 5, 6, 1948.

[61] *Cong. Record,* 84 Cong., 2 Sess., 4515–16 (March 12, 1956).

among the South's most respected and influential leaders. In declaring that they would "use all lawful means to bring about a reversal" of the decision, they vowed to "refrain from disorders and lawless acts." But Senator Harry F. Byrd, Sr., was already developing a plan of "massive resistance" that in due course would compromise the principles of law and order to which he and his colleagues claimed to be committed.[62]

While it is not possible to assess the impact of the southern manifesto on subsequent developments, there can be no gainsaying that it set the stage and tone for the resistance that followed during the next decade or so. The search for alternatives to desegregated schools led to a veritable spate of maneuvers ranging from pupil placement to the closing of some public schools and the establishment of private all-white schools. The path of massive resistance led to the establishment of white citizens' councils and violent confrontations with blacks who had resorted to various forms of protest and demonstration against noncompliance with the decisions in their communities.

It is not the interracial confrontations, important and tragic as they were, that are of prime significance in this discussion. It is the South's confrontation with change, its response in defending what it regarded as a perfect society, that is instructive. The massive resistance, the fire hoses, police dogs, and the electronic cattle prods were, in a real sense, a desperate but futile confrontation with the inexorable forces of change. It all added up to the hopeless defense of a position that, in terms of the nation's laws and its expressed social philosophy, was illogical and indefensible.

The futility of this defense lay in the failure to take into account the myths and fallacies that were the basis of the white South's conception of its perfect society. It failed to recognize the inherent inconsistencies and contradictions in its argument that it could enjoy a social order that was founded on the exploitation of a group that was an integral part of that social order. It failed to see that in arrogating to a few the privileges and rights that belonged to the many, it was depriving itself of the resources that could do so much to create the social order that had, for so long, proved elusive. Its inflexibility had resulted in driving out much of its best talents, white as well as black, that could not flourish or even survive where confrontation with change meant unreasoned and unreasonable resistance to free expression and experimentation. It had also resulted in the development of techniques to defy and circumvent both law and custom. Its obsession was to maintain a government, an economy, an arrangement of the sexes, a relationship of the races, and a social system that had never existed,

---

[62] J. Harvie Wilkinson III, *Harry Byrd and the Changing Face of Virginia Politics, 1945–1966* (Charlottesville, 1968), 113–54.

as Paul M. Gaston has suggested, except in the fertile imagination of those who would not confront either the reality that existed or the change that would bring them closer to reality.[63]

One would hope that a region whose experience and talents had proved to be so ample in so many ways—in the creative arts, in certain aspects of the science of government, and in the capacity to transform so many phases of its economic order—might yet be able to confront fundamental changes in its social order. For only by such confrontation, tempered by a healthy recognition of the importance of change, can the South expect to survive as a viable and effective unit in the body politic and to point the way toward the ordering of a truly vital social organism where men and women, black and white, can live together in their common search for a better society.

[68] Gaston, *The New South Creed: A Study in Southern Mythmaking* (New York, 1970).

8

The Search for Southern Identity

C. Vann Woodward

Not unrelated to the quest for a central theme in southern history
is the search for southern identity. With regard to the problem of
identity, however, the American South has proven itself ambivalent
—it has sought a distinct regional identification and the label of
the "most American" of regions. Arguments supporting both positions have been drawn in terms of geography, race, climate, economics, and culture. C. Vann Woodward, one of the great special-
ists on the history of the South, here analyzes the South's "identity
crisis" in terms of a regional heritage at variance with the myths
of nationalism. A deft handling of "mythology" in both its regional
and national manifestations allows Professor Woodward to draw
attention to one of the grandest ironies of the collective southern
experience. Juxtaposed against the American legends of success,
victory, and innocence, Woodward contends the South's history has
rather provided the region with the "un-American" fate of poverty,
defeat, and guilt. Ironically, and in the end, the South would appear
to be unique precisely because it *is* part of America. The South's
unique and clearly identifiable qualities draw their significance only
in terms of the American experience.

The time is coming, if indeed it has not already arrived, when the Southerner will begin to ask himself whether there is really any longer very much
point in calling himself a Southerner. Or if he does, he might well wonder
occasionally whether it is worth while insisting on the point. So long as

"The Search for Southern Identity" from *The Burden of Southern History*, by C.
Vann Woodward. Baton Rouge: Louisiana State University Press, 1960. Reprinted
by permission of the publisher.

he remains at home where everybody knows him the matter hardly becomes an issue. But when he ventures among strangers, particularly up North, how often does he yield to the impulse to suppress the identifying idiom, to avoid the awkward subject, and to blend inconspicuously into the national pattern—to act the role of the standard American? Has the Southern heritage become an old hunting jacket that one slips on comfortably while at home but discards when he ventures abroad in favor of some more conventional or modish garb? Or is it perhaps an attic full of ancestral wardrobes useful only in connection with costume balls and play acting—staged primarily in Washington, D.C.?

Asking himself some similar questions about the New England heritage, Professor George W. Pierson of Yale has come forth with some disturbing concessions about the integrity of his own region. Instead of an old hunting jacket, he suggests that we call New England "an old kitchen floor, now spatter-painted with many colors." He points out that roughly six out of every ten Connecticut "Yankees" are either foreign-born or born of foreign or mixed parentage, while only three have native forebears going as far back as two generations, and they are not necessarily New England forebears at that. "Like it or not," writes Pierson, "and no matter how you measure it—geographically, economically, radically or religiously, there is no New England Region today." It has become instead, he says, "an optical illusion and a land of violent contrast and change." And yet in spite of the wholesale and damaging concessions of his essay, which he calls "A Study in Denudation," he concludes that, "as a region of the heart and mind, New England is still very much alive."

One wonders if the Southerner, for his part, can make as many damaging admissions of social change and cultural erosion as our New England friend has made and come out with as firm a conclusion about the vitality of his own regional heritage. More doubt than assurance probably comes to mind at first. The South is still in the midst of an economic and social revolution that has by no means run its course, and it will not be possible to measure its results for a long time to come. This revolution has already leveled many of the old monuments of regional distinctiveness and may end eventually by erasing the very consciousness of a distinctive tradition along with the will to sustain it. The sustaining will and consciousness are also under the additional strain of a moral indictment against a discredited part of the tradition, an indictment more uncompromising than any since abolitionist times.

The Southerner may not have been very happy about many of those old monuments of regional distinctiveness that are now disappearing. He may, in fact, have deplored the existence of some—the one-horse farmer, one-crop agriculture, one-party politics, the sharecropper, the poll tax, the white primary, the Jim Crow car, the lynching bee. It would take a blind

sentimentalist to mourn their passing. But until the day before yesterday
there they stood, indisputable proof that the South was different. Now that
they are vanished or on their way toward vanishing, we are suddenly aware
of the vacant place they have left in the landscape and of our habit of
depending upon them in final resort as landmarks of regional identification.
To establish identity by reference to our faults was always simplest, for
whatever their reservations about our virtues, our critics were never reluctant to concede us our vices and shortcomings.

It is not that the present South has any conspicuous lack of faults, but
that its faults are growing less conspicuous and therefore less useful for
purposes of regional identification. They are increasingly the faults of other
parts of the country, standard American faults, shall we say. Many of
them have only recently been acquired—could, in fact, only recently be
afforded. For the great changes that are altering the cultural landscape of
the South almost beyond recognition are not simply negative changes, the
disappearance of the familiar. There are also positive changes, the appearance of the strikingly new.

The symbol of innovation is inescapable. The roar and groan and dust
of it greet one on the outskirts of every Southern city. That symbol is the
bulldozer, and for lack of a better name this might be called the Bulldozer
Revolution. The great machine with the lowered blade symbolizes the
revolution in several respects: in its favorite area of operation, the area
where city meets country; in its relentless speed; in its supreme disregard
for obstacles, its heedless methods; in what it demolishes and in what it
builds. It is the advance agent of the metropolis. It encroaches upon rural
life to expand urban life. It demolishes the old to make way for the new.

It is not the amount of change that is impressive about the Bulldozer
Revolution so much as the speed and concentration with which it has
come and with which it continues. In the decade of the forties, when
urbanization was growing at a swift pace on the country as a whole, the
cities of the South's fifty-three metropolitan areas grew more than three
times as fast as comparable cities in the rest of the country, at a rate of
33.1 percent as compared with 10.3 percent elsewhere. For every three city
dwellers in the South at the beginning of that decade there were four at
the end, and for every five farm residents there were only four. An over-
whelmingly rural South in 1930 had 5.5 millions employed in agriculture;
by 1950, only 3.2 millions. A considerable proportion of these Southerners
were moving directly from country to suburb, following the path of the
bulldozer to "rurbanization" and skipping the phase of urbanization entirely. Rural Negroes, the most mobile of all Southerners, were more likely
to move into the heart of the urban areas abandoned by the suburban
dwellers. In the single decade of the forties the South lost a third of its
rural-farm Negro population. If the same trend were continued through

the present decade, it would reduce that part of the colored population to about one-fifth of the Negroes living in the region.

According to nearly all of the indices, so the economists find, economic growth of the South in recent years greatly exceeds the rate maintained in the North and East. The fact is the South is going through economic expansion and reorganization that the North and East completed a generation or more ago. But the process is taking place far more rapidly than it did in the North. Among all the many periods of change in the history of the South it is impossible to find one of such concentration and such substantive impact. The period of Reconstruction might appear a likely rival for this distinction, but that revolution was largely limited to changes in legal status and the ownership of property. The people remained pretty much where they were and continued to make their living in much the same way. All indications are that the bulldozer will leave a deeper mark upon the land than did the carpetbagger.

It is the conclusion of two Southern sociologists, John M. Maclachlan and Joe S. Floyd, Jr., that the present drive toward uniformity "with national demographic, economic, and cultural norms might well hasten the day when the South, once perhaps the most distinctively 'different' American region, will have become in most such matters virtually indistinguishable from the other urban-industrial areas of the nation."

The threat of becoming "indistinguishable," of being submerged under a national steamroller, has haunted the mind of the South for a long time. Some have seen it as a menace to regional identity and the survival of a Southern heritage. Premonitions of the present revolution appeared during the industrial boom that followed the First World War. Toward the end of the twenties two distinctive attempts were made by Southerners to dig in and define a perimeter of defense against further encroachment.

One of these entrenchments was that of the twelve Southerners who wrote *I'll Take My Stand*. They sought to define what they called "a Southern way of life against what may be called the American or prevailing way," and they agreed "that the best terms in which to represent the distinction are contained in the phrase, Agrarian *versus* Industrial." Agrarianism and its values were the essence of the Southern tradition and the test of Southern loyalty. Their credo held that "the whole way in which we live, act, think, and feel," the humanist culture, "was rooted in the agrarian way of life of the older South." They called for "anti-industrial measures" which "might promise to stop the advances of industrialism, or even undo some of them."

Even in 1930 the agrarians were prepared to admit "the melancholy fact that the South itself has wavered a little and shown signs of wanting to join up behind the common or American industrial ideal." They admonished waverers among the younger generation that the brave new South they contemplated would "be only an undistinguished replica of the usual industrial community."

Three decades later the slight "wavering" in the Southern ranks that disturbed the agrarians in 1930 would seem to have become a pell-mell rout. Defections came by the battalion. Whole regiments and armies deserted "to join up behind the common or American industrial ideal." In its pursuit of the American Way and the American Standard of Living the South was apparently doing all in its power to become what the agrarians had deplored as "only an undistinguished replica of the usual industrial community." The voice of the South in the 1950's had become the voice of the chamber of commerce, and Southerners appeared to be about as much absorbed in the acquirement of creature comforts and adult playthings as any other Americans. The twelve Southerners who took their stand in 1930 on the proposition that the Southern way stands or falls with the agrarian way would seem to have been championing a second lost cause. If they were right, then our questions would have already been answered, for the Southerner as a distinctive species of American would have been doomed, his tradition bereft of root and soil. The agrarian way contains no promise of continuity and endurance for the Southern tradition.

Two years before the agrarian pronouncement appeared, another attempt was made to define the essence of the Southern tradition and prescribe the test of Southern loyalty. The author of this effort was the distinguished historian, Professor Ulrich B. Phillips. His definition had no reference to economic institutions but was confined to a preoccupation with race consciousness. The essential theme of continuity and unity in the Southern heritage, wrote Professor Phillips, was "a common resolve indomitably maintained" that the South "shall be and remain a white man's country." This indomitable conviction could be "expressed with the frenzy of a demagogue or maintained with a patrician's quietude," but it was and had been from the beginning "the cardinal test of a Southerner and the central theme of southern history."

Professor Phillips' criterion of Southernism has proved somewhat more durable and widespread in appeal than that of the agrarians. It is not tied so firmly to an ephemeral economic order as was theirs. Nor does it demand—of the dominant whites, at least—any Spartan rejection of the flesh pots of the American living standard. Its adherents are able to enjoy the blessings of economic change and remain traditionalists at the same time. There are still other advantages in the Phillipsian doctrine. The traditionalist who has watched the Bulldozer Revolution plow under cherished old values of individualism, localism, family, clan, and rural folk culture has felt helpless and frustrated against the mighty and imponderable agents of change. Industrialism, urbanism, unionism, and big government conferred or promised too many coveted benefits. They divided the people and won support in the South, so that it was impossible to rally unified opposition to them.

The race issue was different. Advocates and agents of change could be denounced as outsiders, intruders, meddlers. Historic memories of resistance and cherished constitutional principles could be invoked. Radical prejudices, aggressions, and jealousies could be stirred to rally massive popular support. And with this dearly bought unity, which he could not rally on other issues, the frustrated traditionalist might at last take his stand for the defense of all the defiled, traduced, and neglected values of the traditional order. What then is the prospect of the Phillipsian "cardinal test" as a bulwark against change? Will it hold fast where other defenses have failed?

Recent history furnishes some of the answers. Since the last World War old racial attitudes that appeared more venerable and immovable than any other have exhibited a flexibility that no one would have predicted. One by one, in astonishingly rapid succession, many landmarks of racial discrimination and segregation have disappeared, and old barriers have been breached. Many remain, of course—perhaps more than have been breached —and distinctively Southern racial attitudes will linger for a long time. Increasingly the South is aware of its isolation in these attitudes, however, and is in defense of the institutions that embody them. They have fallen rapidly into discredit and under condemnation from the rest of the country and the rest of the world.

Once more the South finds itself with a morally discredited Peculiar Institution on its hands. The last time this happened, about a century ago, the South's defensive reaction was to identify its whole cause with the one institution that was most vulnerable and to make loyalty to an ephemeral aspect which it had once led in condemning the cardinal test of loyalty to the whole tradition. Southerners who rejected the test were therefore forced to reject the whole heritage. In many cases, if they were vocal in their rejection, they were compelled to leave the South entirely and return only at their peril. Unity was thus temporarily achieved, but with the collapse of the Peculiar Institution the whole tradition was jeopardized and discredited for having been so completely identified with the part abandoned.

Historical experience with the first Peculiar Institution ought to discourage comparable experiments with the second. If Southernism is allowed to become identified with a last ditch defense of segregation, it will increasingly lose its appeal among the younger generation. Many will be tempted to reject their entire regional identification, even the name "Southern," in order to dissociate themselves from the one discredited aspect. If agrarianism has proved to be a second lost cause, segregation is a likely prospect for a third.

With the crumbling of so many defenses in the present, the South has tended to substitute myths about the past. Every self-conscious group of any size fabricates myths about its past: about its origins, its mission, its righteousness, its benevolence, its general superiority. But few groups in the New World have had their myths subjected to such destructive analysis as those of the South have undergone in recent years. While some Southern historians have contributed to the mythmaking, others have been among the leading iconoclasts, and their attacks have spared few of the South's cherished myths.

The Cavalier Legend as the myth of origin was one of the earlier victims. The Plantation Legend of ante bellum grace and elegance has not been left wholly intact. The pleasant image of a benevolent and paternalistic slavery system as a school for civilizing savages has suffered damage that is probably beyond repair. Even the consoling security of Reconstruction as the common historic grievance, the infallible mystique of unity, has been rendered somewhat less secure by detached investigation. And finally, rude hands have been laid upon the hallowed memory of the Redeemers who did in the Carpetbaggers, and doubt has been cast upon the antiquity of segregation folkways. These faded historical myths have become weak material for buttressing Southern defenses, for time has dealt as roughly with them as with agrarianism and racism.

Would a hard-won immunity from the myths and illusions of Southern sectionalism provide some immunity to the illusions and myths of American nationalism? Or would the hasty divestment merely make the myth-denuded Southerner hasten to wrap himself in the garments of nationalism? The danger in the wholesale rejection of the South by the modern Southerner bent on reaffirming his Americanism is the danger of affirming more than he bargains for.

While the myths of Southern distinctiveness have been waning, national myths have been waxing in power and appeal. National myths, American myths have proved far more sacrosanct and inviolate than Southern myths. Millions of European immigrants of diverse cultural backgrounds have sought and found identity in them. The powerful urge among minority groups to abandon or disguise their distinguishing cultural traits and conform as quickly as possible to some national norm is one of the most familiar features in the sociology of American nationalism. European ethnic and national groups with traditions far more ancient and distinctive than those of the South have eagerly divested themselves of their cultural heritage in order to conform.

The conformist is not required nor expected to abandon his distinctive religion. But whether he remains a Protestant, a Catholic, or a Jew, his religion typically becomes subordinate or secondary to a national faith. Foreign observers have remarked that the different religions in America resemble each other more than they do their European counterparts. "By every realistic criterion," writes Will Herberg in his study of American religious sociology, "the American Way of Life is the operative faith of the American people." And where the mandates of the American Way of Life conflict with others, they take undisputed sway over the masses of all religions. Herberg describes it as "a faith that has its symbols and its rituals, its holidays and its liturgy, its saints and its sancta," and it is common to all Americans. "Sociologically, anthropologically, if one pleases," he writes, the American Way of Life "is the characteristic American religion, undergirding American life and overarching American society despite all indubitable differences of region, section, culture, and class." Differences such as those of region and section, "indubitable" though he admits them to be, he characterizes as "peripheral and obsolescent."

If the American Way of Life has become a religion, any deviation from it has become a sort of heresy. Regionalism in the typical American view is rather like the Turnerian frontier, a section on the move—or at least one that should keep moving, following a course that converges at not too remote a point with the American Way. It is a season's halt of the American caravan, a temporary encampment of an advancing society, eternally on the move toward some undefined goal of progress. If the encampment of regionalism threatens to entrench or dig in for a permanent stand, it comes to be regarded as "peripheral and obsolescent," an institutionalized social lag.

The same urge to conformity that operates upon ethnic or national minorities to persuade them to reject identification with their native heritage or that of their forebears operates to a degree upon the Southerner as well. Since the cultural landscape of his native region is being altered almost beyond recognition by a cyclone of social change, the Southerner may come to feel as uprooted as the immigrant. Bereft of his myths, his peculiar institutions, even his familiar regional vices, he may well reject or forget his regional identification as completely as the immigrant.

Is there nothing about the South that is immune from the disintegrating effect of nationalism and the pressure for conformity? Is there not something that has not changed? There is only one thing that I can think of, and that is its history. By that I do not mean a Southern brand of Shintoism, the worship of ancestors. Nor do I mean written history and its interpretation, popular and mythical, or professional and scholarly, which have changed often and will change again. I mean rather the collective experience of the Southern people. It is in just this respect that the South remains the most distinctive region of the country. In their unique historic experience as Americans the Southerners should not only be able to find the basis for continuity of their heritage but also make contributions that balance and complement the experience of the rest of the nation.

At this point the risks of our enterprise multiply. They are the risks of spawning new myths in place of the old. Awareness of them demands that we redouble precautions and look more cautiously than ever at generalizations.

To start with a safe one, it can be assumed that one of the most conspicuous traits of American life has been its economic abundance. From early colonial days the fabulous riches of America have been compared with the scarcity and want of less favored lands. Immense differentials in economic welfare and living standards between the United States and other countries still prevail. In an illuminating book called *People of Plenty,* David Potter persuasively advances the thesis that the most distinguishing traits of national character have been fundamentally shaped by the abundance of the American living standard. He marshals evidence of the effect that plenty has had upon such decisive phases of life as the nursing and training of babies, opportunities for education and jobs, ages of marriage and childbearing. He shows how abundance has determined characteristic national attitudes between parents and children, husband and wife, superior and subordinate, between one class and another, and how it has molded our mass culture and our consumer oriented society. American national character would indeed appear inconceivable without this unique experience of abundance.

The South at times has shared this national experience and, in very recent years, has enjoyed more than a taste of it. But the history of the South includes a long and quite un-American experience with poverty. So recently as 1938, in fact, the South was characterized by the President as "The Nation's Economic Problem No. 1." And the problem was poverty, not plenty. It was a poverty emphasized by wide regional discrepancies in living standard, per capita wealth, per capita income, and the good things that money buys, such as education, health, protection, and the many luxuries that go to make up the celebrated American Standard of Living. This striking differential was no temporary misfortune of the great depression but a continuous and conspicuous feature of Southern experience since the early years of the Civil War. During the last half of the nineteenth and the first half of the twentieth centuries, when technology was multiplying American abundance with unprecedented rapidity, the South lagged far behind. In 1880 the per capita wealth of the South, based on estimated true valuation of property, was $376 as compared with $1,186 per cápita in the states outside the South. In the same year the per capita wealth of the South was 27 percent of that of the Northeastern states. That was just about the same ratio contemporaneously existing between the per capita wealth of Russia and that of Germany.

Generations of scarcity and want constitute one of the distinctive historical experiences of the Southern people, an experience too deeply embedded in their memory to be wiped out by a business boom and too deep not to admit of some uneasiness at being characterized historically as a "People of Plenty." That they should have been for so long a time a "People of Poverty" in a land of plenty is one mark of enduring cultural distinctiveness. In a nation known around the world for the hedonistic ethic of the American Standard of Living, the Southern heritage of scarcity remains distinctive.

A closely related corollary of the uniquely American experience of abundance is the equally unique American experience of success. During the Second World War Professor Arthur M. Schlesinger made an interesting attempt to define the national character, which he brought to a close with the conclusion that the American character "is bottomed upon the profound conviction that nothing in the world is beyond its power to accomplish." In this he gave expression to one of the great American legends, the legend of success and invincibility. It is a legend with a foundation in fact, for much can be adduced from the American record to support it and explain why it has flourished. If the history of the United States is lacking in some of the elements of variety and contrast demanded of any good story, it is in part because of the very monotonous repetition of successes. Almost every major collective effort, even those thwarted temporarily, succeeded in the end. American history *is* a success story. Why should such a nation not have a "profound conviction that nothing in the world is beyond its power to accomplish"? Even the hazards of war—including the prospect of war against an unknown enemy with untried weapons—proves no exception to the rule. The advanced science and weaponry of the Russian challenger are too recent to have registered their impact on the legend. The American people have never known the chastening experience of being on the losing side of a war. They have, until very recently, solved every major problem they have confronted—or had it solved for them by a smiling fortune. Success and victory are still national habits of mind.

This is but one among several American legends in which the South can participate only vicariously or in part. Again the Southern heritage is distinctive. For Southern history, unlike American, includes large components of frustration, failure, and defeat. It includes not only an overwhelming military defeat but long decades of defeat in the provinces of economic, social, and political life. Such a heritage affords the Southern people no basis for the delusion that there is nothing whatever that is beyond their power to accomplish. They have had it forcibly and repeatedly borne in upon them that this is not the case. Since their experience in this respect is more common among the general run of mankind than that of their fellow Americans, it would seem to be a part of their heritage worth cherishing.

American opulence and American success have combined to foster and encourage another legend of early origin, the legend of American innocence. According to this legend Americans achieved a sort of regeneration of sinful man by coming out of the wicked Old World and removing to an untarnished new one. By doing so they shook off the wretched evils of feudalism and broke free from tyranny, monarchism, aristocracy, and privilege—all those institutions which, in the hopeful philosophy of the Enlightenment, accounted for all, or nearly all, the evil in the world. The absence of these Old World ills in America, as well as the freedom from much of the injustice and oppression associated with them, encouraged a singular moral complacency in the American mind. The self-image implanted in Americans was one of innocence as compared with less fortunate people of the Old World. They were a chosen people and their land a Utopia on the make. Alexis de Tocqueville's patience was tried by this complacency of the American. "If I applaud the freedom which its inhabitants enjoy, he answers, 'Freedom is a fine thing, but few nations are worthy to enjoy it.' If I remark on the purity of morals which distinguishes the United States," complained Tocqueville, " 'I can imagine,' says he, 'that a stranger, who has been struck by corruption of all other nations, is astonished at the difference.' "

How much room was there in the tortured conscience of the South for this national self-image of innocence and moral complacency? Southerners have repeated the American rhetoric of self admiration and sung the perfection of American institutions ever since the Declaration of Independence. But for half that time they lived intimately with a great social evil and the other half with its aftermath. It was an evil that was even condemned and abandoned by the Old World, to which America's moral superiority was supposedly an article of faith. Much of the South's intellectual energy went into a desperate effort to convince the world that its peculiar evil was actually a "positive good," but it failed even to convince itself. It writhed in the torments of its own conscience until it plunged into catastrophe to escape. The South's preoccupation was with guilt, not with innocence, with the reality of evil, not with the dream of perfection. Its experience in this respect, as in several others, was on the whole a thoroughly un-American one.

An age-long experience with human bondage and its evils and later with emancipation and its shortcomings did not dispose the South very favorably toward such popular American ideas as the doctrine of human perfectibility, the belief that every evil has a cure, and the notion that every human problem has a solution. For these reasons the utopian schemes and the gospel of progress that flourished above the Mason and Dixon Line never found very wide acceptance below the Potomac during the nineteenth century. In that most optimistic of centuries in the most optimistic part of the world, the South remained basically pessimistic in its social outlook and its moral philosophy. The experience of evil and the experience of tragedy are parts of the Southern heritage that are as difficult to reconcile with the American legend of innocence and social felicity as the experience of poverty and defeat are to reconcile with the legends of abundance and success.

One of the simplest but most consequential generalizations ever made about national character was Tocqueville's that America was "born free." In many ways that is the basic distinction between the history of the United States and the history of other great nations. We skipped the feudal stage, just as Russia skipped the liberal stage. Louis Hartz has pointed up the complex consequences for the history of American political thought. To be a conservative and a traditionalist in America was a contradiction in terms, for the American Burke was forever conserving John Locke's liberalism, his only real native tradition. Even the South, in its great period of reaction against Jefferson, was never able fully to shake off the grip of Locke and its earlier self-image of liberalism. That is why its most original period of theoretical inspiration, the "Reactionary Enlightenment," left almost no influence upon American thought.

There is still a contribution to be derived from the South's un-American adventure in feudal fantasy. While the South was not born Lockean, it went through a Lockean phase in its youth. But as Hartz admits, it was "an alien child in a liberal family, tortured and confused, driven to a fantasy life." There *are* Americans, after all, who were not "born free." They are also Southerners. They have yet to achieve articulate expression of their uniquely un-American experience. This is not surprising, since white Southerners have only recently found expression of the tragic potentials of their past in literature. The Negro has yet to do that. His first step will be an acknowledgment that he is also a Southerner as well as an American.

One final example of a definition of national character to which the South proves an exception is an interesting one by Thornton Wilder. "Americans," says Mr. Wilder, "are abstract. They are disconnected. They have a relation, but it is to everywhere, to everybody, and to always." This quality of abstraction he finds expressed in numerous ways—in the physical mobility of Americans, in their indifference or, as he might suggest, their superiority to place, to locality, to environment. "For us," he writes, "it is not *where* genius lived that is important. If Mount Vernon and Monticello were not so beautiful in themselves and relatively accessible, would so many of us visit them?" he asks. It is not the concrete but the abstract that captures the imagination of the American and gives him identity, not the here-and-now but the future. " 'I am I,' he says, 'because my plans characterize me.' Abstract! Abstract!" Mr. Wilder's stress upon abstraction as an American characteristic recalls what Robert Penn Warren in a different connection once described as "the fear of abstraction" in the South, "the instinctive fear, on the part of black or white, that the massiveness of experience, the concreteness of life, will be violated; the fear of abstraction."

According to Mr. Wilder, "Americans can find in environment no confirmation of their identity, try as they may." And again, "Americans are disconnected. They are exposed to all place and all time. No place nor group nor movement can say to them: we are waiting for you; it is right for you to be here." The insignificance of place, locality, and community for Thornton Wilder contrasts strikingly with the experience of Eudora Welty of Mississippi. "Like a good many other [regional] writers," she says, "I am myself touched off by place. The place where I am and the place I know, and other places that familiarity with and love for my own make strange and lovely and enlightening to look into, are what set me to writing my stories." To her, "place opens a door in the mind," and she speaks of "the blessing of being located—contained."

To do Mr. Wilder justice, he is aware that the Southern states constitute an exception to his national character of abstraction, "enclaves or residual areas of European feeling," he calls them. "They were cut off, or resolutely cut themselves off, from the advancing tide of the country's modes of consciousness. Place, environment, relations, repetitions are the breath of their being."

The most reassuring prospect for the survival of the South's distinctive heritage is the magnificent body of literature produced by its writers in the last three decades—the very years when the outward traits of regional distinctiveness were crumbling. The Southern literary renaissance has placed its writers in the vanguard of national letters and assured that their works will be read as long as American literature is remembered. The distinguishing feature of the Southern school, according to Allen Tate, is "the peculiar historical consciousness of the Southern writer." He defines the literary renaissance as "a literature conscious of the past in the present." The themes that have inspired the major writers have not been the flattering myths nor the romantic dreams of the South's past. Disdaining the polemics of defense and justification, they have turned instead to the somber realities of hardship and defeat and evil and "the problems of the human heart in conflict with itself." In so doing they have brought to realization for the first time the powerful literary potentials of the South's tragic experience and heritage. Such comfort as they offer lies, in the words of William Faulkner, in reminding us of "the courage and honor and hope and pride and compassion and pity and sacrifice" with which man has endured.

After Faulkner, Wolfe, Warren, and Welty no literate Southerner could remain unaware of his heritage or doubt its enduring value. After this outpouring it would seem more difficult than ever to deny a Southern identity, to be "merely American." To deny it would be to deny our history. And it would also be to deny to America participation in a heritage and a dimension of historical experience that America very much needs, a heritage that is far more closely in line with the common lot of mankind than the national legends of opulence and success and innocence. The South once thought of itself as a "peculiar people," set apart by its eccentricities, but in many ways modern America better deserves that description.

The South was American a long time before it was Southern in any self-conscious or distinctive way. It remains more American by far than anything else, and has all along. After all, it fell the lot of one Southerner from Virginia to define America. The definition he wrote in 1776 voiced aspirations that were rooted in his native region before the nation was born. The modern Southerner should be secure enough in his national identity to escape the compulsion of less secure minorities to embrace uncritically all the myths of nationalism. He should be secure enough also not to deny a regional heritage because it is at variance with national myth. It is a heritage that should prove of enduring worth to him as well as to his country.

9

The Savage South: An Inquiry into the Origins, Endurance, and Presumed Demise of an Image

Fred C. Hobson

In 1964, George B. Tindall published an articled entitled "The Benighted South: Origins of a Modern Image," wherein he discussed the "neo-abolitionist" image of a backward and violent South, recreated and vivified by Henry Louis Mencken and "other Americans," north and south. This essay also supports Tindall's speculation in another 1964 article that "perhaps we shall encounter the central theme of Southern history on the new frontier of mythology." Fred C. Hobson, of the University of Alabama, reexamines the benighted image in a more historically expansive sense; he is particularly concerned with the contemporary perception of the image, now that it has become largely a "historical phenomenon." Hobson drives the myth's pre-abolitionist origins back into colonial times, while at the same time speaking to the myth of a nondistinctive early South. After dealing with abolitionists' contributions, he notes the image's irony as its intensity lessened after the Civil War, when one might reasonably have expected it to heighten. The benighted image also has undergone a historical inversion — from anti-Puritan in early history to Puritan in the 1920s. Hobson argues that southern social reality in the 1980s no longer supports the benighted image as clearly as it once did, even as literature of that genre continues to be popular. He concludes speculatively, offering racial harmony to fill Tindall's earlier concern for the lack of a viable substitute for the negative image. He also asks whether the South has lived down its anti-image — perhaps come full circle to realize its early paradisaical promise. Hobson even — hopefully

From *The Virginia Quarterly Review,* 61 (Summer 1985). Reprinted by permission of the publisher.

facetiously—offers a possible lament for the demise of a myth pregnant with danger, violence, and excitement—to blacks and other victims of the benighted myth's realities, an unwelcome "Hobson's choice."

I

Some 20 years ago in these pages George B. Tindall, in an essay entitled "The Benighted South: Origins of a Modern Image," discussed the growth in the 1920s of the "neo-abolitionist" image of a backward, violent South. In the twenties, as he demonstrated, the South put its ills and prejudices on display for the nation to observe—in lynching bees and Ku Klux Klan activity, hookworm and pellegra and child labor, in the Scopes evolution trial of 1925, the anti-Catholic demagoguery of the Al Smith presidential campaign of 1928, the Gastonia textile violence of 1929—and northern journalists and sociologists flocked south with both messianic mission and devilish glee to tell the rest of the nation about the horrors of life below the Potomac and Ohio. Southern journalists also got into the act, with the result that five crusading editors won Pulitzer Prizes between 1923 and 1929. Tindall's essay was a venture into southern mythology—which, as he announced in another essay published the same year, was a "new frontier in Southern history." That frontier had had its early explorers—Francis P. Gaines and, somewhat later, C. Vann Woodward, among others—but in the early 1960s it was still largely open territory. In the 1980s it is pretty well settled: William R. Taylor and David Bertelson joined Mr. Tindall in the 1960s as early homesteaders, and since that time Paul Gaston, Michael O'Brien, Richard King, Bertram Wyatt-Brown, Daniel J. Singal, and other historians have taken up residence. So have numerous southern literary scholars, sociologists, and journalists.

I would like to return, however, to Tindall's insightful essay on the benighted South, for it seems to me that one might view the subject of southern benightedness somewhat differently in the mid-1980s than one could in the mid-1960s. When he wrote in 1964 of a benighted South, Tindall was still, to some extent, an inhabitant of that South. The 1960s was *another* neo-abolitionist decade, with journalists again rushing south—and television cameras, too, this time—to document southern crimes against progress and humanity. The year Tindall published his essay, 1964, was a particularly violent year—the year of Mississippi's Freedom Summer, of three civil rights murders in Neshoba County, of demonstrations, burnings, and bombings across the Deep South.

In 1985, however, one considers southern benightedness largely as a historical phenomenon. The South has presumably come up from savagery, and one views the southern past from the vantage point of southern equality to the rest of the nation, if not presumed superiority in many areas. The South emerged from the dangerous days of the 1960s better than it entered, and it has been in a frenzy of self-congratulation ever since. It now looks disdainfully on the old and decaying cities of the once-superior North—now dismissed as the Rust Belt, the Frost Belt. All the derisive belts once belonged to Dixie—the Bible Belt, the Hookworm Belt, the Chastity Belt, all products of Mencken's imagination—but now Dixie is in the Sun. The South, its numerous champions hold, is the place where America might finally work: an unspoiled land of success, optimism, harmonious race relations and shining new cities. Whether one believes in the new supremacy of the Sun Belt (or whether one even believes that the Sun Belt really has much to do with the traditional South) is not precisely the point. The point is that this new southern success, even if much of it was imported from the North and West—together with substantial gains in race relations of which the southern states can justifiably be proud—gives the South a new confidence, makes it define itself in a somewhat different manner. It's a long way from the Savage South to the Superior South.

And not only does this newest of Souths view *itself* as superior in many ways—some southerners have always done that—but even outsiders often judge it to be superior. One recalls the "cultural indexes" used in the 1920s by Mencken in the *American Mercury:* the southern states finished dead last in nearly every category. Statistically—it was documented, scientifically—the best southern state was a worse place to live than almost any state outside the South. But now look at the surveys and rankings emanating from New York and Chicago. According to Rand McNally, Greensboro and Knoxville are among the very *best* places to live in the United States. In other surveys, Raleigh-Durham, Winston-Salem, and Atlanta come at or near the top. Brevard, North Carolina, was recently proclaimed the best place to retire to in America, Chapel Hill the most educated American city (with 70 percent college graduates), and so forth. Boosterism is not new to the South—in the 1920s, Dothan, Alabama, pronounced itself the American city of the future—but the difference is that Yankees, using those social and cultural indexes with which they once damned the South, are making these most recent judgments. Dixie is deemed to be warm and pleasant and prosperous: a land of oil, aerospace, agribusiness, real estate, and leisure. It is modern—with shopping malls, amusement parks, chain restaurants and motels, and acres of resort condominiums—but it is modern with the southern accent: it is reputed to be less frantic, more open and honest, and more genuinely religious than the rest of America. It has symphonies, art museums, ballet companies, repertory theaters—and, since 1966, major league sports.

One should not, in fact, underestimate the power of sport in image-making. Ever since antebellum southerners George Fitzhugh and Daniel Hundley claimed that the South produced better sportsmen than the North, southerners have believed that is true and, in the twentieth century, have fought some of their most memorable regional battles in stadiums and coliseums. They have won most of those battles. To the television-addicted American who forms images through witnessing crucial victories in prime time, it is clear that southern universities are the best universities. They produced NCAA football champions in 1978, 1979, 1980, 1981, and 1983; and, more important as a sign of higher civilization to some of us, college basketball—once an urban game, dominated by St. Johns, CCNY, and Philadelphia's Big Five and enshrined in Madison Square Garden, Boston Garden, and the Palestra—was until this spring ruled by southern teams. Southern universities were national champions in 1980, 1982, and 1983, and Houston and Virginia reached the Final Four in 1984. True, Georgetown and the Big East dominated collegiate basketball this year, but the South—particularly the Atlantic Coast Conference South—is expected to rise again in 1986. And if northern imports and black southerners are the stars on most of these Dixieland teams, that would seem to strengthen further the case of the southern apologist: northerners want to come here, and blacks want to stay here.

To contend that the new southern image is misleading, that it is based on superficiality, is to miss the point. Football standings, not graduate-program rankings, define universities in the public eye. Skyscrapers are more eye-catching than laboratories and library stacks; and when one approaches Atlanta on I-20 from the west and sees its shining towers fifteen miles away, he believes he has seen Byzantium. Certainly, the new image is misleading and attributes to the South a sort of virtue and energy that it does not fully deserve. I do not know who invented air conditioning, but I would contend that he, as much as anyone else, is responsible for the new image of a superior South—and I would bet that he was not a southerner. Indeed, the South still fares poorly in many of Mencken's social and cultural indexes, ranking high in poverty and homicides and infant mortality, low in the number of volumes on library shelves. In that state, North Carolina, rated the best place to live, the politics of racism endures. In that city, Greensboro, that Rand McNally ranked the most livable place of all in 1984, the Klan still resorts to violence—although now on city streets, not in cow pastures.

But in a larger sense, Peachtree Street has replaced Tobacco Road, and one cannot deny the power of public relations. Southern *is* chic, as we are

constantly reminded: it is associated with authenticity, unpretentious-
ness, country music, good times, a slower pace of life. What once was
avoided is now embraced: several are the Yankee-born-and-bred Ph.D.'s
I know who have taken academic positions in Dixie, fallen in love with
its folk culture, and, within a year or two, are not only eating cornbread
and black-eyed peas but saying "fixing to" and "might could" and
"hey" instead of "hi." And most of my Southern-bred students at the
University of Alabama—the campus where, just twenty-one years ago,
George Wallace stood in the schoolhouse door—don't even know they
are supposed to be from a benighted land. They know only that they are
from a state that is among the best at what America, circa 1985, seems to
prize most—football, religion, beauty queens, and patriotism.

It is, then, this loss of the *consciousness* of being benighted—or being
considered benighted by outsiders; or, in some cases, of ever having been
considered benighted—that intrigues me. It is in this way that the
southern temper has radically changed. I am not so foolish as to proclaim
on this account the end of southern distinctiveness. Historical grave-
yards are full of those who have prophesied in such manner, have insisted
that this time we truly do have a different South with us. Hardly are the
words out of one's typewriter than any number of South-watchers (and all
of us have a professional interest, after all, in seeing that the South
remains distinctive) are reminding us that the prognostication is, at best,
premature. So it is not the loss of southern distinctiveness I am talking
about, but rather the demise of one powerful southern image, the savage
or benighted. As that image fades, it is time to take stock of it, time for a
summing up, or at least (as this essay proposes to be) a preliminary
inquiry. Just as—Richard M. Weaver once wrote—one writes an apolo-
gia for a culture and an era just as that era draws to a close, perhaps one
should also investigate the origins and long endurance of a powerful
perception just as that perception is diminishing.

II

The image of southern benightedness did not begin with the abolitionists. It is as old as the South itself, older in fact than any region known as
"the South"—and thus two centuries older than William Lloyd Garrison. From the earliest days, the southern colonies were perceived as
being more primitive and violent and (as David Bertelson has shown)
lazier than the other American colonies. By the 1630s it was generally
assumed, and not only by New England Puritans, that the settlers of
Virginia were deficient in morality and in piety. One early writer
attributed the problems of Jamestown to the fact that many of its

founders had not "been reconciled to God" but rather were "most miserable, covetous men . . . murderers, thieves, adulterers, idle persons. . . ." By the mid-seventeenth century, Virginia and Maryland were so often maligned that John Hammond was moved to write *Leah and Rachel* (1656) in order to refute the assumption that the two colonies were a "nest of rogues, whores, dissolute and rooking persons." But even Hammond, Hugh Jones, Robert Beverley, and other apologists for the southern colonies conceded that the early colonists were guilty of sloth. Jones contended that Virginians were "climate-struck." And William Byrd, writing in the next century, agreed that the Jamestown settlers "detested work more than famine."

One must begin, however, by acknowledging a certain irony of colonial southern history: that the slothful, irreligious, and dissolute southern colonies *began* as a Southern Eden—a garden which, because improperly tended, proved to be more curse than blessing. "Earth's only paradise," Michael Drayton had written of Virginia in 1619; a "Garden of Eden," William Symonds had proclaimed in a London sermon in 1609; and early visitors to the colony—not always promoters—had described it in similar terms. (New England, by contrast, was often described as a barren wilderness, sometimes—as in Bradford's *History of Plymouth Plantation*—a "hideous and desolate wilderness.") But in the Virginia Eden lay the seeds of a barbarous South, for the fertile soil, the warm climate, and the long growing season contributed to that idleness about which observers complained, and idleness provided time for dissipation, vice, and violence. Numerous colonial writers found other disadvantages in Virginia's apparent assets: the warm climate brought "cruel diseases, as swellings, fluxes, burning fevers," and the prosperous plantation economy soon called for the importation of black slaves. By 1730 slaves made up at least one-third of the population of the southern colonies.

When visitors in the early eighteenth century remarked on the great number of Negroes in the southern colonies, however, it usually was not slavery to which they objected—but rather the slave. As Winthrop Jordan and others have shown, eighteenth-century Europeans, following Linnaeus's studies in classifying man, placed the Negro at the bottom of the earth's people, nearest the beasts. Other commentators, more given to religion than to science, solemnly affirmed that the Negro was the descendant of Ham and bore his curse. In either case, the Negro was assumed to be vastly inferior to the white European and his concentrated presence in the southern colonies was said to degrade the entire southern civilization. By the mid-eighteenth century, then—even more than in the seventeenth—the southern colonies were associated widely with irreligion, licentiousness,and sexual indulgence. The South was indeed assumed to be savage.

It was not until the 1750s and 1760s that writers in any numbers, usually Quakers, began to assert that slavery *itself* might be immoral — and that the region in which the vast majority of slaves were held was even more benighted for that reason. To these writers, slavery was not simply harmful for the civilization that possessed it; rather, to them, slavery was sin. John Woolman recorded in his *Journal* his impressions of a journey in 1746 to Maryland, Virginia, and North Carolina: "I saw in these southern provinces so many vices and corruptions, increased by this slave trade and this way of life, that slavery appeared to me as a dark gloominess hanging over the land; and though now many willingly run into it, yet in future the consequences will be grievous to posterity."

Most Americans, it goes without saying, did not read Woolman and the Quakers, and most in the late eighteenth century were little disturbed by slavery. But the image of a savage South controlled by dissolute planters was nonetheless becoming prevalent, and that image was increasingly at odds with the mythology of a new nation which had fought a revolution to attack aristocratic privilege and establish a representative government. In the late eighteenth and early nineteenth centuries, not only northern writers — who were often something other than dispassionate observers during an era when North and South struggled for control of the new nation — but also English and European travelers and residents remarked on the primitive quality of southern life. Crèvecoeur, Tocqueville, Thomas Ashe, Harriet Martineau, Charles Dickens, Mrs. Trollope — most, particularly the English — found fault with American life in general, but all were critical often harshly so, of the American South: its violence, cultural backwardness, and general shabbiness and disorder. In *Letters from an American Farmer* (1782), Crèvecoeur spoke of South Carolina as the richest province in the northern hemisphere, with "inhabitants . . . the gayest in the hemisphere": "The rays of the sun seem to urge them on irresistibly to dissipation and pleasure." Yet, "while all is joy, festivity, and happiness in Charles Towne, would you imagine that scenes of misery overspread in the country? Their ears by habit are become deaf, their hearts are hardened; they neither see, hear nor feel for the woes of their poor slaves. . . ." Crèvecoeur then presented a devastating picture of the slave South, a picture harsher by far than those painted by eighteenth-century New Englanders.

Thomas Ashe, an Englishman traveling along the western frontier in 1806, found a different sort of benightedness. Southern society was in a state of "shameful degeneracy" and was guaranteed to produce "turbulent citizens, abandoned Christians, inconstant husbands, unnatural fathers, and treacherous friends." Martineau, in *Society in America* (1837), similarly painted a picture of a primitive, violent South, degraded by "that tremendous curse, the possession of irresponsible power (over slaves). . . ." Two years later Mrs. Trollope spoke of southerners as a "people so besotted by their avarice as to be insensible to the sure approach of the vengeance which all others so plainly see approaching them. . . ." Three years later, Dickens wrote of his thoughts as he traveled through Virginia: "where slavery sits brooding . . . there is an air of ruin and decay abroad, which is inseparable from the system. . . . Gloom and dejection are upon all." Tocqueville, writing about the same time, was in some ways kinder to the southern states but still could not escape the conclusion that the American South was a doomed civilization: the "evils" of slavery and the "indolence of the inhabitants of the South" were so ingrained that there appeared to be no solution (not even emancipation) for the southern dilemma.

Demonstrably, then, there existed a powerful and prevailing image of a savage South long before and apart from Garrison and the militant New England abolitionists. That image was deeply rooted before they began to raise their voices in the 1830s. No one can deny, however, that the anti-South invective was carried to a new level by the abolitionists, whose number, modest before the congressional debate over the Missouri Compromise in 1819 and 1820, began to swell not long after that. Garrison pictured a "blood-stained" South guilty of "driving women into the field, like a beast, under the lash of a brutal overseer . . . stealing infants . . . trafficking in human flesh." Wendell Phillips described the South as "a daily system of Hell," Theodore Weld as a society given to "dissipation, sensuality, brutality, cruelty, and meanness. . . ." To the New England abolitionists, as to the eighteenth-century Quakers, slavery was sin. How would southern slaveholders and their apologists, asked Garrison, "be able to bear the awful retributions of Heaven, which must inevitably overwhelm them, unless they speedily repent?"

If the voices of Garrison, Philips, Weld, Lewis Tappan, Gerrit Smith, and other leaders of the abolitionist movement were heeded by few Americans in the 1830s and 1840s, and the antislavery newspapers *The Liberator* and *The Emancipator* were not widely read, the works of more popular writers—Lowell, Whittier, Harriet Beecher Stowe—carried greater influence. The vivid description in Lowell's *Biglow Papers* of the "grasping, over-reaching, nigger-drivin' States"—or Whittier's indictment of a southern system which held "two millions of God's creatures in bondage," or Stowe's depiction of slavery in *Uncle Tom's Cabin*—moved readers as Garrison and Phillips could not. So did narratives by Frederick Douglass, Solomon Northup, James W. C. Pennington, and other ex-slaves which became bestsellers in the mid-nineteenth century. What reader, in an age of sentimental novels, could fail to be moved by stories of family separation, kidnapping, and beatings — or fail to indict the civilization that sanctioned such horrors?

III

Another of the many ironies of southern history is that the northern perception of a savage South was modified by a war in which southerners killed and maimed more than a hundred thousand Union soldiers: southern defeat in the Civil War led to the mythology of a southern Lost Cause — the death of a noble and gracious civilization — that by the 1880s and 1890s was embraced by the North as well as the South. The perception of southern savagery was not altered immediately, of course. Shortly after Appomattox, the northern reading public turned eagerly to harshly anti-southern books by Whitelaw Reid, Sidney Andrews, and J. T. Trowbridge, as well as to numerous articles on the barbarism of southern prisoner-of-war camps, bitter anti-South essays in *Harper's Weekly,* and, somewhat later, *Sherman's Memoirs* (1875). But by the late 1870s, one finds the beginning of an era of regional good feeling, characterized by relative harmony in politics and business and by local color in literature. If this good feeling was occasionally disturbed by Thomas Nast's cartoons and by the novels of Albion Tourgée and, later, Charles W. Chesnutt (and one can hardly calculate the damage done to southern pride and honor by Mark Twain), such anti-South expression between 1877 and 1915 was the exception, not the rule. As the plantation school of southern fiction became popular, the South came to assume the role of a pastoral never-never land in the eyes of a rapidly growing and industrializing North.

North-South hostilities resumed shortly after World War I for a number of reasons. The war opened up the South, and northern soldiers and reporters who traveled through or were based there returned home ready to talk and write of it. The tenor of the iconoclastic 1920s — an attack on the provinces that also extended to the Middle West — played a major role in the southern assault as well. But, most important, the South, through a series of events and atrocities, called attention to itself in so dramatic a fashion as to provoke the wrath and ridicule of northern reporters and writers. Events such as the Scopes trial were nearly prototypic, bringing to the surface tensions between the South and the outside world and dramatizing what the Northeast considered to be southern benightedness. As a result, Mencken and the *American Mercury,* W. E. B. Du Bois and the *Crisis,* Frank Tannenbaum and Walter F.

White (in books entitled *Darker Phases of the South* and *Rope and Faggot*), and numerous writers for the *Nation* and the *New Republic* (in essays such as "Mississippi: Heart of Darkness") reintroduced the notion of southern savagery. For the first time in great numbers, southerners joined in the attack. Journalists such as Gerald W. Johnson of North Carolina, Grover Hall of Alabama, and Julian and Julia Harris of Georgia followed the lead of Mencken, and novelists such as T. S. Stribling of Tennessee emulated Sinclair Lewis and ushered in what might now be called the short, touted reign of southern realism.

When one examines the neo-abolitionist assault on the South in the 1920s, both from within and from without, one finds a curious phenomenon: after a forty-year respite from northern slings and arrows, the nature of southern benightedness had appeared to change. The South from its beginnings to the Civil War had been considered benighted because it was reputed to be irreligious, sexually promiscuous, and given to strong drink and inadequate moral seriousness. But in the 1920s southern benightedness assumed a different, even antithetical character: to critics such as Mencken, Dixie was benighted, in large part, not because it was irreligious but rather because it was excessively religious; not because it was given to strong drink but rather because it was prohibitionist; not because it was sexually indulgent but rather because it was sexually prudish (in literature as well as in life); and not because it was lacking moral seriousness but rather because it, more than any other American region, possessed a life-denying moral seriousness which refused to acknowledge the aesthetic or any other approach to life. The South, formerly the home of the Cavalier, was now presumed—and not only by Mencken—to be the home of American Puritanism. To what extent had the South in fact changed (certainly somewhat through nineteenth-century religious revivals and the rise of genteel Victorian culture), and to what extent the point of view of its detractors? What, after all—beyond violence and racial oppression, which were constants both antebellum and postbellum—constituted savagery or benightedness? Was it a quality to be measured solely through social indexes and standards of high culture?

This is one of many questions surrounding the perception of southern savagery, and before bringing my discussion to that second decade of neo-abolitionism, the 1960s, I should like to consider the motivation of those writers who, from the seventeenth century on, have pronounced the South savage. For one must assume that the reasons for the southern indictment have gone beyond a hatred of slavery and racial oppression, or even indignation over poverty and anti-intellectualism—since racial oppression, poverty, and anti-intellectualism have flourished outside the South as well. The motivation of black writers—Douglass, Du Bois,

Walter F. White, Richard Wright—might appear to be relatively clear: one considers the rage, but also the fascination, of the oppressed for the oppressor. The motivation of English and European travelers might seem equally clear: no matter how intrigued by America, these writers felt culturally superior, particularly to those sections that failed to live up to their idea of civilization—that is, particularly the still largely frontier South.

Even with New England and other northeastern writers, the question of motivation can be answered at a certain level: the South and New England were economic and political rivals from the beginning, and regional criticism often served larger political ends. And beyond that, has not the northeastern disdain for the South, at least since 1800, been in part simply an example of the almost universal disdain felt by the populated, industrialized, moneyed, and sophisticated part of any nation for its provinces, its hinterland—the disdain of the Parisian for the rest of France, of the Prussian for the south of Germany, or the Londoner for Scotland or Ireland or the north of England? Such an assumption is complicated, of course, by competing southern claims to superiority, for many antebellum southerners in fact considered themselves superior to their northern rivals, a sense of superiority that, at first at least, was something other than a defense mechanism. Indeed, claims of cultural superiority by antebellum southerners such as George Fitzhugh and Edmund Ruffin served to infuriate northern detractors who believed that southern claims were clearly fraudulent. Southern pride had always been a target for northern critics. In 1746 John Woolman, on his trip into Virginia and North Carolina, remarked on the "unseemly pride" of the southern slaveholder. Later commentators from Mark Twain to Mencken liked nothing better than exposing shams and frauds, and they believed they found no greater frauds than in the South. Any civilization that made exaggerated claims for itself exposed itself to charges from without.

But one must consider other factors in the making of the northern perception of a savage South. To what extent did tensions in northern society at particular points of social and cultural transition cause northerners, particularly New Englanders, to look south for targets? To what extent did the image of a cruel, despotic South that emerged in the North in the late 1850s and early 1860s rise from the fact that the North, if it was to fight a war, had to convince itself that it was undertaking a holy crusade to rid the republic not only of slavery but also sin and corruption? Finally, to what extent has the South served as scapegoat for the nation's sins? New England traders, after all, had brought slaves to the American South; New England industrialists and merchants had profited from slavery; New Englanders as a people were hardly immune to racial prejudice; and, in the 1830s and 1840s, a condemnation of southern chattel slavery helped to draw attention away from the "wage-slavery" of northern factories. One has always looked abroad for ills to be remedied, heathen to be converted: in the early twentieth century, at a time when northern reformers and teachers and public health workers were heading south, the southern church was sending missionaries to China.

Most important, one must ask to what extent and precisely how the Puritan legacy of New England—in evidence at least as late as Henry Adams—has affected its attitude toward the South: its attitude toward southern indolence (since, to the Puritans, sloth was sin); toward the lack of regard for community in the colonial South; toward southern disorganization and social fragmentation; toward a southern life lived in the country amid lush nature (since, to the Puritans, towns and cities contained civilization); toward the southerner's professed love of leisure and frivolity; toward his tendency to prize piety less than sociability and intellect less than the habit of command; and, finally, toward the southerner's presumed inability to put reins on appetite and emotion? To what extent did the Puritan's horror of sexual license enter in? Was the South, in the antebellum New England mind, tainted both by the presence of debauched, lascivious planter *and* virile, libidinous Negro? To the antebellum northern mind, particularly the New England mind, was the South simply impure, unclean?

Remarks by outsiders up until the time of the Civil War would suggest as much. Numerous colonial observers wrote harshly of southern miscegenation. "The enjoyment of a negro or mulatto woman is spoken of as quite a common thing," wrote one northern traveler in 1773. "No reluctance, delicacy or shame is made about the matter." The rhetoric of those latter-day Puritans, the abolitionists, suggests a preoccupation with the carnality of the South. "One great brothel," Wendell Phillips called the southern states. Garrison complained of the "incest, pollution and adultery" in the South, and blasted the slaveholder as "the remorse-less scourger of Woman of the South." Lowell spoke of "the selling of Christian girls for Christian harems." And so forth. What the abolition-ists wrote of the South in the early and mid-nineteenth century was not far removed from what William Bradford, in the *History of Plymouth Plantation,* had written about the hedonists of Merry Mount. It was not slavery alone to which the abolitionists objected.

IV

But, of course, what I have written above assumes that Puritanism was always in the North, irreligion in the South, whereas, as we have seen, the roles were widely assumed to be reversed in the twentieth century. In fact, however, Mencken's charge that American Puritanism had moved from New England to the South by the 1920s is suspect—for Mencken never really understood Puritanism, and what he and his fellow South-baiters saw when they looked across the Potomac was hardly the rigorous, intellectual Puritanism of the early Massachusetts Bay but rather, in most cases, a sort of raw Southern Calvinism masquerading under that name. For this reason the revelation of Mencken's disciple, Wilbur Cash, that Puritanism and hedonism ran parallel in the southern character is not really so striking as it might at first appear—for the emotional Southern Calvinism of which Cash wrote, a religion of camp meetings and emotional conversions, was really another form of hedonism in itself.

In any case, the 1920s assumptions about southern religion, race, and general benightedness remained in force for nearly the next half-century, the difference being that after the 1920s it was chiefly southern writers, not northern ones, who reinforced and popularized the image. After reading T. S. Stribling, Erskine Caldwell, and William Faulkner, Gerald Johnson announced in the *Virginia Quarterly Review* of January 1935 that he had witnessed a "Horrible South": "these are the merchants of death, hell, and the grave, these are the horror-mongers-in-chief." The new southern fiction, full of murder, suicide, rape, incest, lynchings, castrations, miscegenation, and insanity, presented a South even more savage than that the abolitionists had described in the 1840s or the sociologists had turned up in the 1920s, and Caldwell and Faulkner were hailed in national magazines as southern "realists." Thus Southern Gothic had its birth, and Carson McCullers and Flannery O'Connor—and in a quite different way, Lillian Smith—became its leading practitioners in the 1940s. McCullers and O'Connor relied chiefly on imagination. But when Richard Wright wrote of the horrors of Dixie in *Uncle Tom's Children* (1938) and the autobiographical *Black Boy* (1945), he *was,* to a great extent, writing realism.

In the 1940s and 1950s one found much outside southern fiction to support the perception of southern benightedness, although it was not until the early 1960s that the South found itself again in the national spotlight. If at first one sees the 1960s as a replay of the 1920s and 1930s—with Birmingham, Selma, Oxford, and Neshoba County assuming the earlier roles of Dayton, Gastonia, Elizabethton, and Scottsboro—one soon discovers that there was one distinct difference: this time the white South was taking its last racial stand, was about to change for good. Atlanta, a hundred and fifty miles east of Birmingham, recognized the poor public relations of racial savagery and, in conscious reaction to the old image, proclaimed itself "The City Too Busy to

Hate." Hollywood filmmakers in the sixties, however, were still more intrigued with southern savagery than southern harmony, and so were most southern writers. If the 1960s repeated the 1920s, Jesse Hill Ford and William Bradford Huie assumed the roles of Stribling and Clement Wood. Ford's *The Liberation of Lord Byron Jones* (1965) and Huie's *The Klansman* (1967) contained all the old ingredients—murder, rape, miscegenation, lynching—played out against the background of the civil rights movement.

Ford and Huie wrote a sort of neo–Southern Gothic, and that tradition was to continue in the 1970s and 1980s in the work of Cormac McCarthy, Harry Crews, and Barry Hannah. A work such as McCarthy's *Child of God* (1973), a tale of murder and necrophilia more lurid than anything Caldwell ever invented—or, in a more contemporary vein, Hannah's *Ray* (1980)—assure us that the Savage South still lives in imaginative literature. The problem for the neo-Gothic novelist is that southern social reality, *representative* reality, no longer supports this fiction. It never did fully, of course. Even in the 1920s the South was not so violent, or at least not in the same proportion, as the fiction of Stribling and the early Faulkner suggested it was. But in the 1920s and 1930s the writer, observing life around him and himself feeling the pressure of what Cash later called the savage ideal, could easily *imagine* a South that, in one of its moods, was as savage as the fictional world he created. The 1960s— with bombings and beatings, Klan rallies and civil rights murders—is the last decade of which that could be said. After that, southern savagery in literature appears, if not contrived, at least removed from the social base which gives rise to the fiction.

But what has succeeded southern savagery? "In fact," George B. Tindall wrote in 1964, "it must be said that the twentieth-century South has not produced a positive and viable myth of its own identity powerful enough to challenge the image of a benighted South." Has it still not produced that myth? It has not, if we perceive that "positive and viable myth" to be the myth of Sun Belt success—for the Sun Belt mythology, as we have seen, is more imported than indigenous. Neither Donald Davidson nor Wilbur Cash would recognize it. But the South has perhaps produced a powerful positive myth if that myth is, as Leslie Dunbar expressed it in 1961, the promise of the world's "finest grand example of two races of men living together."

I move to final considerations. Just what change has the transition from savagery to presumed superiority worked on the southern psyche —the psyche of a region that had been conditioned by shame and guilt and failure and defeat but is now suddenly considered a success? Is there a kind of benightedness, or at least implied inferiority, in Dixie's current preoccupation with self-congratulations and positive public relations?

Or has the South, in its passion for promotion, simply come full circle? The southern colonies began, after all, as a paradise for promoters, John Smith chief among them. Now, nearly four centuries later, has the American South—liberated by air conditioning from the heat and humidity which seventeenth-century observers saw as the source of most of its woes; liberated from its other curse, slavery and racial segregation, by external interference and internal good will—has this South now become the good land its earliest boosters promised it to be? Of course it has not fully. Just as it was never as bad as advertised in its days of benightedness, it is hardly as good as advertised now.

It may appear of little consequence to anyone but South-watchers, filmmakers, professional southerners, and readers of modern Gothic fiction, but I am moved to ask a final question: Can a superior South be nearly as *interesting* as a savage one? Can a land of shopping malls, amusement complexes, and resort condominiums hold the fascination that a land of demagogy, night-riding, and lynching bees held? It was surely not a freshly scrubbed South of racial harmony, clean industry, and agrarian piety that Shreve McCannon had in mind when he exclaimed to Quentin Compson in *Absalom, Absalom!*, "Jesus, the South is fine isn't it? It's better than the theatre, isn't it? It's better than Ben Hur, isn't it?" Did the mystique of the South rest on its danger, its theatricality, its racial intrigue, even violence? To black southerners and others whose lots have improved in proportion to the decline of southern savagery, this should appear to be a frivolous question indeed.

10

Myth Against History: The Case of Southern Womanhood

Sara M. Evans

Sexual and racial mythologies are national phenomena in American history. They have, however, played a unique and more lasting role in southern history than in the history of any of the country's other regions. "Down there" it seemed necessary to sink the roots of sexism and racism deeper in order to buttress the Plantation Myth and to rationalize the roles within it ascribed to women, both white and black. As the South developed into the eighteenth and nineteenth centuries, the presence of large numbers of black women allowed southerners to divide Western women's mythic duality between the races. White women reflected the good and pure; black women the bad and impure. As these color-coded myths developed and became more pervasive, they further clouded the realities of all southern women. In this article, Sara M. Evans of the University of Minnesota sketches the hardening of southern womanhood's stereotypes through the antebellum period, which led to a peculiarly southern version of the Victorian Cult of True Womanhood. Professor Evans also outlines the realities of southern womanhood and follows developments during and after the Civil War as white and black women, at first "advancing independently along somewhat parallel lines" (to use David Potter's phrase) moved toward more independence and involvement. Areas covered here include agriculture, industrialization, populism, progressivism, suffragism, and

From *The Encyclopedia of Southern History,* ed. David C. Roller and Robert W. Twyman (Baton Rouge: Louisiana University Press, 1979). Reprinted by permission of the publisher. I am indebted to Anne Firor Scott who first suggested that I write this article and to Jacqueline Dowd Hall who gave invaluable counsel in the early stages of its conception.

social welfare developments of the 1920s and beyond. Much of this
activity on the part of both white and black women came as a result of
personal religious commitment and through religiously oriented institutions. Professor Evans also emphasizes growing interracial cooperation during the twentieth century, which came to focus in the 1950s and
contributed to the feminist revival of the 1960s in the South. In the
process, however, the reality of southern womanhood's move "from
pedestal to politics" was obscurred and obstructed historically by the
South's conservatism, which to a large extent was based on its sexist
and racist mythologies.

Until recent years the idea of "womanhood" in the South was inextricably linked in both history and fiction with the notion of the "southern
lady" or her younger counterpart, the "southern belle." Few southern
women actually lived the life of the lady or fully embodied her essential
qualities: innocence, modesty, morality, piousness, delicacy, self-sacri-
ficial devotion to family, and . . . whiteness. Yet all southern women
have been affected by the fusion of sexual imagery with the racial caste
system. Southern colonists brought with them the fundamental Western
myths about female nature which embodied a polarization between the
virgin, pure and untouchable, and the prostitute, dangerously sexual.
This dichotomy, associated with images of light and dark, good and evil,
gradually took on concrete reality with the emergence of a white planter
class based upon a racial slave labor system.

The role of the white lady which emerged in the eighteenth and
nineteenth centuries and the dual imagery of the black woman as whore
and mammy revealed more about the needs of white planters than about
the actual lives of women, white or black. The white lady, revered and
sexually repressed, guaranteed the purity of the white race and the
future of white civilization. As the symbol of white men's power she was
carefully placed on a moral pedestal within the privacy of the home, well
out of the realm of politics and public power. Sexual relations between
white women and black men violated the most potent social taboo in
southern culture. On the other hand, the white man's guilt-ridden sexual
access to black women represented a reenactment of the power relationships of slavery. Yet responsibility for the rape of black women was laid
at the feet of the victim, who, it was said, was naturally promiscuous.
Finally, the black mammy became the nurturant, all-giving mother
figure, beloved because she threatened neither hierarchy of race nor sex.

By the middle of the nineteenth century the myth of the Southern lady
had become a pillar of the southern defense of slavery. Thus the fusion of
race and sex created a southern version of the Victorian Cult of True
Womanhood. These dual images of black and white women, which

served to maintain the racial caste system and a hierarchical social order, persisted into the twentieth century. Defense of the lady justified racial violence and possibly served as an expiation of white male guilt. And rigid enforcement of the most conservative definitions of sex roles ensured that women would not extend their moral duties beyond the home.

Such myths, clearly, obscured as much as they revealed. The reproductive roles of housewife and mother defined all women, whether they were slaves, wives of yeoman farmers, industrial workers, or plantation mistresses. Yet such roles did not separate them significantly from the basic work of economic production in an economy which remained primarily rural and agrarian from the earliest colonization to World War II.

As slaves, black women provided much of the field labor which enriched Southern society, and they furnished most of the household labor on which the upper-class life-style depended. At the same time they were the central figures in creating and maintaining a unique form of black family structure geared to the exigencies of life under slavery. While they tended the children of the white planter class, they also provided their own children with the emotional support and social skills required for survival and passed on a rich subcultural heritage. Long-term monogamous relationships, highly valued if rare, were characterized by a degree of sexual equality unknown in white society. Southern black women were probably an important source of resistance to the values of white society, and in a few striking cases, such as Harriet Tubman and the Underground Railroad, they led active resistance to the slave system.

Most adult white women before the Civil War were the wives of yeoman farmers. Their families owned few if any slaves. Like black women their lot was one of constant hard work. "Women's work" included gardening, caring for cows and poultry, spinning, weaving, sewing, baking, preserving, and cheese making as well as the routine duties of meal preparation, housecleaning, and child-rearing. Though field work was considered unseemly for a white woman, such social taboos often weakened in the face of grim necessity. In the early Colonial period an acute labor shortage resulted in a wide range of public roles for women who ran shops, printing presses, and taverns, or served their neighbors as lawyers or doctors. Political uprisings such as Bacon's Rebellion involved women not only as passive hostages, but also as talented rebel orators. In seventeenth-century Maryland, Mistress Margaret Brent wielded considerable political influence and became the first female settler to demand the suffrage. In South Carolina Eliza Lucas pioneered the growing and processing of indigo.

The emergence of the aristocratic lady in the eighteenth and nineteenth centuries rendered such public activity increasingly disreputable. Yet even the ladies of the upper classes had little time for leisure. Most sewed, cooked, cleaned, gardened, tended the sick. On large plantations they administered and supervised the work of an army of household servants. Though they were denied access to a true education and had few legal or political rights, their domestic domain lay at the heart of southern economic life, the plantation. Their administrative duties required the constant exercise of authority in the home while from their pedestals they pretended ignorance of the miscegenation around them.

During and after the carnage of the Civil War women took over and ran farms, shops, and plantations and flocked to cities where they provided a significant war-industry labor force. With a new sense of competence, many would be reluctant to yield to patriarchal authority at the war's end. During the Reconstruction era, while upper-class white men attempted to regain social and political control of southern society through political pressure and KKK terrorism, women directed much of the actual work of "reconstructing" the ravaged economy. On many plantations and farms, war widows had no choice but to forge ahead alone. On others, women simply continued to act with the assurance and authority gained during the wartime experience. Thus white women's self-perceptions diverged increasingly from the prescriptions of delicacy and submission despite the resurrection of a romanticized "Old South" after 1880.

After the war, black women, with black men, plunged into the backbreaking labor of subsistence farming, but they dreamed of economic independence and education for their children. When paid labor was virtually unavailable to black men, women and girls were able to find employment as domestic servants. Necessity required greater equality between the sexes in both black and white farm families caught in the crop-lien system than in middle- and upper-class families. No historian has fully examined the role of women in the Populist movement, but a number of works hint at the probability that one might find there southern women in their most politically active roles since the seventeenth century.

If women performed much of the work of reconstructing southern agriculture after the Civil War, so too did women from the southern Piedmont and Appalachian mountains contribute to the development of an industrializing "New South." In 1890 the labor force of four leading textile states was forty percent women and twenty-five percent children. Such labor represented a continuation of their usual lot of long hours at grueling tasks. On the other hand, it meant a relocation of family from farm to mill town, separation from children for ten to fourteen hours a day, and no lessening of the basic labor of housework. Such a setting might have entailed a readjustment of marital relations as women and men coped with the fact that women could obtain mill jobs more easily than their husbands. In the sporadic, bloody, and rarely successful labor struggles which erupted in the following decades, women like Ella Mae Wiggins of the Gastonia Strike in North Carolina frequently played leading roles in mobilizing revolt. They receded into the background, however, when it came time to elect officers or to hire union organizers. Though they were not "ladies," they could stretch the boundaries of their sphere only so far and no farther.

For both white and black women of the growing middle classes in the late nineteenth and early twentieth centuries, the pathway from domesticity to public political activity lay through the church. In missionary societies beginning in the 1870s, and later in the WCTU, women's clubs, and the YWCA, they began to carve out autonomous arenas in which they developed skills, social concerns, and a new self-image. Direct contact between black and white women's groups was rare, but as home missionary societies built settlement houses or worked for child labor reforms, their constituents inevitably confronted the realities of poverty and racial discrimination.

Southern suffragists drew on the reform activity sparked by such new experiences, but their efforts encountered an immense tide of reaction as repressive racial and sexual imagery accompanied the rise of lynching in the 1890s. The growth of suffragism in the South led by racial moderates like Laura Clay of Kentucky and extremists like Kate Gordon of Mississippi may have encouraged a trend toward conservatism and racism in the national suffrage movement. No Deep South states passed the Nineteenth Amendment, but many suffragists continued to work in a variety of reform efforts to curb the abuses of child labor and to shorten the hours of working women. Some, like Lucy Randolph Mason, went on to become labor activists.

The emergence of a black middle class after the Civil War created new roles for black women as professionals and church activists as well. These women pursued a separate strand of progressive reform in the South. Beginning in 1895 Ida B. Wells-Barnett pioneered in the struggle against lynching. In 1908 the Neighborhood Union in Atlanta initiated a settlement-house movement among blacks geared toward generating grass-roots leadership as well as serving the poor. In addition, although black women's role in the struggle for black education has only begun to be unearthed, the leadership of women like Lucy Laney, Charlotte Hawkins Brown, Septima Poinsetts Clark, and Mary McCloud Bethune indicates their great importance.

By the 1920s the two strands of female reform activity began to come together through the avenues of church societies, the YWCA, and the Commission on Interracial Cooperation. In the 1930s the Association of Southern Women for the Prevention of Lynching led by Jesse Daniel Ames reflected the response of a few white women to the prodding of their black sisters.

The second half of the twentieth century marked a turning point in the roles and lives of southern women. While the family remained a central institution in southern culture, it was forced to adapt to new needs and circumstances. The twin processes of industrialization and urbanization provided a new context within which the older images of the pristine "lady" and her "dark sister" were rapidly giving way. Mobility from farm to city placed strains on kinship networks and accented the self-sufficiency of the nuclear family unit. Rapidly broadening educational opportunities and an expanding industrial economy, moreover, widened the employment options of both women and blacks. Thus, black and white women met each other less as mistress and servant and more as co-workers in schools, offices, and factories.

In the midst of such changes, traditional southern conservatism on both sexual and racial equality came under sharp attack. Like the earlier efforts at social reform, the movements of the 1950s and 1960s were spearheaded by southern women whose belief in social justice drew on religious commitment. The southern civil rights movement drew on the tireless work of women like Ella Baker and Septima Clark and local leaders such as Rosa Parks and Fannie Lou Hamer. Following in the footsteps of pioneers like Lillian Smith and Anne Braden, young white women who joined the challenge to segregation and racial discrimination began to question the whole complex of racial and sexual mythology. As a result, they pioneered the feminist revival of the 1960s.

Thus we have the paradox of southern womanhood. The meshing of sexual and racial symbolism throughout southern history created a mythology which functioned as a powerful weapon against social change. This helps to explain the persistence of Victorian definitions of femininity in southern culture. Yet it has obscured the reality that social and economic change in the South has also been built on the labors of southern women.

11

The Ever-Vanishing South

Charles P. Roland

The American South's reputation for regional distinctiveness, vis-à-vis the nation at large, is, in itself, nearly legendary. Yet in some quarters of recent scholarship, the view is taking hold that the once-enduring South is facing its demise: new theory has it that "the Cracker has begun to crumble." Recent findings seemingly support what in some circles is called "massification," "assimilation," or "convergence" — the notion that, in the face of interregional migration, resultant demographic shifts, federally mandated civil rights legislation, the homogenization of American culture via the mass media, the imperatives of industrial urbanization, and the apparent transregional ideological consensus manifested in recent presidential elections, the American nation and its former sections are fast becoming near mirror images of one another. The sure temptation in the face of such arguments is perhaps to reread Harry Ashmore's *Epitaph for Dixie*, John Egerton's *The Americanization of Dixie*, or to agree with the New South journalist Henry Watterson's oft-quoted remark that the South is but a rhetorical anachronism, "simply a geographic expression." However, in the considered judgment of Charles P. Roland, Alumni Professor of History at the University of Kentucky, persistent differences of a significant sort between the South and the North—or, if one prefers, the South and the non-South—continue. Despite stories of convergence, and so on, the suspicion remains strong that regional cultural differences are, in fact, not significantly diminishing. Contrary evidence indicates a durable, persistent, enduring South still to be reckoned with. Arguments that the traditional South is, alas, "gone with the wind,"

From the *Journal of Southern History,* 48 (February 1982), 3–20. Copyright 1982 by the Southern Historical Association. Reprinted by permission of the Managing Editor.

is no longer "a nation within a nation," ignore the South's sub-cultural persistence in the midst of a seeming singularly choreo-graphed national culture. The south continues to affirm differences of mind, spirit, language, religion, folk culture, and economics.

Most observers of the modern South emphasize the so-called transfor-mation of the region during the last few decades. What they mean by this expression is the disappearance of regional distinctiveness: the growing resemblance of the region to the rest of the nation; the merging of the South into the American mainstream.

The prospect of a southern transformation is usually looked upon as being highly desirable, especially by the liberal journalists and college professors who do the bulk of the writing on the subject. The South has traditionally been regarded as the black sheep of the American commu-nity—a willful, delinquent child who has somehow failed to shape up to the national standards. A few years ago this idea was portrayed whim-sically, but perceptively, by a *New Yorker* magazine cartoon showing a fashionably attired matron with a sour look on her face, turning down a bookstore clerk's suggestion of a volume on a certain southern state, with the comment: "I'm sorry for Mississippi, but I just don't like to read about it."[1] Clare Boothe Luce intended no whimsy when she wrote in the preface of her popular social satire *Kiss the Boys Good-bye,* saying: "We are not, perhaps, sufficiently aware that Southernism is a particular and *highly matured* form of Facism . . . ."[2] Only a few months ago the *Manchester Guardian Weekly* chose to refer to the American South as a "neurotic region."[3]

C. Vann Woodward tells us that a major factor in the South's identity is its historic failure to share fully in the great national traditions of success, affluence, and innocence.[4] Southerners were set apart as those Americans who wore the scarlet letters of guilt for having committed the two unpardonable sins of slavery and secession. Even more igno-minious, perhaps, they were the only Americans who had known the travail and humiliation of being conquered and subjected to military occupation. Howard Zinn explained what he called the "Southern

---

[1] Quoted in John S. Reed, *The Enduring South: Subcultural Persistence in Mass Society* (Lexington, Mass., Toronto, and London, 1972), 1. This paper is developed from an address by the author entitled "The Persistent South," given in 1978 at The Citadel: The Military College of South Carolina, Charleston, S.C.

[2] Clare Boothe Luce, *Kiss the Boys Good-bye* (New York, 1939), x.

[3] *Manchester Guardian Weekly,* November 9, 1980

[4] C. Vann Woodward, *The Burden of Southern History* (Baton Rouge, 1960), 16–21.

Mystique" as being largely a distillation of most of the nation's worst traits, along with a few of its best, he added generously.[5] Unquestionably, one of the most familiar images in the American mind has been that of what George B. Tindall has called the "Benighted South"—a land of persistent racial prejudice, religious bigotry, endemic poverty, and a cluster of other presumably un-American attitudes and conditions.[6]

What of the great transformation said to have occurred in the South in recent times? Before turning to this question, perhaps it would be worthwhile to point out that the very idea of southern transformation is not nearly so new as may be supposed from all the talk about it. In 1941, before the occurrence of any of the wartime or postwar events that are thought to be eradicating regional distinctiveness, a renowned social analyst, Wilbur Joseph Cash, felt obliged to reply to those who said the South already was a mere figment of the imagination, that it existed only as a geographical division of the United States. Cash disagreed. The South, he said, was "not quite a nation within a nation, but the next thing to it."[7]

Indeed, the idea and the fact of southern change, or transformation, are extremely old. A so-called New South was proudly proclaimed a few years after the Civil War by an entire covey of young southern boosters, chief among whom was the Atlanta journalist and raconteur Henry Woodfin Grady. Their New South was a South said to be refashioned in the likeness of the victorious North: a South of industry, commerce, and hustle—a South outdoing the Yankees at their own game yet retaining the charm and graciousness of the Old South. Or, to look a bit farther back, the North during the Civil War and Reconstruction had its own vision of southern transformation. The South, rid of the serpent of slavery, was to be remade into a Garden of Eden, or at least into a New England below the Potomac, which was another way of saying about the same thing. Actually, it seems to have been a northern army officer who coined the very expression "The New South."[8] In brief, what may be overlooked in the present enthusiasm for recent southern transformation is that at the time of World War II the South had already experienced more than three centuries of change, some of it of the most radical nature imaginable, without losing its regional distinctiveness.

[5] Howard Zinn, *The Southern Mystique* (New York, 1964), 218.

[6] George B. Tindall, "The Benighted South: Origins of a Modern Image," *Virginia Quarterly Review,* XL (Spring 1964), 281–94.

[7] Wilbur J. Cash, "Preview to Understanding," in *The Mind of the South* (New York, 1941), viii.

[8] Holland Thompson, *The New South: A Chronicle of Social and Industrial Evolution* (New Haven, 1920), 7.

Yes, the South has undergone immense change since World War II, much of it traceable directly or indirectly to the war itself. Perhaps it is no exaggeration to say the region was fated to be affected almost as much by World War II as by the Civil War. Many of the recent changes have been exactly the opposite of those wrought by the Civil War. The South emerged from that experience crushed, bankrupt, demoralized; it emerged from World War II intact, prosperous, confident. Yet some of the recent changes were remarkably similar to those growing out of the Civil War and Reconstruction, for they involved the relationship of the southern states to the federal government and of whites to blacks in the South.[9]

The South since World War II has experienced what may fairly be called revolutions in its economy, politics, and race relations. In 1940 the region was predominantly rural and agricultural; by 1981 it was heavily industrialized, and less than five percent of the total population actually made their livings on farms. Since World War II the South has enjoyed a prosperity beyond the dreams of former times. In 1940 the section was known politically as the Solid South: solid, that is, in its fealty to the Democratic party. In 1972 every southern state voted for the Republican presidential candidate; after a swing back to a native-son Democrat in 1976, an overwhelming majority of the region's states four years later turned Republican again. Southern blacks in 1940 were rigidly segregated from whites, except as menials, both by law and custom, and, with minor exceptions, the blacks were systematically excluded from voting or holding public office. By 1980, as the result of massive federal intervention and black protest demonstrations, southern institutions, at least officially, were thoroughly desegregated, and southern blacks were voting by the millions. Thousands of them held public office, including a few in the United States Congress and the mayoral positions of such prominent southern metropolises as Richmond, Atlanta, Birmingham, and New Orleans. A southern Rip Van Winkle, awakening after thirty years, would not believe his eyes.

This, of course, is the situation that has caused many thinkers to believe the South as an identifiable region is extinct, or almost so. This explains the utterance of such expressions as "The Vanishing South" or "The Disappearing Sectional South" and the selection of such titles as *Into the Mainstream,* "Been Down Home So Long It Looks Like Up to Me," or *An Epitaph for Dixie.*[10]

But Dixie has survived a long array of epitaphs and of epitaph writers,

[9] Charles P. Roland, *The Improbable Era: The South since World War II* (Lexington, Ky., 1975), 169.

[10] George B. Tindall, "Beyond the Mainstream: The Ethnic Southerners," *Journal of Southern History,* XL (February 1974), 3, 3n, 4.

and many things indicate that the epitaphs being composed today may still be premature. Cash warned his readers against adopting hasty conclusions from superficial observation indicating the disappearance of the South. He drew an analogy between the South and a venerable English church with its Gothic facade and towers. Look into the nave, aisle, and choir, he said, and one finds there the old mighty Norman arches; look into the crypt, and one may even find stones hewn by the Saxons, brick made by the Romans.[11] Descend today into the crypt of the southern psyche, I suspect, and there one will discover many ancient emotions, loyalties, and traits of unmistakably southern origin.

Even in those aspects of regional affairs that have been most obviously affected by recent forces—that is, the economy, politics, and race relations—even in these, many old landmarks are still highly visible. Take the economy. Accurate as the reports of the southern prosperity are, the South today actually remains economically behind the rest of the country. The regional economy is still very much a colonial economy. Most of the stock in the great corporations dominating it belongs to outsiders; regional industry is still disproportionately extractive and subsidiary; the southern per capita income and wealth are still significantly below those of the nation at large. Much of the oil, coal, and timber of the region has always been controlled by nonsoutherners, a control that seems not to be relaxing. A recent issue of the Louisville *Courier-Journal* calls attention to the continuing engrossment of Kentucky coal rights by companies from afar. A corporation with headquarters in California, acting through a Kentucky affiliate, has consummated the largest of these recent purchases.[12]

A steady rise in southern incomes since World War II has significantly narrowed the economic gap between southerners and nonsoutherners. But the gap is not closed. Figures on per capita personal income in 1980 show every southern state except Texas below the national average. The poorest southern state, and also the poorest American state, Mississippi, falls almost thirty-one percent below the national average, and almost forty percent below that of the wealthiest states of the Northeast, Midwest, or Far West.[13] In the late 1930s President Franklin Delano Roosevelt called the South the nation's "economic problem number one." Such a statement today would be hooted down. Nevertheless, the South has not yet attained full membership in what used to be known as the Affluent American Society.

[11] Cash, "Preview to Understanding," x.

[12] Louisville *Courier-Journal,* December 18, 1977.

[13] "Revised State Personal Income, 1969–80," *Survey of Current Business,* LXI (July 1981), 31.

Let us look at recent southern politics. A number of new southern
congressmen elected in the early 1970s tended to be more liberal in their
voting than their senior regional colleagues. The wave of congressional
reform that took place then threatened to destroy one of the South's most
cherished agencies of political influence, the congressional seniority
system. For various reasons, some of them personal, such guardians of
southern interests as Representative Felix Edward Hebert (Louisiana),
Representative William Robert Poage (Texas), and Representative Wilbur
Daigh Mills (Arkansas) lost their positions as chairmen of powerful
committees in the House of Representatives.

But the leopard's spots by no means disappeared. No drastic shake-up
occurred in the Senate, and in a short time the new southern members of
the House began to sound and vote suspiciously like the old ones.
According to the *Congressional Quarterly,* the nucleus of opposition in
both houses to the more liberal parts of President James Earl ("Jimmy")
Carter's program still came from the South.[14] So formidable were the
operations of Senator Russell Billiu Long of Louisiana (then chairman of
the Senate Finance committee) that some observers ruefully spoke of
him as the "fourth branch" of the federal government. At the core of a
so-called Conservative Forum of Democratic congressmen, who since
the Republican success in the 1980 elections are asserting themselves,
appear none other than the once-liberal junior members from the South.
Lest anyone forget their regional identity, they have taken a name that
originally was conferred in derision upon their predecessors. They call
themselves the Boll Weevils.[15] Most ironic of all, and most illustrative of
the staying power of traditional southern politics, is the rise to the
chairmanship of the Senate Judiciary Committee of James Strom Thurmond of South Carolina, former Dixiecrat, Democrat-turned-Republi-
can, and Nixon supporter, who threatens to emerge as the South's new
"fourth branch" of the federal government.

What about the role of blacks in current southern politics? Unquestionably it has been spectacular; the blacks have made great gains and
can never again be canceled out of the regional political equation. But the
limits of black political power are also visible. Except in those localities
where they are heavily concentrated by de facto segregation, they have
usually been defeated in their bids for office. When a prominent black
ran for the governorship of Mississippi in 1970, he not only failed
to draw more than a token handful of liberal white votes, but he also
lost an alarming proportion of the black votes. True, in presidential
politics the black votes have become far more important than in local

[14] Louisville *Courier-Journal,* January 16, 1978; April 27, 1981.
[15] *Ibid.,* December 3, 1980.

politics. In 1976 they were decisive in forming, with a portion of the white votes, a coalition that carried most of the South for Carter. But this was a precarious victory. A majority of the whites opposed Carter then, and in 1980 this majority became strong enough to defeat him in all but his native state of Georgia. This outcome, plus the omens drawn from southern history, suggests that the white-black bond in regional presidential politics is a fragile one.

Finally, race relations today. Here one sees the sharpest change of all from the way of the pre–World War II South. But legal desegregation has not by any means wiped out the color line. Only through massive court-ordered programs of busing has significant integration come about in the most desegregated of southern institutions, the public schools, and even this accomplishment has been virtually nullified in many instances by resegregation through the flight of the whites to the suburbs or the withdrawal of their children to private schools. In Atlanta, for example, where the school system a few years ago was hailed as a model of orderly desegregation, the public schools are now ninety percent black. They are approaching the condition of the Washington, D.C., schools, which are reported to be ninety-six percent black.

It is not, however, in economic, political or racial affairs (at least not in official racial affairs) that the endurance of the South as a distinctive region is most pronounced. Rather, it is in the subtler areas of the mind and spirit, and even of the senses, of the eye, ear, tongue, and palate, that the South continues to affirm its differentness most effectively.

Southern religion would stand at or near the top of the list of distinguishing southern characteristics. The famed essayist and lampoonist Henry Louis Mencken derisively called the South "The Bible Belt." Shortly after World War II, Mississippian Hodding Carter wrote more sympathetically of southern religion: "Though the citadels crumble," he said, "the South remains the great western-world stronghold of Protestant, fundamentalist Christianity. . . . That thing called the old-time religion is in the blood of most of us, and if it is laughed at, the laughter has as accompaniment an almost inescapable inner, esoteric warning that the ways of God are not to be mocked by man."[16] The South today continues to represent the nation's strongest commitment to biblical literalism and orthodox Protestantism. The Southern Baptist church (the largest Protestant denomination in the country, with over twelve million members) is the foremost manifestation of this sectional religious outlook. It has been called the "folk church" of the South. A critic has parodied the Southern Baptists' faith in an eternal life of bliss

---

[16] Hodding Carter, *Southern Legacy* (Baton Rouge, 1950), 27, 28–29.

after this life of troubles by describing their conviction in these terms: "Hang on, there's a better life coming." To which the targets of this gibe have replied with bumper stickers (or some of them have) saying: "God said it. I believe it. That settles it."[17]

Most other denominations in the South hold views similar to those of the Southern Baptists, even if they proclaim them somewhat less vehemently. Public-opinion surveys indicate that southerners are likelier than nonsoutherners to believe in the immorality of the soul and the promise of reward and threat of punishment after death and to believe that religion holds the answers to the great problems of the world.[18] A larger proportion of students in southern colleges than in colleges elsewhere consider religion a relevant part of their lives. Psychologists even detect in southerners a greater tendency to depend upon prayer rather than technology for protection against tornadoes. If anyone believes the South has ceased to be a Bible Belt, he ought to make a Sunday automobile trip across the region with his radio tuned to one local station after another as he goes.

So pervasive is orthodox religion in the South, so intimate its connection with the other elements of life, that one scholar has given it the name "Culture-Protestantism."[19] Southern churches have persistently rejected the illusion of human perfectibility, the promise of a heaven on this earth. The leading character in Robert Penn Warren's novel *All the King's Men* appropriately says he has fully understood the inherent sinfulness of man since the Sunday school training of his rural Louisiana boyhood.[20]

This Calvinistic skepticism toward human possibilities carries over into the region's attitude toward all sorts of programs for the improvement of society. Thus, it is consistent with regional theology to condemn such proposals as that of a guaranteed annual wage as a violation of the Apostle Paul's injunction: "If any would not work, neither should he eat." The religious outlook often becomes public policy, for southern churches and the state and local authorities usually form so close a liaison that neither is aware of its existence; both honestly denounce a union of church and state as a subversion of American principles. State legislatures and other governing bodies reflect more directly than elsewhere the church attitudes on sex, divorce, abortion, equal rights for women, pornography, drugs, alcohol, education, child-rearing, parental

---

[17] Roland, *The Improbable Era,* 126.

[18] Reed, *The Enduring South,* 57–81.

[19] Samuel S. Hill, "The South's Culture-Protestantism," *Christian Century,* LXXIX (September 12, 1962), 1094–96.

[20] Robert Penn Warren, *All the King's Men* (New York, 1946), 358.

authority, dress, and general behavior.[21] The celebrated Moral Majority that claimed so much media time and space during the 1980 presidential campaign spoke more often than not with a decided southern accent.

After the defeat of the Confederacy a southern preacher said: "If we cannot gain our *political,* let us establish, at least, our *mental* independence."[22] There are those today who believe this exhortation has been carried out through the region's churches.

If the southern white churches have sustained a sense of sectional independence, both they and the black churches have sustained a sense of racial independence. A British observer in the South during Reconstruction described the withdrawal of the blacks then occurring from the white churches as an extension of emancipation.[23] It has remained thus to this day. The great majority of southern congregations are still completely black or white, or almost so, apparently by mutual consent. The saying holds true that the hour from eleven to twelve on Sunday morning is the most segregated time of the week in the South. The black churches played a vital role in the civil rights struggle of the 1950s and 1960s, yet nowhere is southern religious orthodoxy stronger.

The most acclaimed form of the South's cultural expression is its creative literature. Mencken once flippantly called the region "The Sahara of the Bozart" — a literary and artistic desert. Hardly had he coined this epithet when the South flowered into a remarkable literary renaissance that reached its peak in the Southern Gothic novels of Missippian William Faulkner. Set in the imaginary Yoknapatawpha County, Mississippi, they pictured a hell on earth of murder, lynching, mutilation, rape, deceit, incest, and miscegenation. Beneath the sound and fury of Faulkner's prose was a renunciation of modern American materialism, exploitiveness, and rootlessness and a yearning for the realization of the nobler ideals of the old southern aristocracy. At Vanderbilt University a group of poets, including John Crowe Ransom, Allen Tate, Donald Davidson, and Robert Penn Warren, defended traditional southern values in a magazine entitled *The Fugitive.* In 1930 these four poets joined with eight other writers, together known as the Agrarians, to bring out the controversial volume *I'll Take My Stand,* which contained a prescient warning of the dangers lying in wait for a progressive, industrial society. Ransom captured the spirit of the work in a single brilliant line, saying such a society was constantly engaged in

---

[21] Roland, *The Improbable Era,* 128 (quotation), 136.

[22] Rollin G. Osterweis, *The Myth of the Lost Cause, 1865–1900* (Hamden, Conn., 1973), 118.

[23] Quoted in Gunnar Myrdal, *An American Dilemma: The Negro Problem and Modern Democracy,* 2 vols. (New York, 1944), II, 860–61.

a losing war with nature, a war in which the society won only what he called "Pyrrhic victories . . . at points of no strategic importance."[24]

Other southerners during the last half-century have enriched American literature with works that vary from the high romance of Margaret Mitchell's *Gone with the Wind* to the stark, ribald, tragic satire of Erskine Caldwell's *Tobacco Road*. The outpouring of southern letters has not diminished since World War II. Perhaps the two most distinguished figures of the postwar period are Robert Penn Warren of Kentucky (transplanted eventually to Yale University) and Eudora Welty of Mississippi. Warren has spanned more fully than any other writer the entire era from the beginning of the Southern Renaissance to the present. Having interpreted the region's experience in many novels and essays and in some of the most powerful verse ever written in America, he stands with Faulkner at the summit of southern letters. Miss Welty also has been active during most of the period, producing novels and short stories that capture with remarkable fidelity the countless nuances of southern thought and speech. She exercises the region's most delicate literary touch.

Notwithstanding their diversity in mode and outlook, all southern writers share certain qualities that set them apart from others. The southerners place unusual emphasis on the very points most emphasized in southern life itself. These are family, history, race, religion, and a sense of place, of concreteness, and of the imperfectibility of man. One could never say of a novel by Faulkner what C. Vann Woodward has said of the work of a famed twentieth-century nonsouthern writer, Ernest Hemmingway: that is, "a Hemmingway hero with a grandfather is inconceivable. . . ."[25] Reynolds Price speaks of the influence on his own works of the surrounding North Carolinians of both races who, he says, could converse intelligibly and easily with their great-grandparents.[26] Southern fiction swarms with grandfathers and grandmothers, great-grandfathers and great-grandmothers, and so on *ad infinitum*. The strengths and weaknesses of the present generation are seen as a legacy from its forebears.

Allen Tate pointed out that regional writers reflect a sense of history as something more than what is written in books; that they see it as a force actually operating on society. Southerners, said Tate, possess a knowledge of history carried to the heart. One of Faulkner's characters puts it

[24] John Crowe Ransom, "Reconstructed but Unregenerate," in Twelve Southerners, *I'll Take My Stand: The South and the Agrarian Tradition* (New York, 1930), 15.

[25] Woodward, *The Burden of Southern History*, 31.

[26] Reynolds Price, "Dodo, Phoenix, or Tough Old Cock?" in H. Brandt Ayers and Thomas H. Naylor, eds., *You Can't Eat Magnolias* (New York, 1972), 75.

this way: "The past is never dead. It's not even past."[27] In discussing the career of Katherine Ann Porter—a writer of Texas birth and southern upbringing—Robert Penn Warren says her works are "drenched in historical awareness."[28] Henry Steele Commager says it is "possible to study the Civil War period in contemporary Southerners . . . [because] they retain the psychology and vocabulary of that period."[29] To the accusation that southerners continue to live in the past, the poet Miller Williams replies: "Not so, the past continues to live in southerners."[30]

So strong is the southern sense of place that the actions in southern novels cannot be imagined to have happened anywhere but where they did happen. There is an organic, symbiotic relationship between place and theme. Eudora Welty employs redundancy to emphasize the importance of place in her novels. It, she says, "is the named, identified, concrete, exact and exacting, and therefore credible, gathering-spot of all that has been felt, is about to be experienced, in the novel's progress."[31]

Another of Faulkner's characters demonstrates humorously the southern sense of concreteness by explaining the difference between how a southerner and a northerner go about establishing a goat ranch. The southerner does it unceremoniously when his herd of goats grows so large it can no longer be accommodated in the barnyard or on the front porch. The northerner begins with no goats at all but with a pencil and piece of paper to reckon how many yards of fence and how many acres of land are needed for a given number of imaginary goats. The southerner never has the problem of making the number of goats match the length of fence or amount of land. They never matched, and he doesn't expect them to. If, on the other hand, after the northerner has set up his business he is unable to make them all match, he resorts to pencil and paper again. Now, said Faulkner's speaker, instead of a goat ranch, the northerner has an "insolvency."[32]

Katherine Anne Porter explained the southern sense of concreteness by saying southerners cannot comprehend murder, for example, as an abstract thing. One should note here that, according to this principle, a southerner would never say what the young gang leader in the movie *The*

---

[27] Quoted in Woodward, *The Burden of Southern History,* 36.

[28] Robert Penn Warren, "The Genius of Katherine Anne Porter," *Saturday Review,* VII (December 1980), 11.

[29] New York *Times,* April 26, 1971, p. 37:6.

[30] Miller Williams, "The Dominance of Southern Writers," *LSU Alumni News,* XLI (September 1965), 3.

[31] Quoted in Frederick J. Hoffman, *The Art of Southern Fiction: A Study of Some Modern Novelists* (Carbondale, Ill., 1967), 13–14.

[32] William Faulkner, *The Hamlet* (New York, 1940), 90–91.

Godfather said to his distressed fiancée about a certain recent killing: that there was nothing personal about it. "A good southerner," continued Miss Porter, "doesn't kill anybody he doesn't know."[33]

Above all, southern writers dwell upon the inherent weakness and sinfulness of man. In other words, their themes are essentially religious, however secular they may appear to be. The critic Cleanth Brooks says of the southern writer: "He is not disposed to dissolve evil into nothing either by interpreting it as the temporary pressure of a hostile environment or by transforming it onto any other external thing that can be liquidated by one's voting the right way at the polls or by paying for its removal on the psychoanalyst's couch."[34]

The writer whose works since World War II most explicitly reveal the effect of southern religion is the late Flannery O'Connor of Georgia. In two novels and an assortment of short stories she used southern religious fundamentalism of spectacular intensity to satirize the emptiness of modern rationalism. One of her characters, in a God-versus-science argument, dismisses the marvels of the jet age with the sneer: "I wouldn't give you nothin' for no airplane. A buzzard can fly."[35]

Miss O'Connor's tart discourses on southern literature are classics of their own, and they aptly illustrate the regional mind. Once when asked why southern writers are so preoccupied with the grotesque, she replied that every southern theme is called grotesque by nonsouthern critics, unless it actually is grotesque. Then, she said, it is "called photographic realism."[36] On another occasion she wrote: "Whenever I'm asked why Southern writers particularly have a penchant for writing about freaks, I say it is because we are still able to recognize one." "To be able to recognize a freak," she continued, "you have to have some conception of the whole man, and in the South the general conception of man is still, in the main, theological. . . . I think it is safe to say that while the South is hardly Christ-centered, it is most certainly Christ-haunted. The Southerner . . . is very much afraid that he may have been formed in the image . . . of God."[37]

The most renowned southern novelist to emerge in the past two decades is Walker Percy of Louisiana. Literary critics sometimes call him an Existentialist. If he is indeed an Existentialist, he is unmistaka-

---

[33] Quoted in Hoffman, *The Art of Southern Fiction*, 6.

[34] Cleanth Brooks, "Regionalism in American Literature," *Journal of Southern History*, XXVI (February 1960), 41.

[35] Flannery O'Connor, *The Violent Bear It Away* (New York, 1960), 173.

[36] Quoted in Melvin J. Friedman and Lewis A. Lawson, eds., *The Added Dimension: The Art and Mind of Flannery O'Connor* (New York, 1966), 243.

[37] Quoted in Sister Kathleen Feeley, *Flannery O'Connor: Voice of the Peacock* (New Brunswick, N.J., 1972), x.

bly a Southern Existentialist. According to Cleanth Brooks, Percy has consciously tried to avoid writing the "southern novel." Yet all the telltale southern literary characteristics abound in his works. "I know of no present novelist who is more 'southern' in every sort of way . . . ," says Brooks. "As an observer of the southern scene, . . . [Percy] can scarcely be bettered as he describes the sights, smells, and sounds of the French Quarter in New Orleans; or the chatter and posturings of a concourse of automobile sales in Birmingham; or the precise differences in manner and accent between a damsel from Winchester, Virginia, a girl from Fort Worth, and a big, strapping drum majorette from Alabama."[38]

To a reader who is familiar with New Orleans and the nearby Gulf Coast of Mississippi, Percy's first novel, *The Moviegoer,* is a haunting exercise in the sense of place. At the same time, through the experiences of an aimless young movie addict, the story points up the sense of displacement that threatens much of modern American life. Percy's later works are aimed, in part, at the sexual and general behavioral license of today. "Whether or not Percy fancies himself as a writer of the southern novel," says Brooks, "his southern heritage has stood him in good stead as he deals with his chosen theme, the alienation within man's soul." In this respect, concludes Brooks, Percy is in the direct line of Ransom, Tate, Warren, and Faulkner.[39] Also, one might add, Percy is in the direct line of his cousin and father by adoption, the late William Alexander Percy—poet, essayist, and conservative Mississippi planter-aristocrat.

The same qualities that distinguish the writings of southern white authors are also found in those of southern black authors, though they have deliberately avoided trying to turn themselves into "black Faulkners." For understandable reasons many of the southern literary characteristics, such as the emphasis on race and violence, loom even larger in black literature than in white literature. Alex Haley's universally known work of "faction," as he calls it (part fact, part fiction), his book *Roots,* is an arresting study in the sense of place and family, as well as of race, violence, and almost every other theme particularly associated with southern letters. It is, of course, possible that the author of *Roots* could have been born and reared anywhere in the United States. But Haley is, in fact, a Tennessean. Probably, the author of *Roots* had to be a black from the South. Ernest J. Gaines, born in Louisiana and perhaps the most prominent of the recent black novelists, explains the inspiration for his

---

[38] Cleanth Brooks, "The Crisis in Cultures as Reflected in Southern Literature," in Louis D. Rubin Jr., ed., *The American South: Portrait of a Culture* (Baton Rouge and London, 1980), 188.

[39] *Ibid.,* 188–89.

work thus: "My body left Louisiana [he lives in California] but my soul did not."[40]

Though southerners have never won critical acclaim in the visual and performing arts comparable to that in literature, they have nevertheless made their mark in these media. The works of such modern southern or southern-born playwrights as Tennessee Williams, Lillian Hellman, and Paul Green show a close affinity for southern letters. Green could well have been speaking for Faulkner in saying: "Our very existence as a people here in the South has been something of an epic tragic drama—a sort of huge and terrifying Job story, if the truth were acknowledged."[41] The southern folk arts, or popular arts, including black spirituals, blues, and jazz, and white balladry, hillbilly, Gospel, and country music, also reflect the peculiarities of the southern experience and temperament.

Innumerable traits of everyday life, desirable and undesirable, continue to distinguish southerners. For example, the South still has the highest illiteracy rate in the nation. Nor do all the illiterates object to their condition. One of them, a cantankerous eighty-three-year-old, rallied his questioner with the declaration: "I guess I made it O.K., didn't I? . . . After all . . . a man's got a right not to read, ain't that right?"[42]

Violence and widespread possession of firearms are still hallmarks of the region. It maintains the highest homicide rates in the nation. On the other hand, there remains a sense of manners that causes even the hippiest and wooliest of students to reply with a "Yes, Ma'am," or a "No, sir." One is reminded of Cash's description of the graceful manners of the old plantation gentry and how these manners were reflected in what he called the "level-eyed" courtesy and ease of bearing of the ordinary folk.[43] Someone has said, to emphasize the irony, that a southerner will remain polite until he is angry enough to kill. A heartless southern murderer in one of Flannery O'Connor's short stories apologizes for being shirtless in the presence of the women who are about to become his victims. He courteously invites them to their deaths with the words, "Would you mind stepping back in them woods there?"[44]

Southern speech still features its drawling vowels, still calls a small stream of water a creek instead of a crick, and still says "You all" when addressing more than one person. Southern speech shows little sign of

[40] Quoted in *People Weekly,* IX (June 19, 1978), 94.

[41] Paul Green, "Symphonic Outdoor Drama," in Robert W. Howard, ed., *This Is the South* (Chicago, New York, and San Francisco, 1959), 251.

[42] New York *Times,* July 19, 1971, pp. 15:4–5.

[43] Cash, *The Mind of the South,* 70.

[44] Quoted in Josephine Hendin, *The World of Flannery O'Connor* (Bloomington, 1970), 38.

surrendering to the crisp stage diction of the television announcers or to the exhortations of the speech instructors. When southern-born movie stars return home on visits, I am told, they quickly lapse into the local vernacular and inflection. Nor does southern cooking seem to have yielded to the injunctions of the nutritionists. Southern "soul food," which for centuries before it got this name was eaten by whites and blacks alike, is now challenging the national taste buds in such forms as fried chicken (Kentucky and' otherwise) and even fried catfish, once considered by nonsoutherners to be the basest of edibles, if edible at all.

If the Redneck or Cracker of an earlier, rural South are disappearing as national stereotypes, they are being replaced by the southern Good Ole Boy: a figure who, according to a partly serious, partly whimsical, and even a partly affectionate description, is distinguishable by his uncouthness, his ruttishness, his beer belly, and his manner of mounting a bar stool—leading with the crotch.[45] Billy Carter, the Good Ole Boy, and Jimmy Carter, the born-again Christian, represented equally authentic national images of the modern South.

Finally, the South still retains a homogeneity and folksiness that seem about gone elsewhere. Having received little of the vast stream of European immigration that poured into the country during the latter half of the nineteenth century and the opening decades of the present century, the South lacks the so-called ethnic mix that makes up the rest of the nation. The South's two main ethnic groups, southern whites and southern blacks, are so large and so long established in the region that their homogeneity is natural and familylike. It does not need to be imposed by the public schools or by an administrative bureaucracy. Walker Percy says all "of white Mississippi . . . is one big kinship lodge."[46] The same could be said of black Mississippi; or of most of the South, white or black.

The region's folksiness defies the forces of urbanization and industrialization that are usually considered deadly to folksiness. Louis D. Rubin, Jr., identifies an extraordinary example of this quality by showing how southerners characteristically convert the impersonal artifacts of modern technology into socializing media. How the men who drive the monster tractor-trailers of American transport, "southern rednecks for the most part," he says, "good ole boys—are not merely watching the multilane road unfold before them. They are busily gossiping away with each other [on their CB radios], and with every motorist who comes

[45] Florence King, *Southern Ladies and Gentlemen* (New York, 1975), 91–93.
[46] Walker Percy, "Mississippi: The Fallen Paradise," *Harper's Magazine*, CCXXX (April 1965), 170.

along and wants to talk. . . . Driving along the interstate highway has, in short, been transformed into a social occasion!"[47]

Despite the conventions that preserve a large measure of racial segregation in the personal affairs and everyday life of the region, the relationship between the races is so ancient and so close that the sociological phenomenon known as "cultural pluralism" is hardly recognizable in the South. Indeed, a recent public opinion survey indicates that the outlook of southern whites and southern blacks is closer together on most points than that of southern and nonsouthern whites.[48]

If the South is growing more and more to resemble the rest of the nation, the rest of the nation is also growing more and more to resemble the South. The humiliation of defeat in the Vietnam War and of Watergate, the revelations of the misuse of the Federal Bureau of Investigation, the Central Intelligence Agency, and the Internal Revenue Service by presidents of both parties and of both liberal and conservative political and social persuasion, and the recognition of nationwide problems of poverty, racism, air and water pollution, and energy depletion: all have tarnished the national image of success, affluence, and innocence, have reaffirmed the eternal verity of universal human weakness, and have narrowed the philosophical gap between the North and South even as other forces are narrowing the material gap.

Perhaps the most conspicuous illustration of the trend toward a national consensus occurred in the 1976 election of a Southern Baptist from the Deep South to the presidency of the United States, a thing that as late as a dozen years earlier would have been unthinkable, and which, incidentally, may now again be unthinkable. The nationwide popularity of such television shows as "The Waltons" indicates that a Benign South has, to a degree, taken its place alongside the Benighted South in the popular imagination. The wittiest line in Jack Temple Kirby's work *Media-Made Dixie,* and a most perceptive line, is the one that identifies Jimmy Carter as "John-Boy Walton grown up."[49]

A frequently heard expression nowadays goes: "At last the South has rejoined the United States." Not so, says David Herbert Donald, ". . . the United States has finally decided to rejoin the South."[50] More

[47] Louis D. Rubin, Jr., "The American South: The Continuity of Self-Definition," in Rubin, ed., *The American South,* 20–21.

[48] Reed, *The Enduring South,* 83.

[49] Jack Temple Kirby, *Media-Made Dixie: The South in the American Imagination* (Baton Rouge and London, 1978), 172.

[50] New York *Times,* August 30, 1976, p. 23:2

guardedly, John Egerton says that while Dixie is being Americanized, America is being southernized.[51]

Egerton's observation is true even in the strict demographic meaning. During and after World War II millions of southerners migrated to the cities of the North and Far West, carrying their southern ways with them. There are today, for example, Southern Baptist churches scattered throughout these nonsouthern parts of the country. But for the last fifteen or twenty years also even greater numbers of northerners have been moving to the South, which seems about to become the nation's pivotal population area. Not all these immigrants are at first comfortable in their new home. There is the gasp of consternation the first time little Billy or little Jane comes in from the playground talking southern; the furrowed brow over the sudden prospect of acquiring a southern religious fundamentalist as a son-in-law or daughter-in-law. One hears of occasional efforts to establish some sort of compound to keep the natives at safe distance. You are doubtless familiar with Flannery O'Connor's story of the northerner in Atlanta who sold his house in the suburbs there to another northerner, reassuring him with these words: "You'll like this neighborhood. There's not a Southerner for two miles."[52]

But, as a rule, the newcomers and the natives soon establish amicable relations. Most of the newcomers are conservative in their political, economic, and social views to begin with, or, if not conservative, they are at least discreet in expressing their views, else they probably wouldn't have moved South in the first place. Also, the South throughout its entire history has demonstrated a remarkable capacity to absorb newcomers and convert them into southerners. Like China, it has conquered its conquerors. Many of the southern leaders in secession and the Civil War were either northern-born migrants to the Land-o'-Cotton or their children or grandchildren. The present newcomers, or their offspring, will eventually become indistinguishable from other southerners.

It would, of course, be foolish to deny that southern attributes are being diluted or diffused at a steady rate. Many of the changes are, of themselves, good. Who would complain over the recent increase in southern productivity and prosperity? Someone has said we ought not be so fond of our disabilities that we are unwilling to give them up when the time comes. But also we ought not forget that every gain has its price. Flannery O'Connor once lamented: "The anguish that most of us have observed for some time now has been caused not by the fact that the

---

[51] The theme of John Egerton's *The Americanization of Dixie: The Southernization of America* (New York, 1974).

[52] Quoted in Friedman and Lawson, eds., *The Added Dimension*, 246.

South is alienated from the rest of the country, but by the fact that it is not alienated enough, that every day we are getting more and more like the rest of the country, that we are being forced out, not only of our many sins but of our few virtues."[53] The warnings of the Vanderbilt Agrarians have never been more timely, especially for southerners, than they are now. Southerners ought to beware of committing themselves more deeply than they are already committed to a war against nature that will bring them hollow triumphs only — "Pyrrhic victories . . . at points of no strategic importance."

Even so, the South today is still discernibly the South. Carl N. Degler concluded his recent interpretive survey of the southern experience, *Place over Time,* with these words: "In short, neither in the realm of social fact nor in the realm of psychological identity has the South ceased to be distinctive, despite the changes of the twentieth century."[54] There is cause to believe the region's unique combination of political, religious, cultural, ethnic, and social traits, reinforced as they are by geography and history, myth and folklore, and convention and inertia, will for a good while yet keep it distinctive.

[53] Quoted, *ibid.,* 79.
[54] Carl N. Degler, *Place over Time: The Continuity of Southern Distinctiveness* (Baton Rouge and London, 1977), 126.

Bibliography

Abbott, Shirley, "Southern Women and the Indispensable Myth," *American Heritage,* 34 (December 1982), 82–91.

Adams, Richard P., "Faulkner and the Myth of the South," *Mississippi Quarterly,* 14 (1961), 131–37.

Alden, John R., *The First South* (Baton Rouge, 1961).

Alexander, Thomas B., Stanley Engerman, Forrest McDonald, Grady McWhiney, and Edward Pessen, "Antebellum North and South in Comparative Perspective: A Discussion," *American Historical Review,* 85 (1980), 1150–66.

————, "Persistent Whiggery in the Confederate South, 1860–1877," *Journal of Southern History,* 27 (1961), 305–29.

Atkinson, Maxine P., and Jacqueline Boles, "The Shaky Pedestal: Southern Ladies Yesterday and Today," *Southern Studies,* 24 (1985), 398–406.

Axtell, James, "White Legend: The Jesuit Missions in Maryland," *Maryland Historical Magazine,* 81 (1986), 1–7.

Ballard, Michael B., *A Long Shadow: Jefferson Davis and the Final Days of the Confederacy* (Jackson, Miss., 1986).

Bargainnier, Earl F., "The Myth of Moonlight and Magnolias," *Louisiana Studies,* 15 (1976), 5–20.

Belz, Herman, "Twentieth-Century American Historians and the Old South: A Review Essay," *Civil War History,* 31 (1985), 171–80.

Berlin, Ira, "Time, Space, and the Evolution of Afro-American Society on British Mainland North America," *American Historical Review,* 85 (1980), 44–78.

Berry, Mary F. and John W. Blassingame, *Long Memory: The Black Experience in America* (New York, 1982).

Berthoff, Rowland, "Celtic Mist over the South," *Journal of Southern History,* 52 (1986), 523–46.

Bickley, R. Bruce, Jr., "Joel Chandler Harris and the Old and New South: Paradoxes of Perception," *Atlanta Historical Journal,* 30 (1986), 9–31.

Blassingame, John W., *Black New Orleans, 1860–1880* (Chicago, 1973).

————, *The Slave Community: Plantation Life in the Antebellum South* (rev. ed., New York, 1979).

————, "Using the Testimony of Ex-Slaves: Approaches and Problems," *Journal of Southern History,* 41 (1975), 473–92.

Boles, John B., and Evelyn Thomas Nolen, *Interpreting Southern History: Historiographical Essays in Honor of Sanford W. Higginbotham* (Baton Rouge, 1987).

Boney, F. N., "The South's Peculiar Intuition," *Louisiana Studies,* 12 (1973), 565–77.

—————, *Southerners All* (Macon, Ga., 1984).

Boorstin, Daniel J., "The Vision and the Reality," in *The Americans: The Colonial Experience* (New York, 1966).

Boskin, Joseph, *Sambo: The Rise and Demise of an American Jester* (New York and Oxford, 1986).

Bradford, M. E., "What We Can Know for Certain: Frank Owsley and the Recovery of Southern History," *Sewanee Review,* 78 (1970), 664–69.

Breen, T. H., " 'Making a Crop': Tobacco and the Tidewater Planters on the Eve of Revolution," *Virginia Cavalcade,* 36 (1986), 53–65.

Bridenbaugh, Carl, *Myths and Realities: Societies of the Colonial South* (New York, 1963).

Brooks, Cleanth, "Faulkner and History," *Mississippi Quarterly,* 25 (1972), 3–14.

Brownell, Blaine A., "If You've Seen One, You Haven't Seen Them All: Recent Trends in Southern Urban History," *Houston Review,* 1 (1979), 63–80.

Byrd, Edward L., "The Old South as a Modern Myth: An Interpretive Essay," *Red River Valley Historical Review,* 1 (1974), 55–65.

Campbell, Edward D. C., *The Celluloid Society: Hollywood and the Southern Myth* (Knoxville, 1981).

Censer, Jane Turner, "Planters and the Southern Community: A Review Essay," *Virginia Magazine of History and Biography,* 94 (1986), 387–408.

Cider, Gerald, "When Parrots Learn to Talk, and Why They Can't: Domination, Deception, and Self-Deception in Indian-White Relations," *Comparative Studies in Society and History,* 29 (1987), 3–23.

Clinton, Catherine, *The Plantation Mistress: Woman's World in the Old South* (New York, 1982).

Cobb, James C., "From Muskogee to Luckenbach: Country Music and the 'Southernization' of America," *Journal of Popular Culture,* 16 (1982), 81–91.

Cole, Wayne S., "America First and the South," *Journal of Southern History,* 22 (1956), 36–47.

Connelly, Thomas L., *The Marble Man: Robert E. Lee and His Image in American Society* (New York, 1977).

—————, and Barbara L. Bellows, *God and General Longstreet: The Lost Cause and the Southern Mind* (Baton Rouge, 1982).

Cords, Nicholas, and Patrick Gerster, eds., "The Mythology of the South," in *Myth and the American Experience,* vol. 1 (New York, 1978), 88.

Cotterill, Robert S., "The Old South to the New," *Journal of Southern History,* 15 (1949), 3–8.

Cressy, David, "Elizabethan America: 'God's Own Latitude?," *History Today,* 36 (1986), 44–50.

Cunliffe, Marcus, *Soldiers and Civilians: The Martial Spirit in America, 1775–1865* (Boston, 1968), 335–84.

Current, Richard N., "Fiction as History: A Review Essay," *Journal of Southern History,* 52 (1986), 77–90.

Danoff, Clarence H., "Four Decades of Thought on the South's Economic Problems," in Melvin Greenhut and W. Tate Whitman, eds., *Essays in Southern Economic Development* (Chapel Hill, 1964), 7–68.

Davenport, Garvin F., Jr., *The Myth of Southern History: Historical Consciousness in Twentieth-Century Southern Literature* (Nashville, 1970).

_____, "Thomas Dixon's Mythology of Southern History," *Journal of Southern History,* 36 (1970), 350–67.

David, Paul A., Herbert Gutman, Richard Such, Peter Temin, and Gavin Wright, *Reckoning with Slavery: A Critical Study in the Quantitative History of American Negro Slavery* (New York, 1976).

Davis, David Brion, *The Problem of Slavery in the Age of Revolution, 1770–1823* (Ithaca, 1975).

_____, *The Problem of Slavery in Western Culture* (Ithaca, 1966).

_____, *Slavery and Human Progress* (New York, 1984).

Davis, Michael, *The Image of Lincoln in the South* (Knoxville, 1972).

Dawson, Jan C., "The Puritan and the Cavalier: The South's Perception of Contrasting Traditions," *Journal of Southern History,* 44 (1978), 597–614.

Dazey, Mary Ann, "Truth in Fiction and Myth in Political Rhetoric: The Old South's Legacy," *Southern Studies,* 25 (1986), 305–10.

DeConde, Alexander, "The South and Isolationism," *Journal of Southern History,* 24 (1958), 332–46.

Degler, Carl, "Dawn without Noon," in *Out of Our Past: The Forces That Shaped Modern America* (New York, 1984), 228–57.

_____, "The Foundations of Southern Distinctiveness," *Southern Review,* 13 (1977), 225–39.

_____, *Neither Black nor White: Slavery and Race Relations in Brazil and the United States* (New York, 1971).

_____, *The Other South: Southern Dissenters in the Nineteenth Century* (New York, 1974).

_____, *Place over Time: The Continuity of Southern Distinctiveness* (Baton Rouge, 1977).

_____, "Remaking American History," *Journal of American History,* 67 (1980), 7–25.

_____, "Rethinking Post–Civil War History," *Virginia Quarterly Review,* 57 (1981), 250–67.

_____, "The South in Southern History Textbooks," *Journal of Southern History,* 30 (1964), 48–57.

_____, "Thesis, Antithesis, Synthesis: The South, the North and the Nation," *Journal of Southern History,* 53 (1987), 3–18.

_____, "Why Historians Change Their Minds," *Pacific Historical Review,* 45 (1976), 167–84.

Dillon, Merton L., *Ulrich Bonnell Phillips: Historian of the Old South* (Baton Rouge, 1985).

Donald, David, "The Confederate as a Fighting Man," *Journal of Southern History,* 35 (1959).

————, "The Scalawag in Mississippi Reconstruction," *Journal of Southern History,* 10 (1944), 447–60.

Dykeman, Wilma, "The Southern Demagogue," *Virginia Quarterly Review,* 33 (1957), 558–68.

Durant, Susan S., "The Gently Furled Banner: The Development of the Myth of the Lost Cause, 1865–1900" (unpublished Ph.D. dissertation, University of North Carolina, 1972).

Durden, Robert, "A Half-Century of Change in Southern History," *Journal of Southern History,* 51 (1985), 3–14.

Eaton, Clement, *The Waning of the Old South Civilization* (New York, 1969).

Egerton, John, *The Americanization of Dixie: The Southernization of America* (New York, 1974).

Engerman, Stanley, L., "The Antebellum South: What Probably Was and What Should Have Been," *Agricultural History,* 44 (1970), 127–42.

————, "A Reconsideration of Southern Economic Growth, 1770–1860," *Agricultural History,* 49 (1975), 343–61.

————, and Eugene D. Genovese, eds., *Race and Slavery in the Western Hemisphere: Quantitative Studies* (Princeton, 1975).

Estaville, Lawrence E., Jr., "Changeless Cajuns: Nineteenth-Century Reality or Myth?," *Louisiana History,* 28 (1987), 117–40.

Evans, William McKee, "From the Land of Canaan to the Land of Guinea: The Strange Odyssey of the 'Son of Ham'," *American Historical Review,* 85 (1980), 15–43.

Evitts, William J., "The Savage South: H. L. Mencken and the Roots of a Persistent Image," *Virginia Quarterly Review,* 49 (1973), 597–611.

Faust, Drew G., "Christian Soldiers: The Meaning of Revivalism in the Confederate Army," *Journal of Southern History,* 53 (1987), 63–90.

————, *The Ideology of Slavery: Proslavery Thought in the Antebellum South, 1830–1860* (Baton Rouge, 1981).

Ferris, William, "The Dogtrot: A Mythic Image in Southern Culture," *Southern Quarterly,* 25 (1986), 72–85.

Fishwick, Marshall, "Robert E. Lee: The Guardian Angel Myth," *Saturday Review,* March 4, 1961, 17–19.

Floan, Howard R., *The South in Northern Eyes, 1831–1861* (Austin, 1958).

Fogel, Robert W., and Stanley L. Engerman, *Time on the Cross: The Economics of American Negro Slavery* 2 vols. (Boston, 1974).

Fox-Genovese, Elizabeth, "Scarlet O'Hara: The Southern Lady as New Woman," *American Quarterly,* 33 (1981), 391–411.

Franklin, John Hope, "Mirrors for Americans: A Century of Reconstruction History," *American Historical Review,* 85 (1980), 1–14.

————, "The North, the South, and the American Revolution," *Journal of American History,* 62 (1975), 5–23.

————, "Southern History: The Black-White Connection," *Atlanta Historical Journal,* 30 (1986), 7–18.

Frederickson, George, *The Black Image in the White Mind: The Debate on Afro-American Character and Destiny* (New York, 1971).

————, "Masters and Mudsills: The Role of the Planter Ideology of South

Carolina," *South Atlantic Urban Studies,* 2 (1978), 73–88.

Gaines, Francis Pendelton, *The Southern Plantation: A Study in the Development and Accuracy of a Tradition* (New York, 1924).

Gara, Larry, *The Liberty Line: The Legend of the Underground Railroad* (Lexington, 1967).

Genovese, Eugene D., *In Red and Black: Marxian Explorations in Southern and Afro-American History* (New York, 1971).

————, *Roll, Jordan, Roll: The World the Slaves Made* (New York, 1974).

————, "Yeoman Farmers in a Slaveholders' Democracy," *Agricultural History,* 49 (1975), 331–42.

————, and Elizabeth Fox-Genovese, "The Religious Ideals of Southern Slave Society," *Georgia Historical Quarterly,* 70 (1986), 1–16.

————, "The Slave Economies in Political Perspective," *Journal of American History,* 66 (1979), 7–23.

Gerster, Patrick G., and Nicholas J. Cords, "The Mythology of the South," in *Myth in American History,* (New York, 1977), 110–36.

————, "The Northern Origins of Southern Mythology," in Charles R. Wilson, ed., *The Encyclopedia of Southern Culture* (Chapel Hill, 1988).

Gilmore, Al-Tony, ed., *Revisiting Blassingame's* The Slave Community: *The Scholars Respond* (Westport, Conn., 1978).

Goldfield, David R., *Promised Land: The South since 1945* (Arlington Heights, Ill., 1987).

Gomez, Jewelle, "Black Women Heroes: Here's Reality, Where's the Fiction?," *Black Scholar,* 17 (1986), 8–13.

Govan, Thomas P., "Was the Old South Different?," *Journal of Southern History,* 21 (1955), 447–55.

Grantham, Dewey W., Jr., "The Contours of Southern Progressivism," *American Historical Review,* 86 (1981), 1009–34.

————, "Regional Imagination: Social Scientists and the American South," *Journal of Southern History,* 34 (1968), 3–32.

————, ed., *The South and the Sectional Image: The Sectional Theme since Reconstruction* (New York, 1967)

————, "South to Posterity," *Mid-West Quarterly,* 8 (1966).

————, "The Southern Bourbons Revisited," *South Atlantic Quarterly,* 60 (1961), 286–95.

Green, Fletcher, "Democracy in the Old South," *Journal of Southern History,* 12 (1946), 3–23.

————, *The Role of the Yankee in the Old South* (Athens, Ga., 1973).

————, "The South and Its History," *Current History,* 35 (1958), 287–91.

Gross, Seymour L., and Eileen Bender, "History, Politics and Literature: The Myth of Nat Turner," *American Quarterly,* 23 (1974), 487–518.

Gundersen, Joan R., "The Double Bonds of Race and Sex: Black and White Women in a Colonial Virginia Parish," *Journal of Southern History,* 52 (1986), 351–72.

Gutman, Herbert G., *The Black Family in Slavery and Freedom* (New York, 1976).

————, *Slavery and the Numbers Game* (Urbana, 1975).

————, "The World Two Cliometricians Made," *Journal of Negro History,* 60 (1975), 53–227.

Gwin, Minrose C., *Black and White Women of the Old South: The Peculiar Sisterhood in American Literature* (Knoxville, 1985).

Hackney, Sheldon, "The South as a Counter Culture," *American Scholar,* 42 (1973), 283–93.

Hagler, D. Harland, "The Ideal Woman in the Antebellum South: Lady or Farmwife?," *Journal of Southern History,* 46 (1980), 405–18.

Hall, John A., "Disillusioned with Paradise: A Southern Woman's Impression of the Rural North in 1862," *Southern Studies,* 25 (1986), 204–7.

Hanna, William F., "A Gettysburg Myth Exploded," *Civil War Times Illustrated,* 24 (1986), 43–47.

Harlan, Louis R., *Booker T. Washington: The Making of a Black Leader, 1856–1901* (New York, 1972).

————, *Booker T. Washington: The Wizard of Tuskegee, 1901–1915* (New York, 1983).

Herskovits, Melville, *The Myth of the Negro Past* (Boston, 1958).

Herring, George C., and Gary R. Hess, "Regionalism and Foreign Policy: The Dying Myth of Southern Internationalism," *Southern Studies,* 21 (1981), 247–77.

Hill, Samuel S., ed. *Encyclopedia of Religion in the South* (Macon, 1984).

————, *Southern Churches in Crisis* (New York, 1967).

————, "The South's Culture—Protestantism," *Christian Century,* 79 (1962), 1094–96.

Hines, Linda O., "White Mythology and Black Duality: George Washington Carver's Response to Racism and the Radical Left," *Journal of Negro History,* 62 (1977), 134–46.

Hobson, Fred C., Jr., *Serpent in Eden: H. L. Mencken and the South* (Chapel Hill, 1974).

Hofferber, Michael, "Bronze Heroes," *Civil War Times Illustrated,* 26 (1987), 32–37.

Hofstadter, Richard, "Ulrich B. Phillips and the Plantation Legend," *Journal of Negro History,* 29 (1944), 109–24.

Holzer, Harold, "Confederate Caricature of Abraham Lincoln," *Illinois History Journal,* 80 (1987), 23–36.

Inscoe, John C., *"The Clansman* on Stage and Screen: North Carolina Reacts," *North Carolina Historical Review,* 64 (1987), 139–61.

Issac, Rhys, "Evangelical Revolt: The Nature of the Baptists' Challenge to the Traditional Order in Virginia, 1765–1775," *William and Mary Quarterly,* 31 (1974), 345–68.

————, *The Transformation of Virginia, 1740–1790* (Chapel Hill, 1974).

Johannsen, Robert W., *To the Halls of the Montezumas: The Mexican War in the American Imagination* (New York, 1985).

Johnson, Michael P., "Mary Boykin Chesnut's Autobiography and Biography: A Review Essay," *Journal of Southern History,* 47 (1981), 585–92.

Jones, Anne Goodwyn, *Tomorrow Is Another Day: The Woman Writer in the South, 1859–1936* (Baton Rouge, 1980).

Karanikas, Alexander, *Tillers of a Myth: Southern Agrarians as Social and Literary Critics* (Madison, 1966).

Keyserling, Hermann, "The South—America's Hope," *Atlantic Monthly,* 144 (1929), 605–8.

Klement, Frank L., "Civil War Politics, Nationalism, and Postwar Myths," *Historian,* 38 (1976), 419–38.

King, Richard H., *A Southern Renaissance: The Cultural Awakening of the American South, 1930–1955* (New York, 1980).

Kirby, Jack Temple, *Media-Made Dixie: The South in the American Imagination* (Baton Rouge, 1978).

Kolchin, Peter, "Reevaluating the Antebellum Slave Community: A Comparative Perspective," *Journal of American History,* 70 (1983), 579–601.

Kondert, Nancy T., "The Romance and Reality of Defeat: Southern Women in 1865," *Journal of Mississippi History,* 35 (1973), 141–52.

Kulikoff, Allan, "The Colonial Cheseapeake: Seedbed of Antebellum Southern Culture?," *Journal of Southern History,* 45 (1979), 513–40.

————, "The Origins of Afro-American Society in Tidewater Maryland and Virginia, 1700–1790," *William and Mary Quarterly,* 35 (1978), 226–59.

————, *Tobacco and Slaves: The Development of Southern Cultures in the Chesapeake, 1680–1800* (Chapel Hill, 1986).

Land, Aubrey C., "The American South: First Epiphanies," *Journal of Southern History,* 50 (1984), 3–14.

Lemons, J. Stanley, "Black Stereotypes as Reflected in Popular Culture, 1880–1920," *American Quarterly,* 29 (1977), 102–16.

Lerche, Charles O., Jr., *The Uncertain South: Its Changing Patterns of Politics and Foreign Policy* (New York, 1964).

Leslie, Kent Anderson, "A Myth of the Southern Lady: Antebellum Proslavery Rhetoric and the Proper Place of Women," *Sociological Spectrum,* 6 (1986), 31–49.

Levesque, George A., "Biracialism, the 'Central Theme' Thesis and the Emergence of Southern Sectionalism," *Journal of Black Studies,* 6 (1975), 158–74.

Levine, Lawrence W., *Black Culture and Black Consciousness: Afro-American Folk Thought from Slavery to Freedom* (New York, 1977).

Litwack, Leon F., *Been in the Storm So Long: The Aftermath of Slavery* (New York, 1979).

Lowe, Richard, "Another Look at Reconstruction in Virginia," *Civil War History,* 32 (1986), 56–76.

McArthur, Judith N. "Myth, Reality and Anomaly: The Complex World of Rebecca Hagerty," *East Texas Historical Journal,* 24 (1986), 18–32.

McCardell, John, *The Idea of a Southern Nation: Southern Nationalists and Southern Nationalism, 1830–1860* (New York, 1979).

McDonald, Forrest, and Grady McWhiney, "The South from Self-Sufficiency to Peonage: An Interpretation," *American Historical Review,* 85 (1980), 1095–118.

————, "The Antebellum Southern Herdsman: A Reinterpretation," *Jour-*

nal of Southern History, 41 (1975), 147–66.

Mackintosh, Barry, "George Washington Carver: The Making of a Myth," *Journal of Southern History,* 42 (1976), 507–28.

McPherson, James M., "Antebellum Southern Exceptionalism: A New Look at an Old Question," *Civil War History,* 29 (1983), 230–44.

McWhiney, Grady, "Jefferson Davis—The Unforgiven," *Journal of Mississippi History,* 42 (1980), 113–27.

———, *Southerners and Other Americans* (New York, 1973).

———, and Francis Simkins, "The Ghostly Legend of the KKK," *Negro History Bulletin,* 14 (1951), 109–12.

———, and Forrest McDonald, "Celtic Origins of Southern Herding Practices," *Journal of Southern History,* 51 (1985), 165–82.

Marius, Richard, "Musing on the Mysteries of the American South," *Daedalus,* 13 (1984), 143–76.

Mathis, Ray, "Mythology and the Mind of the New South," *Georgia Historical Quarterly,* 60 (1976), 228–38.

May, Robert E., "Dixie's Martial Image: A Continuing Historical Enigma," *Historian,* 40 (1978), 213–34.

———, *"Gone with the Wind* as Southern History: A Reappraisal," *Southern Quarterly,* 17 (1978), 51–64.

Mayo, Bernard, *Myths and Men* (New York, 1963).

Middleton-Keirn, Susan, "Magnolias and Microchips: Regional Subcultural Constructions of Femininity," *Sociological Spectrum,* 6 (1986), 83–107.

Miller, John Chester, *The Wolf by the Ears: Thomas Jefferson and Slavery* (New York, 1977).

Miller, Randall M., "The Man in the Middle: The Black Slave Driver," *American Heritage,* 30 (October 1979), 40–49.

Moore, John Hebron, "Two Cotton Kingdoms," *Agricultural History,* 60 (1986), 1–16.

Morgan, Chester M., *Redneck Liberal: Theodore G. Bilbo and the New Deal* (Baton Rouge, 1985).

Morgan, Edmund S., *American Slavery-American Freedom: The Ordeal of Colonial Virginia* (New York, 1975).

Mowry, George E., *Another Look at the Twentieth-Century South* (Baton Rouge, 1973).

Nagel, Paul C. "Reconstruction: Adams Style," *Journal of Southern History,* 52 (1987), 3–18.

Napier, John Hawkins III, "The Militant South Revisited: Myths and Realities," *Alabama Review,* 33 (1980), 243–65.

Nash, Gary B., "The Image of the Indian in the Southern Colonial Mind," *William and Mary Quarterly,* 29 (1972), 197–230.

Noggle, Burl, "Variety and Ambiguity: The Recent Approach to Southern History," *Mississippi Quarterly,* 16 (1963–64) 21–35.

O'Brien, Mathew C., "John Esten Cooke, George Washington, and the Virginia Cavaliers," *Virginia Magazine of History and Biography,* 84 (1976), 259–65.

O'Brien, Michael, "C. Vann Woodward and the Burden of Southern Liberalism," *American Historical Review,* 78 (1973), 589–604.

————, *The Idea of the American South, 1920–1941* (Baltimore, 1979).

————, "The Lineaments of Antebellum Southern Romanticism," *Journal of American Studies,* 20 (1986), 165–88.

Osterweiss, Roland G., *The Myth of the Lost Cause, 1865–1900* (Hamden, Conn., 1973).

————, *Romanticism and Nationalism in the Old South* (New Haven, 1949).

Owsley, Frank L. and Harriet C. Owsley, "The Economic Basis of Society in the Lake Ante-Bellum South," *Journal of Southern History,* 6 (1940), 24–45.

Payne, Ladell, "Willie Stark and Huey Long: Atmosphere, Myth or Suggestion," *American Quarterly,* 20 (1968), 580–95.

Perry, Richard L. "The Front Porch as Stage and Symbol in the Deep South," *Journal of American Culture,* 8 (1985), 13–18.

Peskin, Allan, "Was There a Compromise of 1877?," *Journal of American History,* 60 (1973), 63–75. Reply by C. Vann Woodward, "Yes, There Was a Compromise of 1877" (same citation).

Pessen, Edward, "How Different from Each Other Were the Antebellum North and South?," *American Historical Review,* 85 (1980), 1119–49.

Peterson, Thomas Virgil, *Ham and Japheth: The Mythic World of Whites in the Antebellum South* (Metuchen, N.J., 1978).

Potter, David, "On Understanding the South," *Journal of Southern History,* 30 (1964), 451–62.

————, *The South and the Sectional Conflict* (Baton Rouge, 1968).

Pyron, Darden Asbury, "*Gone with the Wind* and the Southern Cultural Awakening," *Virginia Quarterly Review,* 62 (1986), 565–87.

Rainard, R. Lyn, "The Gentlemanly Ideal in the South, 1660–1860: An Overview," *Southern Studies,* 25 (1986), 295–304.

Reed, John Shelton, *The Enduring South: Subcultural Persistence in Mass Culture* (Chapel Hill, 1974).

————, *One South: An Ethnic Approach to Regional Culture* (Baton Rouge, 1982).

————, *Southerners: The Social Psychology of Sectionalism* (Chapel Hill, 1983).

Rogers, Gayle J., "The Changing Image of the Southern Woman: A Performer on a Pedestal," *Journal of Popular Culture,* 16 (1982), 60–67.

Roland, Charles P., *The Improbable Era: The South since World War II* (Lexington, 1975).

————, "The South, America's Will-o'-the Wisp Eden," *Louisiana History,* 11 (1970), 101–19.

Roller, David C., and Robert W. Twyman, eds., *The Encyclopedia of Southern History* (Baton Rouge, 1979).

Rozwenc, Edwin C., "Captain John Smith's Image of America," *William and Mary Quarterly,* 16 (1959), 27–36.

————, ed., *The American South: Portrait of a Culture* (Baton Rouge, 1980).

Rubin, Louis D., Jr., "The Historical Image of Modern Southern Writing,"

Journal of Southern History, 22 (1956), 147–66.

————, "The South and the Faraway Country," *Virginia Quarterly Review,* 38 (1962), 444–59.

Scarborough, William K., *The Overseer: Plantation Management in the Old South* (Baton Rouge, 1966).

Scott, Ann Firor, "The 'New Women' in the South," *South Atlantic Quarterly,* 61 (1962), 473–83.

————, "The Progressive Wind from the South, 1906–13," *Journal of Southern History,* 29 (1963), 53–70.

————, *The Southern Lady: From Pedestal to Politics* (Chicago, 1970).

————, "Women in a Plantation Culture: Or What I Wish I Knew about Southern Women," *South Atlantic Urban Studies,* II (1978), 24–33.

————, "Women's Perspectives on the Patriarchy in the 1850's," *Journal of American History,* 61 (1974), 52–64.

Seidel, Kathryn Lee, *The Southern Belle in the American Novel* (Tampa, 1985).

Sellers, Charles G., Jr., ed., *The Southerner as American* (Chapel Hill, 1960).

————, "Who Were the Southern Whigs?," *American Historical Review,* 59 (1954), 335–46.

Shapiro, Edward S., "Frank L. Owsley and the Defense of Southern Identity," *Tennessee Historical Quarterly,* 36 (1977), 75–94.

Shaw, Barton C., "Henry W. Grady Heralds 'The New South'," *Atlanta Historical Journal,* 30 (1986), 55–66.

Shore, Laurence, "The Poverty of Tragedy in Historical Writing on Southern Slavery," *South Atlantic Quarterly,* 85 (1986), 147–64.

Simkins, Francis B., "The Everlasting South," *Journal of Southern History,* 13 (1947), 307–22.

————, "The South," in Merrill Jensen, ed., *Regionalism in America* (Madison, 1951), 147–72.

————, "Tolerating the South's Past," *Journal of Southern History,* 21 (1955), 3–16.

Simpson, John A., "The Cult of the 'Lost Cause'," *Tennessee Historical Quarterly,* 34 (1975), 350–61.

Singal, Daniel Joseph, "Ulrich B. Phillips: The Old South as the New," *Journal of American History,* 54 (1977), 871–91.

Skaggs, Merrill Maguire, "Roots: A New Black Myth," *Southern Quarterly,* 17 (1978), 42–50.

Smiley, David L., "The Quest for the Central Theme in Southern History," *South Atlantic Quarterly,* 71 (1972), 307–25.

Smith, Henry Nash, *Virgin Land: The American West as Symbol and Myth* (Cambridge, 1970).

Smith, Stephen A., *Myth, Media, and the Southern Mind* (Fayetteville, 1985).

————, "The Old South Myth as a Contemporary Southern Commodity," *Journal of Popular Culture,* 16 (1982), 22–29.

Soapes, Thomas F., "The Federal Writer's Project Slave Interviews: Useful Data or Misleading Source," *Oral History Review,* (1977), 33–38.

Sosna, Morton, "The South Old and New: A Review Essay," *Wisconsin*

Magazine of History, 55 (1972), 231–35.

Spruill, Julia Cherry, *Women's Life and Work in the Southern Colonies* (New York, 1973).

Stampp, Kenneth M., "Rebels and Sambos: The Search for the Negro's Personality in Slavery," *Journal of Southern History,* 37 (1971), 367–92.

Stephenson, Wendell Holmes, "The South Lives in History," *Historical Outlook,* 23 (1932).

Tate, Allen, "Faulkner's 'Sanctuary' and the Southern Myth," *Virginia Quarterly Review,* 44 (1968), 418–27.

Thornton, Kevin Pierce, "Symbolism at Old Miss and the Crisis of Southern Identity," *South Atlantic Quarterly,* 86 (1987), 254–68.

Tindall, George B., "The Benighted South: Origins of a Modern Image," *Virginia Quarterly Review,* 40 (1964), 281–94.

———, *The Disruption of the Solid South* (New York, 1973).

———, *The Ethnic Southerner: Beyond the Mainstream* (Baton Rouge, 1976).

———, "The SunBelt Snow Job," *Houston Review,* 1 (1979), 3–13.

Trelease, Allen W., "Who Were the Scalawags?," *Journal of Southern History,* 29 (1963), 445–68.

Van Deburg, William L., *The Slave Driver: Black Agricultural Labor Supervisors in the Antebellum South* (Westport, Conn., 1979).

Vandiver, Frank E., "Jefferson Davis—Leader without Legend," *Journal of Southern History,* 43 (1977), 3–18.

Van West, Carroll, "Perpetuating the Myth of America: Scottsboro and Its Interpreters," *South Atlantic Quarterly,* 80 (1981), 36–48.

Van Steeg, Clarence L., "Historians and the Southern Colonies," in Ray A. Billington, ed., *The Reinterpretation of Early American History* (San Marino, Calif., 1966).

Walters, Ronald G., "The Erotic South: Civilization and Sexuality in American Abolitionism," *American Quarterly,* 72 (1973), 177–201.

Ward, John William, *Andrew Jackson: Symbol for an Age* (New York, 1962).

Warren, Robert Penn, *The Legacy of the Civil War: Meditations on the Centennial* (New York, 1964).

Watson, Richie Devon, Jr., *The Cavalier in Virginia Fiction* (Baton Rouge, 1985).

Whitridge, Arnold, "The John Brown Legend," *History Today,* 7 (1957), 211–20.

Williams, D. Alan, "The Virginia Gentry and the Democratic Myth," in Howard H. Quint, Dean Albertson, and Milton Cantor, eds., *Main Problems in American History* (Homewood, Ill., 1972), 25–33.

Williams, T. Harry, *Romance and Realism in Southern Politics* (Athens, Ga. 1961).

Williamson, Joel, "The Oneness of Southern Life," *South Atlantic Urban Studies,* 2 (1978), 78–89.

Wilson, Charles Reagan, *Baptized in Blood: The Religion of the Lost Cause, 1865–1920* (Athens, Ga., 1980).

———, "The Death of Bear Bryant: Myth and Ritual in the Modern

South," *South Atlantic Quarterly,* 86 (1987), 282–95.

————, ed., *The Encyclopedia of Southern Culture* (Chapel Hill, 1988).

Wood, Peter H., *Black Majority: Negroes in Colonial South Carolina from 1670 through the Stono Rebellion* (New York, 1974).

————, "'I Did the Best I Could for my Day': The Study of Early Black History during the Second Reconstruction, 1960–1976," *William and Mary Quarterly,* 35 (1978), 185–225.

————, "'Taking Care of Business' in Revolutionary South Carolina: Republicanism and the Slave Society," *South Atlantic Urban Studies,* 2 (1978), 49–72.

Woodman, Harold D., "New Perspectives on Southern Economic Development: A Comment," *Agricultural History,* 49 (1975), 374–80.

————, "Sequel to Slavery: The New History Views the Postbellum South," *Journal of Southern History,* 43 (1977), 523–41.

Woodward, C. Vann, "The Aging of America," *American Historical Review,* 82 (1977), 583–94.

————, "The Antislavery Myth," *American Scholar,* 31 (1962), 312–28.

————, "The North and South of It," *American Scholar,* 35 (1966), 647–58.

————, "Southerners versus the Southern Establishment," *Atlanta History,* 31 (1987), 4–11.

————, "Southern Mythology," *Commentary,* 42 (May 1965), 60–63.

————, *The Strange Career of Jim Crow* (New York, 1974).

————, *Thinking Back: The Perils of Writing History* (Baton Rouge, 1986).

————, "Time and Place," *Southern Review,* 22 (1986), 1–14.

————, "Why the Southern Renaissance?," *Virginia Quarterly Review,* 51 (1975), 222–39.

Wright, Gavin, "The Efficiency of Slavery: Another Interpretation," *American Economic Review,* 69 (1979), 219–26.

————, *Old South, New South: An Economic History since the Civil War* (New York, 1985).

Wright, Louis B., *The Dream of Prosperity in Colonial America* (New York, 1965).

————, "Intellectual History and the Colonial South," *William and Mary Quarterly,* 16 (1959), 214–27.

————, "Less Moonlight and Roses," *American Scholar,* 12 (1943), 263–72.

Wyatt-Brown, Bertram, *Southern Honor: Ethics and Behavior in the Old South* (New York, 1982).

Zinn, Howard, *The Southern Mystique* (New York, 1964).

Index

Abolitionist(s), 19, 22, 108, 109, 114
  role in development of southern myths, 6
Adams, Charles Francis, Jr., 56
Adams, Henry, 26, 54
  positive exposure to southern lifestyle, 55
  and attitude toward the South, 144
Addams, Jane, 95
Air conditioning
  as affecting southern lifestyle, 136
All the King's Men (Warren), 162
American Dilemma, An (Myrdal), 26, 49
American Historical Association
  meeting in Durham, N.C. (1929), 8
American Mercury. See Henry Louis Mencken
American Way of Life
  as American religion, 126
Ames, Jesse Daniel
  and antilynching, 93, 154
Aristocracy (southern)
  northern fascination with, 49
Ashmore, Harry, 39
Association of Southern Women for the
    Prevention of Lynching, 154
Atlanta
  image as New South Byzantium, 136
  and school desegregation, 161
Atlantic Coast Conference South (sports), 136

Bacon's Rebellion
  role of colonial women in, 151
Bailey, Thomas A.
  and definition of myth, xiv
Baptist Church (Southern), 161
Bardstown (Federal Hill), 47
Beale, Howard K., 36
Beard, Charles and Mary, 36, 40
Benèt, Stephen Vincent
  quoted, 48
Benighted South, 9, 15, 35
  on development of image during 1920s, 6
  neo-abolitionist image of, 134ff.
Bible Belt, 134
Bilbo, Theodore G., 66
Birth of a Nation, The (Griffith), 55

Black Sambo, 46ff.
Blacks. *See* Negro(es); Slavery (Slaves)
Blair, Emily Newell, 97
Blease, Cole L., 66, 98
Boll Weevils
  as political force, 160
Bourbons (Redeemers), 66, 80, 125
Bradford, William, 138
Brooks, Cleanth, 166, 167
Brown, Joseph E.
  and opposition to female suffrage, 110
Bryan, William Jennings, 66ff.
Bulldozer Revolution, 121ff.
Byrd, Harry F., Sr., 117
Byrd, William
  on sloth in early Jamestown, 138

Cabell, James Branch, 32
Caldwell, Erskine, 164
Calhoun, John C., 35, 37
Carpetbaggers, 125
Carter, Hodding
  on southern organized religion, 111
  on southern religiosity, 161
Carter, James Earl "Jimmy," 160
Caruthers, William Alexander, 46-47
Cash, Wilbur J., xii, xv, 44, 50, 112, 159
  and relationship between southern
      puritanism and hedonism, 145
  on southern identity, 157
Catt, Carrie Chapman, 95
Central theme (in southern history), xiii, xv,
    13, 14, 15, 45
Child labor legislation, 79, 89, 98
Christy, David, 46
Church(es). *See* Religion (southern)
Civil War
  role of women in, 152
Clansman, The (Dixon), 55-56
Clark, David
  as opponent of child labor legislation, 98
Clark, Septima
  leadership in southern women's movement,
    154

185

Clay, Laura
  and women's suffrage, 153
Comer, Braxton Bragg
  and railroad regulation in Alabama, 72
Commager, Henry Steele, 445ff.
Commission form of city government, 78
Confederacy (Confederate States of America)
  literature on, 34
Confederate Veteran, The, 30
  as organ of Old South myth, 21
Congress (federal)
  southern dominance of seniority system,
    160
Conservatism, 10
  defined, 60
Constitution (federal), 104
Cooking (southern), 169
Cooper, James Fenimore, 50
Corrupt practices legislation, 76, 77
Cotton Is King (Christy), 46
Country music, 137
Crèvecoeur, Hector Saint-John de, 139ff.
Currier, Nathaniel, 48

Daniels, Josephus, 68, 69
Davis, Jefferson, 35
Degler, Carl N.
  quoted, 172
Demagogue, 66
Democratic party, 96, 97, 158
  and agrarian movement, 63ff.
  and Bourbons, 37
Demography (southern)
  post–World War II shifts in, 171
"Dixie," 47
Dixon, Thomas, Jr., 55-56
Dodd, William E.
  as author of Statesmen of the Old South,
    35ff.
Donald, David Herbert
  quoted, 170
Drayton, Michael
  on Virginia as Garden of Eden, 138

Eaton, Clement
  on South as northern "colony," 47
Economy (southern), 159ff.
Eden
  South as, 138
Edmunds, Richard Hathaway
  as New South prophet, 23
Education, 21
  during Progressive period, 66, 68
  exclusion of Negroes in, 112
  and desegregation order of 1954, 116
Egerton, John, 171
Eliade, Mircea
  on myth and human nature, xiv

Elkins, Stanley
  as author of Slavery, 14
Emmett, Daniel Decatur, 47

Faithful darkey, 46ff.
Family
  separation of in sentimental fiction, 141
  black, 151
  as central institution in southern culture,
    154
Farmer's Alliance, 62, 63, 65, 73, 90
Faulkner, William, 12, 131, 163, 165
  quoted, ix
  as supportive of southern myths, 3
  on southern savagery, 7
  on north's gullibility for southern myth, 58
Ferguson, Miriam A., 114
Fitzgerald, F. Scott, 47ff., 57ff.
Fitzhugh, George, 108, 136
  as proslavery theorist, 19
Floyd, Joseph S., Jr., 122
Folk culture, 41, 42
Ford, Jesse Hill
  and violent South, 146
Foster, Stephen C., 46ff.
Fourteenth Amendment, 36
French Quarter (New Orleans), 167
Fugitive, The. See Vanderbilt Agrarians
Fugitive poets. See Vanderbilt Agrarians

Gaines, Ernest J., 167
Gaines, Francis Pendleton, xiii, 4, 5, 14, 15,
    19, 21, 22, 26, 48
Garrison, William Lloyd, 22, 137
Gaston, Paul M., 14, 15, 118
  on distinctiveness of southern mythology,
    xv
  on evolution of New South creed to myth, 7
Gastonia (strike)
  women's leadership in, 153
Georgia
  and election of 1980, 161
Glass, Carter, 67
Gone with the Wind (Mitchell), 164
Good Ole Boy
  description of, 169
Gordon, Kate
  and women's suffrage, 153
Grady, Henry W., 7, 18, 22, 27, 31
  and New South image, 157
Granger movement, 61, 62
Green, Paul, 168
Grenback-Labor movement
  as successor to Grange, 62
Griffith, David Wark, 55

Haley, Alex, 167

Hammond, James H., 104, 106
Hammond, John, 138
Harris, Joel Chandler, 18, 19, 21
    as spokesman for sectional reconciliation,
        109, 110
Hartz, Louis, 130
Hellman, Lillian, 168
Hemmingway, Ernest, 164
Henry, Patrick, 18
Herberg, Will
    on American Way of Life, 126
History
    as essence of southernism, 126ff.
History of Plymouth Plantation (Bradford),
    138
Hofstadter, Richard, 38, 41
    and agrarian ideal, 50ff.
Hogg, James Stephen, 67
    and railroad regulation, 73
Home missionary societies, 153
Homer, Winslow, 48
Hundley, Daniel, 136

"Ice Palace, The" (Fitzgerald), 47ff., 57ff.
I'll Take My Stand (1930). See Vanderbilt
    Agrarians
Immigration
    lack of European, in the South, 169
Industrialization
    and women, 154
Intruder in the Dust (1948). See William
    Faulkner
Ives, James Merritt, 48

Jackson, Andrew, 35, 36
    era, 50
Jackson, Stonewall, 34
James, Henry, 26, 31, 54
Jamestown, 137
Jefferson, Thomas, 10, 130
    and agrarian ideal, 35
Johnson, Eastman, 48
Jordan, Winthrop, 138

Kennedy, John Pendleton, 45, 46
    as author of Swallow Barn (1832), 4
Key, V. O., 115
King, Edward
    and Scribner's, 20
King Cotton
    concept of, 46
Kirby, Jack Temple, 170
Ku Klux Klan
    during the 1920s, 93
    activity in North Carolina, 136

Labor movement
    and women, 90

LaFollette, Robert M., 74
    on lack of progressivism in South, 60, 61
League of Women Voters, 92, 93
    in Tennessee, 87
    in North Carolina, 88
Leah and Rachel (Hammond), 138
LeConte, Emma, 109
Lee, Robert E., 34
    cult of, in North, 56
Lee, William Henry Fitzhugh "Roony," 55
Legree, Simon, 46
Leopard's Spots, The (Dixon), 55-56
Levin, Harry
    on debunking myths, 2
Letters from an American Farmer
    (Crèvecoeur), 139ff.
Liberation of Lord Byron Jones, The (Ford),
    146
Link, Arthur S., 10
Literary renaissance. See Vanderbilt Agrarians
    importance of, 131
Locke, John, 130
Long, Senator Russell Billiu, 160
Longstreet, A. B.,
    as author of Georgia Scenes, 5
Lost Cause, 141
    aura of, 34
    in relation to the North, 45
Lucas, Eliza, 151
Luce, Clare Boothe
    quoted, 156

McKelway, Alexander J.
    and child labor reform, 79
Maclachlan, John M., 122
Macune, C. W., 63
Mason, Lucy Randolph, 90, 91, 92, 98, 99
Mason-Dixon line, 51-52, 129
Masters, Edgar Lee, 56
Media-Made Dixie (Kirby), 170
Melville, Herman, 26, 54
Mencken, Henry L., 6, 7, 34, 40, 141
    and Benighted South image, 135
    anti–Bible Belt view, 161
Middle West
    and Benighted image, 141
Mitchell, Margaret, 164
Moral Majority
    and national politics, 163
Moviegoer, The (Percy), 166-67
Murphy, Edgar Gardner
    and child labor laws, 79
"My Old Kentucky Home," 47
My Old Kentucky Home (painting, 1859), 48
Myrdal, Gunnar, 56
    on appeal of Old South myth in North, 26
    and northern fascination with southern
        aristocracy, 49

Myth(s)
definition(s) of, xiv
as new frontier in southern history, 1-15
of faithful darkey, 5, 6
of traditional (agrarian) South, 8, 9
of demagogic South, 10
of proslavery South, 10
of Reconstruction, 10
populist, 33
Puritan, 34
agrarian, 41
of southern womanhood, 83ff.
of the Cavalier, 125
of southern distinctiveness, 125
of American nationalism, 125ff.
of American success and invincibility, 128
of American innocence, 129
of southern lady, 150ff.

Nashville Group. *See* Vanderbilt Agrarians
Negro(es)
as exotic primitive, 28
and southern character, 42
exclusion from some abolitionist societies, 52
and women's progressive movement, 92
free, 114
migration from South, 115
and southern demagogue, 115
and urbanization, 121
as southerners, 130
alleged inferiority of, 138
women, 150
in current southern politics, 160
withdrawal from white churches, 163
Neighborhood Union, the
and setlement-house movement among blacks, 153
Neo-abolitionism
and Benighted South image, 142
New Deal, 115
New England
and slavery, 143ff.
New South, 7, 8, 157
religious opposition to, 110
role of women in, 152
Nineteenth Amendment, 82 passim, 153
and race, 112, 113
Novels (southern Gothic)
and Benighted South image, 163

O'Connor, Flannery, 166, 171
Odum, Howard W., 36
as regional sociologist, 8
Old South
legends of, 18ff.
Owsley, Frank L., 40

on experience with southern stereotypes, 3, 4
on southern yeoman farmer, 4, 5
on southern black women, 105

Page, Thomas Nelson, 18, 21, 22, 24, 29
Paulding, James Kirk, 48
Percy, Walker, 166-67
Percy, William Alexander, 167
Phillips, Ulrich B., xiii, 11, 13, 38, 123
Phillips, Wendell
critique of South, 140
Pickett, Goerge, 34
Pierson, George W.
on New England regionalism, 120
Pinkney, William, 104
Place over Time (Degler), 172
Plantation myth (illusion), 7, 14, 15, 20, 125, 147
on viability of, 4
on development of, 5
on pervasiveness of, 6
Poll tax, 94
Popular election of senators, 78
Populists (People's party), 40
and Tom Watson, 37
as nondemocratic, 41
as successor to Greenback-Labor movement, 62ff.
role of women in, 152
Porter, Katherine Ann, 165ff.
Potter, David M., 44
on nature of Benighted South, 9
on folk culture as central theme, 12
on economic abundance, 127
Poverty
and southern experience, 127
Primary (direct), 112
as feature of southern progressivism, 75ff.
Progressivism, 112

Quakers
on immorality of slavery, 139

Radical Republicans
as a reforming force, 53
Railroads
regulation of, during progressive period, 71ff.
Rankin, John E., 115
Reconstruction, 6, 20, 31, 36, 111, 125
Booker T. Washington's view of, 24, 25
"tragic legend" of, 53ff.
amendments, 109
role of women in, 152
Redeemers. *See* Bourbons
Red scare, 87

Religion (southern), 113, 114, 161ff.
  as force for status quo, 110
Renaissance (southern)
  in literature, 164
Republican party
  resurgence in South, 158
Rivers, L. Mendel, 116
Romance. *See* Myth(s)
Roosevelt, Franklin D., 8, 35
  on southern economy, 159
Roots (Haley), 167
Rubin, Louis, Jr.
  quoted, 169-70
Russell, Richard B., Jr., 116

Savage South. *See* Benighted South
Sayre, Zelda
  as Montgomery "belle," 57
Schlesinger, Arthur, Jr.
  as author of *The Age of Jackson,* 41
  on national character, 128
Schorer, Mark, xiv, 2
Scopes trial (1925), 114, 141
Scott, Anne Firor, 105
Segregation
  and women, 154
Share-cropping, 109
Sheppard-Towner Act, 91, 98
Simkins, Francis Butler, 8
Slavery, 36, 37. *See also* Negro(es)
  U. B. Phillips on, 38
  as perfect economic system, 104ff.
  as sanctioned by Christianity, 108
Smiley, David L.
  on central theme in southern history, 11, 13
Smith, Henry Nash, 2, 14
  definition of myth, xiv
Smith, Hoke, 67, 69, 71
Smith, Lillian
  as leader of southern women's movement, 154
Somerville, Nellie Nugent, 96
South Carolina
  Granger movement in, 61, 62
Southern Council on Women and Children in Industry, 91
Southern distinctiveness
  persistence of, 137ff.
  supposed disappearance of, 156ff.
Southern Summer School for Women Workers in Industry, 90, 91
Speech (southern), 168-69
Stampp, Kenneth, 38, 53
Stowe, Harriet Beecher, 5, 19, 46ff.
Stuart, Jeb, 34
Suffrage(ism)
  women's, 153

Sun Belt
  image of, 135
Sunday Morning in Virginia (painting, ca. 1870), 48

Tate, Allen, 164
  on historical consciousness of southern literature, 12
  on southern literary renaissance, 131
Taylor, William, R., 14, 18, 48-49
  on psychological origins of myth, 15
Tennessee Valley Authority, 94
Thornwell, James Henley
  and religious defense of slavery, 108
Thurmond J. Strom, 160
Tillman, Benjamin, 65
  and Hepburn Bill, 74
Tindall, George B., xiii, 44, 100, 134
  and viability of Benighted South image, 146, 157
Tobacco Road (Caldwell), 164
Tocqueville, Alexis de, 129, 139
  and critique of South, 140
Tourgee, Albion W.
  on Confederate literature, 21, 29
Truman, Harry S
  and civil rights, 116
Tubman, Hariet, 151
Turner, Frederick Jackson, 14, 15n, 35
Twain, Mark
  as critic of Gilded Age, 54
Twelve Southerners. *See* Vanderbilt Agrarians

Underground Railroad, 151
Upshur, Abel P., 106
Urbanization
  and women, 154

Vance, Rupert V.,
  as regional sociologist, 8
Vanderbilt Agrarians, 12, 39, 40, 122, 123, 163, 172
  and myth of the traditional (agrarian) South, 8, 9
  as authors of *I'll Take My Stand,* 9
Victorian Cult of True Womanhood, 150
Violence (southern)
  and manners, 168

Waring, Judge J. Waties, 116
Warren, Robert Penn, 3, 131, 162, 164
Washington, Booker T.
  as black prophet of New South, 24, 25
Washington, D.C.
  and school desegregation, 161
Washington and Lee University, 56
Watson, Thomas, 37

Wecter, Dixon
  and Lee hero worship, 56
Welty, Eudora, 131, 164
Westbrook, John T.
  on southern misconceptions, 3, 5
White, Sue Shelton, 96, 97
Wiggins, Ella Mae, 153
Wilder, Thornton
  on national character, 130, 131
Williams, Tennessee, 168
  on southern decadence, 6
Wilson, Edmund, 19, 20
Wilson, Woodrow, 35, 67, 68, 69
Wirt, William
  as precursor of plantation legend, 18
Woolman, John
  on southern sinfulness, 139
Women
  and perfection of southern society, 104, 105
  in antebellum romance, 110
  as southern lady and southern belle, 150
  black, 150

Women's Christian Temperance Union, 83, 84, 153
Woodward, C. Vann, xiii, 12, 18, 26, 31, 41, 82
  on Tom Watson, 37
  on patterns of biracialism, 39
  on northern zest for southern myths, 50
  on antislavery myth, 51
  and southern identity, 156
World War I
  and beginnings of Benighted South image, 141
World War II
  effect on southern change, 158

Yeoman farmer
  as characteristic antebellum white southerner, 5
YWCA (Young Women's Christian Association), 88, 90, 153

Zinn, Howard
  on southern identity, 156-57

A Note on the Editors

PATRICK GERSTER is a professor of history and American studies at Lakewood Community College, White Bear, Minnesota. He holds a B.A. from the College of St. Thomas and an M.A. and Ph.D. from the University of Minnesota. Co-editor with Nicholas Cords of *Myth and the American Experience* and co-author with Nicholas Cords of *Myth in American History,* he is a five-time fellow of the National Endowment for the Humanities and was a Fulbright lecturer in Denmark.

NICHOLAS CORDS is a professor of history at Lakewood Community College, White Bear Lake, Minnesota. He holds a B.S. from Mankato State University and an M.A. and Ph.D. from the University of Minnesota. Co-editor with Patrick Gerster of *Myth and the American Experience* and co-author with Patrick Gerster of *Myth in American History,* he has received fellowships from the Coe Foundation, the Bush Foundation, and the National Endowment for the Humanities.